American Soul

SPRING JOURNAL BOOKS

ANALYTICAL PSYCHOLOGY & CONTEMPORARY CULTURE SERIES

Series Editor
THOMAS SINGER, M.D.

OTHER TITLES IN THE SERIES

LISTENING TO LATIN AMERICA
EXPLORING CULTURAL COMPLEXES IN BRAZIL, CHILE, COLOMBIA,
MEXICO, URUGUAY, AND VENEZUELA
*edited by Pilar Amezaga, Gustavo Barcellos, Áxel Capriles,
Jacqueline Gerson, and Denise Ramos*

PLACING PSYCHE: EXPLORING CULTURAL COMPLEXES IN AUSTRALIA
edited by Craig San Roque, Amanda Dowd, and David Tacey

ANCIENT GREECE, MODERN PSYCHE: ARCHETYPES IN THE MAKING
edited by Virginia Beane Rutter and Thomas Singer

PSYCHE AND THE CITY: A SOUL'S GUIDE TO THE MODERN METROPOLIS
edited by Thomas Singer

VIOLENCE IN HISTORY, CULTURE, AND THE PSYCHE: ESSAYS
by Luigi Zoja

AMERICAN SOUL
A Cultural Narrative

Ronald Schenk

Spring Journal Books
New Orleans, Louisiana

Published by:
Spring Journal, Inc.
627 Ursulines Street #7
New Orleans, Louisiana 70116
Website: www.springjournalandbooks.com

The author gratefully acknowledges permission from
Spring Journal Books for the following:

Chapter 1 is adapted from
"9/11, the Twin Towers, and the American Soul," originally published in *Archetypal
Psychologies: Reflections in Honor of James Hillman*, edited by Stanton Marlan (2008).

Chapter 11 is adapted from
"Captain America and His Zealous Blast," originally published in *Spring: A
Journal of Archetype and Culture,* vol. 81, *The Psychology of Violence* (2009).

Chapter 13 is adapted from
"The Soul of Terror/The Terror of Soul," originally published in *Spring: A
Journal of Archetype and Culture*, vol. 78, *Politics and the American Soul* (2007).

Cover Image:
"Angel"
John Gast
1871, oil on board, 13 in. x 18 in.
Private collection

Cover design and typography by
Northern Graphic Design & Publishing
info@ncarto.com

Text printed on acid free paper

Library of Congress Cataloging-in-Publication Data Pending

To J. H.
for teaching, guidance, and kindness

minori e' grandi
di questa vita miran nello speglio
in che, prima che pensil, il pensier pandi

small and great
in this life gaze into the mirror
in which, before thou thinkest, thou makest
plain the thought

—Dante, *Paradiso* 15:61–3

Contents

Acknowledgements

This book would not have seen the light of day without the patient, provocative, supportive skills in psychological midwifery of Thomas Singer. His project of bringing insight to the psyche of culture is one of the most important in psychology today. I am grateful for the ongoing support of Nancy Cater over many years in her capacity as publisher of psychological ideas. Jessica Wilbanks provided an editor's eye that helped to bring together and make readable a vast array of thoughts on many subjects expressed through a multitude of modes. Siobhan Drummond performed her task of manuscript editor with sensitive insight into the subject and an excellent eye for detail. I am indebted to Michael Vannoy Adams and Lyn Cowan for reading initial drafts and providing advice and support. I am appreciative for the many years of friendship and encouragement for this project provided by Thomas Moore and James Hollis. Virginia Parker and Edward Countryman gave very helpful ideas regarding their respective fields of accounting and history.

It has been a privilege to present portions of this work to many institutes, societies, and professional groups including the C. G. Jung Educational Center of Houston, the Saybrook Institute Jungian Studies Program, the Department of Mythological Studies at Pacifica Graduate Institute, the Association of Retired Foreign Service Workers of Santa Fe, the Interdisciplinary Colloquium of the Dallas Psychoanalytic Institute, the Council of North American Societies of Jungian Analysis, the International Association of Analytical Psychology, the Academic Council for Jungian Studies, the Jung societies of Buffalo, Dallas, Los Angeles, Philadelphia, Pittsburgh, Santa Fe, Waco, and Washington, DC. Conversations with my son, Ashley, have provided many fruitful ideas for alternative lifestyles and ways of thinking regarding cultural narrative. Finally, I want to thank my wife, Charlotte, for her love during the many years of this book's making.

Introduction
Myth and American Psyche

American Soul is about an idea—that all groups, particularly nations, exist as derived from a unique, essential underlying story or myth. Although America identifies itself primarily through the language and story of democracy, egalitarianism, and humanistic concerns which to an extent have been made manifest, historically America's attitudes and actions have been predominantly marked by a different orientation that is difficult to reconcile with these ideals—blind self-interest, a privileging of an elite section of the population, rampant racism, devouring consumerism, the plundering of energy and natural resources, capitalistic exploitation, overwhelming political influencing by moneyed interests, the savaging of education, the dilution of health care relative to cost, the demise of infrastructure, the alienation of the international community, the stripping away of constitutional rights of individuals, and the continuous reversion to military action for the sake of dominance. All of this is acted out in service to a general denial enabled by the manipulation of language so that terms such as "jobs," "progress," "opportunity," "change," "choice," "security," "action," and "freedom" co-opt final authority while playing on the underlying appetites and anxiety of a gullible population.

The question that arises in addressing American character becomes: How can one explain the sheer ubiquity and vastness of the discrepancy between ideal and practice in many different aspects of American life that has occurred throughout its many decades? One response offered by depth psychology is that foundational assumptions and attitudes, predominant guiding images, and basic action patterns of an individual or group all stem from a fundamental narrative or myth as indicator of core character lying latent in the rhizome of the psyche.

The idea that myth connotes a reality runs counter to the mainstream of modern Western thought, beginning with the rationalism of the seventeenth century, which has tended to equate the word "myth" with "fancy," meaning fallacy, delusion, or a mistaken notion, that which opposes what can be proven as fact or truth through rationality. From this view, all certitude must be grounded in analytic reason. As depth psychology has revealed from its inception, an approach based purely on reason does not hold when applied to the complexity of human nature. The founders of psychoanalysis, Sigmund Freud and Carl Jung, thought that another form of discourse was called for to explain human behavior and its underpinnings in an intangible world they called the unconscious. They turned to myth as a means of expression for this aspect of psychological life—the Oedipal myth for Freud and universal mythology for Jung. With myth as a primary tool, the psychoanalysis of human nature was first applied to the individual psyche and was then expanded to group psychology, including the analysis of culture and national character. This book furthers the analysis of national psyche in relation to an essential American character or soul.

The book suggests that American myth is predominantly derived from the Judeo-Christian tradition, especially the first five books of the Old Testament and the book of Revelation in the New Testament. It explores the historic and contemporary implications of the following motifs: the chosen people, presumed innocence, the journey, the Promised Land, God's blessings and protection, the privileged elite, travail, ambivalence toward the law, and the role of dominance. It goes into many aspects of American life, particularly those that have been experienced as disaster, in order to find openings to the underlying myth that lies in the details of the images presented.

The beginning chapter, "9/11 and the Twin Towers," is a meditation on 9/11 that attempts to convey the dramatic impact upon the nation's psyche elicited by the event through its imagery. Archetypal amplification of the images suggests the idea of an underlying "life" at work in the psyche of the nation, revealing a deeper meaning than topical discussion would indicate. The chapter begins exploring the roots of this event through an investigation of the object of the attack, the twin towers, with the implication that the Port Authority—the building complex and the agency that conceived and constructed the towers—can be viewed as living out a "personality" reflective of the nation as a whole.

The idea of a deeper meaning to 9/11 is elaborated in the second chapter with an initial foray into the concept that America holds a national character. This idea was first and perhaps most profoundly described by a visiting Frenchman in the 1830s, Alexis de Tocqueville. Tocqueville described Americans in terms of self-interest, but a self-interest moderated with an understanding of the need for a window of connection to the world. "[Americans] show with complacency how an enlightened regard for themselves constantly prompts them to assist one another and inclines them willingly to sacrifice a portion of their time and property to the welfare of the state."[1] Tocqueville also foresaw the danger that a democracy such as he found in America might very well lose this "right understanding" of self-interest and close off connection with the world so that the "people" would become a tyrannical body in itself.

The third chapter, "Ronald McDonald: A Mythic Narrative," presents an outline of an underlying mythic image in the form of nine interconnected aspects of American character that find their roots in a Judeo-Christian heritage. Each theme can be found in different aspects of American life from the everyday consciousness of the individual to the more overarching scope of national policy as manifest in the different epochs of the country's history. The purpose of the chapter is to show how different parts of national life, large and small, are founded in a larger-than-life story that repeats itself over and over again in different guises.

Having explored the idea of national character housed in story, the book delves into the country's historical rhetoric to find the foundation of the themes demarcated in the previous chapters. "*Nehemius Americanus*: Puritan Consciousness and American Soul" describes aspects of the Puritan psyche that would form the core of American soul—the sense of being chosen by God, the identification with spiritual dominance, the orientation toward willful action in the world in God's name, and the association of money with spirit. It was out of its Puritan beginnings that America became a theocracy founded in capitalistic hierarchy and oriented toward empire.

"From Puritan to Yankee" explains the shift in American identity from an overtly religious identification with Judeo-Christian values through Puritanism to a related identity based upon a civic religion that merged Christianity with capitalism and a technological/industrial orientation. Two Founding Fathers were preeminent in this transformation, Benjamin Franklin and Alexander Hamilton. Franklin's writings epitomized the shift from formal Puritan values to those of everyday work and business, while Hamilton paved the way for government support of big business.

The pull in the American psyche toward dominance and empire as it manifested in the nineteenth century is considered in "Empire Builder." This was the age of manifest destiny when the energy of the nation was funneled through notions of progress, development, and growth in the service of moral superiority. With a keen sense of mission, expansion without boundaries came to be a core aspect of the nation's character.

"The Cowboy Crusader and the Americanization of the World" investigates three American leaders of the twentieth century, Theodore Roosevelt, Woodrow Wilson, and Ronald Reagan. All of these men embodied the American ideal, articulated by Ralph Waldo Emerson, of the superindependent individual operating out of conviction in his own values yet indirectly seemingly working for the good of the community at large. The term "cowboy crusader" would seem to fit this image, as it implies the spiritual entitlement that governs this figure who acts as if divinely chosen. At the same time the characterization of cowboy implies the kind of reckless abandon so centrally embedded in the American psyche.

After establishing a historical base for the image of a national soul, the book turns to events and aspects of American life that can be considered openings into its character. The first of these is an exploration of the catastrophic floods in New Orleans that decimated the city in 2005. Although the depiction of this event by authorities was of a natural disaster, the fact is that the flood occurred due to poor maintenance of the flood control system by governmental agencies which had been warned of the probability of disaster on numerous occasions. Katrina is seen as representative of a culture that is predominantly oriented toward progress while leaving the core infrastructure unattended. The tragic images of destruction from the flood give symbolic form to the fact that a large portion of the national population—the poor, the elderly, the infirm, and racial minorities—are given a secondary priority.

"The Shell Game," dealing with the collapse of the Enron Corporation, is the first of two chapters that look into America's economic life as emanating from an underlying mythic narrative. The demise of Enron is imagined as a mirror event to the fall of the twin towers with similar dynamics occurring in each case having to do with a grandiose and inflated self-image and a need to dominate. In addition, the psychology of Enron reveals a mythic influence on American corporate life other than that of the Judeo-Christian tradition. The Greek god of the economy and market, Hermes, helps to clarify the trickster-like quality of American business.

"The Tower of Mirrors" explores the financial meltdown of 2008 as part of a series of financial crises that occur over and over due to the privileging of those in the upper echelon of American finance and the attitude that government regulation hinders progress. These underlying assumptions are linked to a Judeo-Christian mentality wherein the market becomes an entry to the Promised Land, and the invisible self-guiding hand of the market becomes like that of God. This configuration is contrasted with that of a culture which presents itself as "other" to American capitalism, that of Islam, in which the banking practices are also seen as derived from an underlying mythology, in this case Sufism.

The book turns to America's defense and foreign policy as "Captain America and His Zealous Blast" provides an extended example of the mindset at work in American actions, especially in relation to the use of bombing directly or indirectly of civilian populations.

An exploration of American foreign policy follows with a historical march through America's attitudes and involvements in relation to Middle Eastern culture with its predominately Muslim orientation. The picture that emerges is mostly divergent from that presented through America's traditional rhetoric of freedom, democracy, and respect for all peoples. Instead, America's interactions with the Middle East have been marked by an uninformed, dismissive, and self-serving approach derived from biblical tradition that has largely alienated the Middle East.

Having set up the groundwork for an understanding of a hostile view toward America on the part of Islamic militants, the book concludes with a return to its beginning subject, 9/11, with an investigation of terrorism itself, "The Soul of Terror/The Terror of Soul." Terrorism is revealed as an archetypal or universal phenomenon rooted in religious zeal which carries a political message through an act of violence based in performance. In this last chapter we leave a predominantly Judeo-Christian underlying narrative for a deeper universal image depicted in religious ritual and in the figure of the Greek god Dionysus, an approach that brings terrorism closer to home.

American Soul is a book based in psychology, and as the psyche is an indefinable concept in itself, it reflects and is reflected by many different disciplines and aspects of cultural life. The book borrows from many areas of culture—history, accounting, architecture, engineering, political science, literature, economics, theology, and sociology—while claiming expertise in none. It rides the horse of history, for example, to seek out predominant patterns, but does not attempt to account for each facet of the country's history, nor does it attempt to balance all aspects of historical and contemporary cultural life through a theory of cyclical emergence or harmony. Rather, the book aims, through a detailed investigation of the nation's rhetoric, to identify predominant historical and cultural patterns that are reflective of an underlying essence. This approach runs afoul of the comfortable position that what makes America unique is its diversity, its identity, a collection of divergent approaches, actions, and attitudes. Instead, the book will take the position that diversity is eventually governed by a common underlying structure. The thesis of the book banks upon religion, but it sees religion—etymologically rooted in the image of "bending back"—within a wide spectrum of larger-than-life forces to which the culture is subject. The sense of religion to which the book refers is that of a civil religion of shared beliefs, images, and ultimate concerns outside of institutional religion and the religious fundamentalism of political extremes.

As a book of psychology, *American Soul* emphasizes one approach to psychology, the delineation of character based on core tendencies or essences. This approach is akin to two other related approaches to culture in depth psychology. One looks at culture through the lens of pathology and sees aberrant behavior or symptoms split off from the central cultural personality which can be changed or corrected. This book instead takes the position that, given the sheer ubiquity of the subject, the depth and breadth of its manifestations, what is often seen as pathological are actually qualities lying within the core of the nation's personality itself. Likewise, with the exception of sections on architecture, economy, and terrorism, which reference archetypes through Greek gods, the book differs from a view that looks at the various behaviors of culture as emanations of a universal collective consciousness—all cultures are inherently alike. Rather, the book takes the position that while any single aspect of American character, such as entitlement and a tendency toward imperialism, is shared by other cultures and nationalities, the entire matrix of tendencies weaves into a single, unique national pattern.

American Soul does not diminish qualities that are distinctly American, such as the propensity for ingenuity, innovation, and enterprise, an eye for the practical and pragmatic, a facility for perseverance and resiliency, a highly developed capacity for hard work, a creative artistic genius, an authentic altruistic empathy, and a profound sense of humor. Rather, the focus of the book is on those aspects of American soul that predominate but are difficult to acknowledge and apprehend. It is an attempt to account for these aspects with an overarching psychological structure, that of myth. The book's mythic view is neither positive or negative, optimistic or pessimistic, hopeful or discouraging, a vote of confidence or an indictment calling for change, all of which are inherently ego-centered and therefore somewhat self-serving. Rather it is an attempt, through a mythic orientation around limits and finitude, to identify a national character for what it is, no matter the coloring tone of this perception. Ultimately, the book's intention is to bring psychological insight into the discussion regarding America's alignment with itself and the world in hopes of deepening the discourse.

Note

1. Alexis de Tocqueville, *Democracy in America*, vol. 2 (New York: Vintage Books, 1990), 122.

1

9/11 and the
Twin Towers

A letter always arrives at its destination.
— Jacques Lacan

After the dust settled, the magnitude of the effect of the terrorist strikes on the World Trade Center on 9/11 emerged: the deaths of thousands, the destruction of billions of dollars of property, an ensuing retaliatory military campaign of untold cost and duration, political crisis throughout the Middle East, and a severe deepening of global economic recession. What remains most indelibly in mind is the sheer immensity and power of the images which inflicted a psychic wound of untold proportion onto a nation . . . each image, some strangely erotic, containing "with savage" its own particular beauty. "Beauty's nothing / but beginning of Terror we're still just able to bear."[1]

A lush orange fire billowing in the sky.

Showers of burning birds.

A rain of bodies, some in flames. Milton's diving corporate angels; Blake's terrified, tumbling souls falling into the hyle; the contorted figures of Bosch's souls plopping on pavement like the frogs of Exodus.

Steady long lines descending endless stairs while burdened rescuers climb in counterpoint, and those who pause become obstructions.

Many in flight on the stairs making choices as to whether to go up or down, ascent ultimately ending in death, descent, in life.

Everywhere the confusion of war, the search for certainty, while the intercom voice of authority instructs individuals to return to their offices—soon to become tombs.

Firefighters and police officers arguing over who is in charge while top-level officials set up their headquarters in the very locations that are most endangered.

Cell phone connections between loved ones "cut out" as . . . what was unimaginable to all except a few firemen and a distant demolitions engineer—the sky falling in a booming tidal wave of collapse amidst a mushrooming cloud.

White-faced, ghostly crowds flee the streets.

"I had not thought death had undone so many."[2]

"Burning burning burning burning."[3]

"London Bridge is falling down falling down falling down."[4]

And then nothing . . . nothing but the weighted presence of absence.

After the crashes, silence . . . an underworld emerging, sirens sounding perpetual alarm; shadowy workers steadfastly sifting in ashen light; search dogs howling at the smell of dead humanity, frustrated in the quest for flesh and bone; gnarled, jagged forms of broken steel looming in the background; permeating putrid smell of emptiness, timeless fire below; finally, small altars and memorials of flowers appearing scattered on sidewalks, body bags replaced by baggies for remains of smudges and fragments to be delivered to the doors of the deceased;

"My name is Ozymandias, King of Kings;
Look on my Works, ye Mighty, and despair!
Nothing beside remains. Round the decay
Of that colossal Wreck, boundless and bare
The lone and level sands stretch far away."[5]

Time bowed down.

The images carried the complexities and paradoxes of a Hollywood epic where acts of genuine selfless heroism interfaced with those of well-intentioned folly.[6] No one could know the scope of the production, organized by a disciplined team of terrorist authors, directors, and actors and brought into being by an unwitting cast and crew of thousands. Nineteen individuals, each armed with only a small box-cutting tool, were able to bring the most powerful nation in history—a country that spends billions each year on defense and security—to its knees. The very symbols of the nation's technological and economic superiority, the jet and the skyscraper, become instruments of its own destruction, revealing the terror of its technology and the violence of its architecture. Jets turned into bombs, skyscrapers into tombstones, and all the while, oil, the life-blood of the nation, fueled the flames that brought the fall.

As American imagination could not deepen to meet the depth of tragedy in the images it was confronted with, it became homogenized, idealizing victims and firefighters and demonizing perpetrators.[7] Self-identification became swept up in a tidal wave of blind patriotism. The national flag became a displaced icon decorating everything from greeting cards to bath towels (one young woman literally wrapping herself in the flag at a parade) while patriotic themes became background for advertisements. Everywhere, unity with country meant connection to God, as the appeal, "God Bless America," rang from the steps of the national capitol building to the seats of stadiums and classrooms. Linking itself to God on the one hand, America identified with money on the other. Buy, stay spending, keep consuming constant. Don't let terrorism bring down the economy. What emerged was the image of a holy trinity—God, country, and economy—inextricably linked in the American consciousness as its governing story.

9/11 could be seen as

- a deconstructive event, the sudden appearance of the other as "the direct experience of the Real," violent transgression penetrating the insular numbness of programmed Western consciousness enveloped in corporate shroud;[8]
- an archetypal event, its imagery reaching through the ages and across cultures to signal the "call from without" of cosmic change;

- a mythic event, a story of the tragic hero whose hubris or inability to see gives rise to a violent fall, enacting sacrifice;
- a biblical event: Babel, Sodom and Gomorrah, Samson and the fall of the Philistines, the collapse of Nebuchadnezzar, the Lord as a refiner's fire, all giving a sense of divine punishment, divinity presenting its earthly form in a cosmic hierarchy[9] . . . But who was David and who was Goliath? asked a boy in a Bronx elementary school.

The events of September 11th could also be viewed in terms of dualistic entities in conflict—a jet-propelled, unstoppable spirit force meeting a towering world of immovable matter—each with its own respective goal of intangible fortune and tangible self-interest. And yet a closer look reveals that dualism fails in this instance, as each "world" actually contains the other.[10] The spiritual world of fundamentalist Islam turns to violent enactment and the American world of global capitalism embraces the spirit of a people "under God."

Extending the exploration of different perspectives on 9/11, the immediate and tangible viewpoints might focus upon the political (what do we do?), the sociological (what did we do as a community in reaction?), or the moral/medical (what is the pathology here?), while the spiritual position would emphasize abstract principles and moral values at work. An alternative analytic perspective can be imagined from the details of the actual physical manifestation of post-9/11 Ground Zero: a hazy, smelly realm of flickering images, shadows and twilight. This description is much like that of the classical underworld of dead souls. It is this underworld that is traditionally home to a third orientation encompassing both spirit and matter, that of *psyche* or soul. The primary expression and mode of understanding psyche is not the abstract moral principle of reason, nor the literal facts of the material world; rather, it is imagination, "seeing through" the concrete phenomenon to a larger meaning. In order to have a psychological understanding of 9/11, we would need to be imaginal in our approach, taking into account the interplay of the facts and the spirit held within them.

Hearkening to a universal tradition, Carl Jung held that the world itself had a soul, *anima mundi*, an autonomous life in which humans participate and which calls for human reflection. The world has its own desire and depth, its own underworld, its own dis-ease through which it makes its appearance and becomes a part of psychology. Soul permeates the world. Each culture, country, and city and each place, object, and event has its own subjectivity, its own essence. For the French psychoanalyst, Jacques Lacan, the idea of *anima mundi* might indicate the other, an encompassing symbolic matrix or structure with its own subjectivity out of which another subjectivity evolves in reciprocal interaction. *Anima mundi* would be the other of human consciousness, and human subjectivity would reflect the life of the world.

The other is the "not me" standing in counter position while watching "me" in my habitual way of seeing and experiencing. When the other, as world, calls to the self through traumatic violence, psychology asks, What does this say about the subject and its condition? What does the world want of the subject? From this psychological position, a place of uncertainty, the psychologist would respond to the fall of the twin towers by seeing it in terms of *anima mundi* and more particularly in terms of the nation and *its* soul as reflected in many aspects of *its* life.

The exploration begins with the object of the attack, the twin towers, and the life or soul of the twin towers building complex and the agency that constructed it, the Port Authority.

The World Trade Center, soaring above the world like classic titan twins, was built in the 1960s and '70s by two brothers who were among the world's wealthiest men, David and Nelson Rockefeller, in conjunction with the Port Authority of New York and New Jersey. The Port Authority was established in 1921 to assess the New York area's transportation needs and build transportation systems that would minimize interstate conflict. In particular, it was mandated to address the problem of transporting goods between docks in Brooklyn and Manhattan and the New Jersey mainland. Over the years the Port Authority took on a personality of its own: "hard driving," "masculine," and militaristic with a culture of competitiveness for "self-promotion" and profit which "encouraged people to get results rather than just 'operate by the rules.'"[11]

As a real estate project, the World Trade Center (WTC) was a diversion from the Port Authority's chartered purpose of facilitating transportation and improving commerce and trade. Originally imagined as a modest building on the east side of Manhattan housing only agencies central to transportation, the WTC became the world's tallest building structure and was ultimately used to lease private office space. The building project was managed by Guy Tozolli, the ambitious former planner of the New York World's Fair who demanded absolute loyalty to what he called "the Program."

The Rockefellers and Tozolli eventually chose a building design emphasizing largess and symbolizing a dominance that would attract both notoriety and money. The idea for building "the tallest building in the world" came from the Port Authority's female public relations director, Lee Jaffe, and from the beginning its symbolic signification was prominent. The rhetoric of the project quickly took on a tone of spiritualized inflation. As one engineer said, "We all thought it was like building the Pyramids. It was the eighth wonder of the world."[12] Describing the attitude with which the WTC was built, one construction manager explained: "We were the elite. There was nothing we couldn't do. There was no challenge that we couldn't tackle. There were no rules we couldn't find a way around—without being illegal—to get the thing done."[13]

From its conception to its destruction, the WTC's size made it a target. Containing 10 percent of the office space in Manhattan, the WTC eventually came to be a mixed blessing. The diversified mini-city of mostly private businesses and agencies quickly came to be seen by the international community as the symbolic center of global capitalism and hence a two-time target for terrorists. For the builders, the towers represented dominance, while to the popular American mind their height gave a sense of spiritual ascendance, similar to a space shuttle's liftoff. To the world outside of the United States, the towers signified arrogance and exceptionalism. Their eventual destroyer, Osama bin Laden, referred to them as "those awesome symbolic towers."[14]

The WTC's construction was opposed by many sectors of the New York business and real estate worlds. Theodore Kheel, a labor mediator, declared that the Port Authority was a "dangerously short-sighted and rigid conservative money machine harnessed to serve, not the public interest, but the private vision of an opportunistic management."[15] For Kheel, the WTC was the "clearest sign of the Port Authority's intellectual bankruptcy and arrogant indifference to the real needs of community."[16] Lawrence Wien, baron of Manhattan real estate, headed the Committee for a Reasonable World Trade Center and prophetically suggested that an airplane might hit the twin towers. *New York Times* architecture critic Ada Louise Huxtable was ambivalent, stating, "The trade-center towers could be the start of a new skyscraper age or the biggest tombstones in the world."[17]

Some architects were appalled by the twin towers. Michael Lewis referred to them as "swagger buildings—arrogant, proud and strutting objects that are physical manifestations of America's competitive culture."[18] In the *Washington Post*, Wolf von Eckardt wrote, "There is the fascination of the tower's ugliness. Man's tallest buildings to date defy their surroundings, man's most wondrous, skyscraping community. The 110-story Brobdingnagian shafts stand with blunt, graceless arrogance at the western edge of Manhattan island, seeming to tilt that wonder with overbearing size and hubris."[19]

Although the WTC was conceived and built ambitiously and aggressively, its architect, Minoru Yamasaki, was a man with a fear of heights who thought of it as a symbol of peace.[20] Tozolli chose Yamasaki in part because he would follow Tozolli's program and in part because Tozolli was impressed by the way Yamasaki's building for the Consolidated Gas Company in Detroit pulled the eye upward, evoking the sense of a medieval cathedral. Tozolli told Yamasaki, "President Kennedy is going to put a man on the moon. You're going to figure out a way to build me the tallest buildings in the world."[21]

Historically, skyscrapers are the descendants of medieval cathedrals and church steeples of the Enlightenment. Skyscrapers have had three distinct architectural periods. Those of the first generation, built at the end of the nineteenth and beginning of the twentieth centuries, were made of iron frames which supported the building from the exterior. This provided a great deal of interior space, but it meant that the skyscrapers' floors were vulnerable to pancaking on top of each other during fires. The second generation consisted of buildings made of steel frames encased in concrete, eliminating the danger of collapse but losing valuable space due to the placement of heavy interior columns. Remaining examples of this type include the Woolworth

Building, once called the "cathedral of commerce," the Empire State Building, which itself survived an airplane crash in 1945, and 90 West Street, which survived the fires that brought the downfall of its neighbor, the World Trade Center.

The WTC's chief engineer, Leslie Robertson, constructed the twin towers in an innovative style, combining aspects of the previous two generations by putting the load-bearing steel pillars on the perimeter buttressed by trusses of flooring, forming a tube-shaped structure of steel frame and concrete surrounding a core of steel reinforcement. Lightweight steel plates between the upright pillars kept the building from swaying too much in high winds. In spite of their height, the towers would be relatively light in weight, ensuring that their monolithic form would evoke a transcendent feeling. Yamasaki liked the aesthetics of the bamboo-pole style and the strength it would provide, while Tozolli liked the large amount of rental space the design made available.

Towers that reach for the heavens universally symbolize spiritual pride and hubris resulting in their fall at the hands of the gods.[22] In the Old Testament, Babel was built by men to make a name for themselves and to allow them to take their place at Yahweh's level. In the ancient Tarot, the image representing the Tower shows a tall stone structure being struck and broken by lightning, its upper floors in flames, and its crown toppled. A king and queen tumble out of the windows, falling headlong through the air. The interpretations of this card include destruction, coming of a new age, the fall of Adam, the materialization of spirit, the fall of the House of Life infested with evil, the demise of Falsehood, trial by fire, the jaws of Dis, the eye of God, the king must die, freedom from old structures, catastrophe, and complete and sudden change.

The symbolism of the twin towers, when paired with America's response to the terrorist attacks, demonstrates the way the well-being of the economy has taken the place of a spirit force or god in the American psyche. This sense of the economy as god is mirrored in the pantheon of the ancient Greeks where the god Hermes was divinity of commerce: the god of the marketplace and all liminal places of transition or trade. He governed over windfall profits, catastrophic losses, and thievery. He was divinity of the favorable moment as well as the calculated risk.

Hermes's altars were called herms. In their primitive form they were stone heaps set up along the roadside where sacrifices could be offered and also pilfered. In their sculpted form, herms were stone columns, four-sided pillars with a head at the top, placed at the entrances to cities and homes. The phallic form of the herms bespoke their significance as indicators of vitality. In this light, the twin towers would be seen as America's double phallic herm honoring America's allegiance to the economy as a psychological divinity.

In constructing the towers, chief engineer Robertson took into account the force of a jet plane slamming into the building. In fact, both towers withstood the impact of a 767, and the structure of the buildings allowed for the escape of most of those 25,000 people working below the impact levels. The collapse of the buildings came about when the intense heat of the burning building, ignited by 10,000 gallons of flaming jet fuel from the fully loaded planes, caused the steel structures to fold. The south tower collapsed because the connectors—which attached the floor trusses to the upright steel pillars on the exterior walls with two bolts each—couldn't hold in the heat of the fire. The north tower caved in when the damaged internal core pillars eventually gave way. It is thought that the major factor in the collapse of both buildings was not so much the architectural design, but the disintegration of the inexpensive foam fire protection that had been either worn away over time or was blown away by the impact of the plane.[23] In addition, the stairwells of both buildings (with the exception of one in the south tower) were either blocked or unprotected from the fire because they were lined with inexpensive drywall rather than the old-fashioned concrete casings, trapping those people on the floors above.

The writer Jack Miles has said that piety, "that set of graceful accepting, and otherwise positive attitudes that one may choose to cultivate toward relationships that are not a matter of choice," is achieved ultimately within the context of danger.[24] The terrorist strikes and the fall of the twin towers made all Americans pious in the sense of addressing the fact of being American. The catastrophe produced many reactions, but they were all founded upon a renewed connection to the public realm of America. Confrontation with the fundamentalism of another culture forced America to look at its own fundament, its ground of basic assumptions about itself.

If the towers reflected an American ideal of spiritual ascendance, political dominance, and economic self-interest, then the lack of priority given to the details of fire prevention maintenance in the internal structure would be indicative of a vulnerability in these values. Furthermore, the mythical meanings inherent in the image of the tower and its fall, as well as the etymology of the word "disaster," literally "separated from the stars," suggests a meaning in the collapse of the twin towers that might tell us of a larger story in their existence. The story might depict the events of 9/11 as a violent opening in American consciousness. Through that opening, it would be possible for America to see the other seeing it. If the towers were glass mirrors through which America could only see itself as dominating power, then their absence would create a void that not only would allow space for a new understanding of what America is but would allow the other in the world to inform America.

It was just this kind of insight into the nation's character that was prophetically provided by a young French tourist who was quite sympathetic to the project of the budding nation almost two centuries ago, Alexis de Tocqueville.

Notes

1. Rainer Maria Rilke, "The First Elegy," *Duino Elegies,* trans. J. B. Leishman and Stephen Spender (New York: W. W. Norton, 1939), 21.

2. T. S. Eliot, "The Waste Land, I. The Burial of the Dead," in *The Complete Poems and Plays 1909–1950* (New York: Harcourt, Brace & World, Inc., 1952), 39.

3. Eliot, "The Waste Land, III. The Fire Sermon," in *The Complete Poems and Plays 1909–1950*, 46.

4. Eliot, "The Waste Land, V. What the Thunder Said," in *The Complete Poems and Plays 1909–1950*, 50.

5. Percy Shelley, "Ozymandias," *Shelley: Poetical Works*, ed. Thomas Hutchinson (New York: Oxford University Press, 1970), 550.

6. Lawrence Wright reports, in his book *The Looming Tower: Al-Qaeda and the Road to 9/11* (New York: Knopf, 2006, 303, 309), that the jihadist architects of 9/11 watched Hollywood movies on videotape to refine their plot.

7. Yet, as one firefighter later said, it was too simplistic to make the event one of heroism or blame: "It was a series of random events that killed thousands and saved hundreds. Not many people did anything right that day, but not many people did anything wrong that day either." Jim Dwyer, et al., "9/11 Exposed . . . ," *The New York Times*, July 7, 2002, A1. Another firefighter declared, "I saved one person that day and that was me, and it was by running for my life." Angus Gillespie, *Twin Towers: The Life of New York City's World Trade Center* (New York: New American Library, 2002), 246.

8. Slavoj Zizek, *Welcome to the Desert of the Real!: Five Essays on September 11 and Related Dates* (New York: Verso, 2002), 5.

9. "And the kings of the earth, who have committed fornication and lived deliciously with her, shall bewail her, and lament for her, when they shall see the smoke of her burning. / Standing afar off for the fear of her torment, saying, Alas, alas that great city Babylon that mighty city! For in one hour is thy judgment come. / And the merchants of the earth shall weep and mourn over her; for no man buyeth their merchandise any more." Revelation 18:9–11.

10. Ironically, one of the victims of 9/11 was John O'Neil, who at the time was security director of the World Trade Center. For years he had worked in the FBI as chief of the counterterrorism unit and early on realized the danger presented by Osama bin Laden, working diligently to track him down. In fact, O'Neil and bin Laden had much in common in their private lives, personalities, and core values while inhabiting two seemingly oppositional worlds. See Wright, *The Looming Tower*, 208, 345–52.

11. Gillespie, *Twin Towers*, 40.

12. James Glanz and Eric Lipton, "The Height of Ambition," *The New York Times Magazine*, September 8, 2002, 42.

13. Gillespie, *Twin Towers*, 63.

14. Daniel Benjamin, "The 1,776-foot-tall Target," *The New York Times*, March 23, 2004, A22.

15. Gillespie, *Twin Towers*, 135.

16. *Ibid.*, 136.

17. Glanz and Lipton, "The Height of Ambition," 34.

18. Gillespie, *Twin Towers*, 265.

19. *Ibid.*, 140.

20. Yamasaki had also served as the architect for one of the world's most despised and failed public housing projects, Pruitt-Igoe in St. Louis, which was explosively demolished shortly after work on the twin towers was completed, paradoxically anticipating the similar demise of its sibling structures.

21. Gillespie, *Twin Towers*, 54.

22. "Anon out of the earth a Fabric huge
Rose like an Exhalation, with the wound
Of Dulcet Symphonies and voices sweet,
Built like a Temple, where Pilasters round
Were set, and Doric pillars overlaid
With Golden Architrave;"

A description of Mammon's tower from *Paradise Lost* (1.710–715), in John Milton, *Complete Poems and Major Prose*, ed. Merritt Y. Hughes (Indianapolis: Bobbs-Merrill Educational Publishing, 1957), 229.

23. Louis DiBono, the head of the company contracted by Tozolli to apply the fire protection, was apparently involved with the Mafia and was murdered by John Gotti for "the sin of disrespect." Here the gangster underworld of America is revealed as the shadowy underpinning of the towers as icons of the ascending spirit.

24. Jack Miles, "In Impious America," *Spring* 52(1992):20–26.

2

Self-Interest
Rightly Understood

Americans . . . are fond of explaining almost all the actions of
their lives by the principle of self-interest rightly understood.
—Alexis de Tocqueville

The events of 9/11 presented America with an occasion to see
itself through the eyes of others seeing it. In 1831, one hundred
and seventy years before 9/11, a thirty-year-old Frenchman,
Alexis de Tocqueville, provided such a view after traveling with a friend
around America ostensibly to investigate its prisons. The work that
emerged from this venture, *Democracy in America,* remains arguably
the best account of a much larger subject, the political ground of a
nation known for its freedoms. Tocqueville wrote, "I confess that
in America I saw more than America; I sought there the image of
democracy itself, with its inclinations, its character, its prejudices,
and its passions, in order to learn what we have to fear or to hope
from its progress."[1] The depth of his insights is matched only by
the breadth of the spectrum of political persuasions that look to
him for validation. Today his work reflects both a stunning
anticipation of the attitude informing the establishment of such
institutions as the World Trade Center *and* the perspective on America
held by twenty-first-century Islamic terrorists.

Tocqueville wrote *Democracy* in two volumes, published five years
apart. The first volume dealt with the workings of political institutions

in America—the structure of government, the principle of the sovereignty of the people, factors at work in maintaining democracy—while the second focused upon cultural values—individualism, pragmatism, physical well-being. In these volumes he ushered in a new idea in political science: the notion that the underlying way of life of a people, its *moeurs* or "habits of the heart" and traditional opinions, were as important as its documented history. In addition, he anticipated future sensibilities in that he wrote not as a detached observer applying method or abstract theory, but rather as a participant observer who had immersed himself in the culture.

During his journey, Tocqueville was impressed by the exaggerated size of the American spectacle—its grand expectations, the scope of freedom in its actions, the larger-than-life scale of its energy—in short, America's resistance to limits and boundaries of any kind. "There is not a country in the world where man more confidently seizes the future," he observed, "where he so proudly feels that his intelligence makes him master of the universe, that he can fashion it to his liking."[2] Tocqueville was most taken, however, with the way this exaggerated energy was devoted to one bond that united the different parts of the national body—self-interest. In fact, Tocqueville invented the term "individualism" to describe the tendency he found in America, where "all feeling [in the individual] is turned towards himself alone."[3]

Tocqueville believed that the starting point for creating an image of a nation's character lay in an investigation of its historical origins. "If we were able to go back to the elements of states and to examine the oldest monuments of their history," he wrote, "I doubt not that we should discover in them the primal cause of the prejudices, the habits, the ruling passions, and in short, all that constitutes what is called the national character."[4] The young Frenchman traced America's particular national character to the manner by which the nation was founded: the sheer determination and "constant self-interested efforts" of the early settlers.[5] He did note, however, that there seemed to be one constraint to the tendency toward self-interest, the adherence to Christianity, especially as engendered through the practice of the founding Puritans.

For Tocqueville, the Puritans established the core image of American settlers as the new children of Israel with predominantly middle-class values struggling to survive in the wilderness of the New

World. "Puritanism . . . was almost as much a political theory as a religious doctrine."[6] The tradition of moral rigor that the Puritans left to their descendants was created when concern for the body politic became interwoven with the necessity of worshipping the Judeo-Christian God. In effect, one earned God's praises through attention paid to the group.

In America it was possible for self-interest to be moderated by an eye toward God as He revealed himself in community. Tocqueville envisioned America, under the influence of Puritan discipline and sensitivity toward the body politic, as holding the potential to embody a utopian ideal, "self interest rightly understood." It is a self-regard that inspires its adherents to assist others, not through acts of self-denial, but rather through small acts of daily sacrifice, awareness of others, and service to community. By keeping open a window of accessibility to the world outside of one's immediate private and familial interests, individuals could become citizens in the true sense of *homo politicus*, members of the political community at large.

As an aristocrat writing for a French audience that had struggled for decades with the concept of government by the people, the notion of self-interest rightly understood gave Tocqueville an encouraging vision of democracy. He saw in American democracy a model of what government of a body called "the people" actually looked like. As John Locke had earlier theorized in *Two Treatises of Government*, this form of government worked through the will of the majority. Locke had rescued the sense of the body politic from Hobbes's fantasy of a destructive mob and made it into a rational, active force through collective agreement to be bound by the decision of the majority. Now Tocqueville was seeing firsthand how this principle could achieve its best form through legislative democracy wherein "the people are . . . the real directing power; and although the form of government is representative, it is evident that the opinions, the prejudices, the interests, and even the passions of the people are hindered by no permanent obstacles from exercising a perpetual influence on the daily conduct of affairs."[7] For Tocqueville, the people had become a form of "Deity . . . the cause and the aim of all things; everything comes from them, and everything is absorbed in them."[8] The Puritan God, existing in latent form in community had become manifest in the body politic itself.

Seeing through Tocqueville's sensibility regarding the people, we can see that he went even further in ascribing an aura to American political life through its specialized focus on the individual. Following the insights of political scientist Sheldon Wolin, one realizes that Tocqueville was essentially seeing in the American individual the birth of modern man, the ultimate vehicle of the Enlightenment project of transferring subjectivity from divine to human consciousness.[9] This project had found its original voice in the thought of the sixteenth-century French philosopher René Descartes. Descartes's inquiries into the nature of God and man had led him to the questions of why the mind of man is prone to err and how can the mind work so as to become a reliable source of inquiry. Descartes's solution to these questions was radical doubt.

For Descartes, everything was uncertain except the fact of one's thinking upon which one could establish certainty of being. "I think, therefore I am." The result was the alienation of consciousness from world and community and the movement of "world" to an internal locus. The mind of the individual became the center of the universe. The external world as inert matter became an object with the potential for human exploitation and profit. Method, the application of technique as an extension of the human mind, became indispensable as a form of inquiry giving rise to the birth of science. Subjectivity—founded on doubt, centering itself in private consciousness, and manifesting itself through method—brought Protestantism, capitalism, and science together as predominant in the configuration through which modern humanity experienced itself. In Wolin's words, "the Cartesian presents a controlled self, translucent, autonomous; its errors traceable and, in principle, corrigible, its possibilities calculable, and its prospects in a mathematized world, infinite."[10] For Tocqueville, democracy was the new form of politics in the Cartesian mold, and the American the prime exemplar of the Cartesian man.

Tocqueville saw that freedom as practiced through this American modern man runs the risk of giving rise to a predominant orientation toward self-interest as determined by the individual. In its American form, self-interest would be equated with private physical well-being and become not only the national "taste," but in a larger sense, the channel in which the great underlying current of human passions finds its course. Political life would inevitably be tied to private material life and political freedom equated with capacity to procure.

> The men of democratic times require to be free in order to procure more readily those physical enjoyments for which they are always longing . . . Americans believe their freedom to be the best instrument and surest safeguard of their welfare . . . they believe . . . that their chief business is to secure for themselves a government which will allow them to acquire the things they covet and which will not debar them from the peaceful enjoyment of those possessions which they have already acquired.[11]

Love of wealth would become the "principle . . . at the bottom of all that the Americans do."[12]

However, even while the predominant inclination of the nation might be the acquisition and enjoyment of the pleasures of material life, in a democratic landscape the possibility exists for an individual with sufficient moral education to confine this passion to limited parameters. "To add a few yards of land to [one's] field, to plant an orchard, to enlarge a dwelling, to be always making life more comfortable and convenient, to avoid trouble, and to satisfy the smallest wants without effort and almost without cost."[13] For Tocqueville a "virtuous materialism" enervating and activating the soul was indeed possible in America.

The forces working against this ideal are truly great. A nation so focused on the preservation of material well-being of the individual will naturally make the workings of the economy and commerce and the notions of productivity and pragmatism the foundations of its belief system. Theory and ethics will become subordinate to means ("how to do") and means secondary to ends. Efficiency and a short-term orientation take priority in achieving well-being as physical comfort.

The antidote to an overly dominant materialism would seem to be religion, and Tocqueville commented that America's religiosity was actually the first thing that captured his attention upon his arrival. What was most noteworthy to him, however, was the way in which spiritual values were accommodated to the pragmatic values of material success. "One sees [Americans] seeking with almost equal eagerness material wealth and moral satisfaction; heaven in the world beyond, and well-being and liberty in this one. Under their hand, political principles, laws, and human institutions seem malleable, capable of being shaped and combined at will."[14] In America, materialism and morality went hand in hand.

Tocqueville saw in American consciousness the tendency to value the useful over the beautiful, as well as the convergence of religious and practical worlds. The result was a quasi-religious faith in technology itself. In a country where means triumph over ends, where the practical triumphs over the theoretical and the aesthetic, and where materialism is imbued with spirituality—in that world methodology/the practical/materialism become merged into a single frame of mind subsumed into a larger-than-life ideology.

When political rights become inextricable from self-interest, the role of government is reduced to avoiding impediments to earning potential produced through technology and inevitably enjoyed by the privileged few. Such a government becomes one of rules and administrative habits, rather than an agency of service to its population. Here lay precisely the danger that Tocqueville saw in democracy and, in particular, American democracy. When the utopian ideal upon which the nation is founded loses the right understanding of self-interest, its "window on the world," an "ignorant and coarse" shadow presents itself and the ideal becomes transformed. Democracy and its individualism would degenerate into the simple selfishness of individuals isolated from community. "It is difficult to foresee to what pitch of stupid excess their selfishness may lead them; and no one can foretell into what disgrace and wretchedness they would plunge themselves lest they should have to sacrifice something of their own well-being to the prosperity of their fellow creatures."[15]

Tocqueville called this specter the "despotism" of democracy, occurring in the American character through the convergence of two impulses—the pursuit of religion and the unfettered striving for personal material gain. The moral world classifies, systematizes, foresees, and decides beforehand, while the political world agitates, disputes, and maintains uncertainty. The individual is passively obedient in the former while scornfully independent in the latter. The two modes advance together, each leaning on the other. Such a mind-set flattens the consciousness of a people to a homogenous state in which the most able-minded individuals avoid government.

The "people," as tyrannical, imposes its beliefs, permeating the thinking of the personal mind with ready-made opinions. Collective consciousness becomes enveloped by a nameless, faceless presence which is in fact totalitarian. Tocqueville: "I know of no country in which there is so little independence of mind and real freedom of discussion as in America."[16]

Tocqueville prophesied that the despotism of democracy in America would utilize the American preoccupation with material well-being, withdraw energy and focus from public to private welfare, and shift America's plurality of involvements and allegiances to a singularity of interest. Eventually, the Cartesian, democratic man would become forgetful of time in terms of history and blind to space in terms of community. He would think of himself in isolation, assuming that his destiny lies solely in his own hands. For Tocqueville, whose grandfather had been beheaded in the Great Terror, this triumph of banality in a collective mediocrity of mind was the true "terror which depresses and enervates the heart."[17]

Tocqueville's image of the utopian paradigm resulting through the shift from "self interest rightly understood" to an enclosed vacuum where the individual is "shut up in the solitude of his own heart," is a paradise of innocence protected by an invisible parental power.[18] "The first thing that strikes the observation is an innumerable multitude of men, all equal and alike, incessantly endeavoring to procure the petty and paltry pleasures with which the fate of all rest; his children and his private friends constitute to him the whole of mankind."[19] Over this population would stand "an immense and tutelary power," gratifying and protecting. This authority might be beneficial if its purpose was to prepare the individual for a truly independent existence, but instead it seeks to maintain its own power by keeping its subjects in a perpetual state of childish dependency.

In short, Tocqueville is describing the shadow of the American character as a Disney World. It is the ubiquitous simplification of the mind through systematic banishment of the other. Historically, this process becomes the American attempt to disnify the world through an imperial or globalizing attitude. The image he has provided echoes biblical themes in terms of a restless, ambitious, conformist, self-interested people with a childlike innocence, perpetually in search of a utopian existence of material well-being imbued with spirituality under the gaze of a singular eye of protective authority. In outlining this form, Tocqueville gives a prelude to a turn toward a more differentiated sense of American soul as cultural narrative derived from aspects of the Judeo-Christian tradition that inform a wide spectrum of national life in terms of both everyday attitudes and far-reaching policies.

Notes

1. Alexis de Tocqueville, *Democracy in America*, 2 vols., the Henry Reeve text as revised by Francis Bowen with an introduction by Daniel Boorstein (New York: Vintage Books, 1990), 14.

2. Quoted in Sheldon Wolin, *Tocqueville between Two Worlds: The Making of a Political and Theoretical Life* (Princeton, NJ: Princeton University Press, 2001), 120.

3. Tocqueville, *Democracy in America*, 2:98.

4. Tocqueville, *Democracy in America*, 1:27.

5. *Ibid.*, 1:34.

6. *Ibid.*

7. *Ibid.*, 1:173.

8. *Ibid.*, 1:58.

9. Wolin, *Tocqueville between Two Worlds*.

10. *Ibid.*, 85.

11. Tocqueville, *Democracy in America*, 2:140–42.

12. *Ibid.*, 2:229.

13. *Ibid.*, 2:132.

14. *Ibid.*, 1:43.

15. *Ibid.*, 2:124.

16. *Ibid.*, 1:263.

17. *Ibid.*, 2:330.

18. Robert Bellah, Richard Madsen, William M. Sullivan, Ann Swidler, and Steven M. Tipton, *Habits of the Heart: Individualism and Commitment in American Life* (Berkeley: University of California Press, 1985), 47.

19. Tocqueville, *Democracy in America*, 2:318.

3

Ronald McDonald:
A Mythic Narrative

The archetypal American is a displaced person—arrived from a
rejected past, breaking into a glorious future, on the move,
fearless himself, feared by others, a killer but cleansing the world
of things that 'need killing,' loving but not bound down by
love, rootless but carrying the center in himself, a gyroscope
direction-setter, a traveling norm.

—Gary Wills

Tocqueville's belief that American character congeals around an
orientation toward self-interest and that democracy carries an
inherent danger of becoming a tyranny of the collective mind
to the detriment of general well-being is borne out by a scan of the
cultural terrain in America.[1] In the second decade of the twenty-first
century, the country finds itself under-covered in regard to medical
care and its public education remains mediocre. America's
infrastructure is in dire need of maintenance, while cost-effective
energy from domestic sources is inadequate. The opportunity for
meaningful work and the equitable distribution of profit and job
benefits is not available to most of the workforce. Attention to the
environment as a factor determining quality of life for all is superficial
and sporadic. The nation's debt places it in a precarious position
economically, and this state of affairs is due chiefly to questionable
tax deductions predominantly favoring only a few, in conjunction with

an engagement in dubious and expensive military pursuits. The sources from which the country truly needs "defense" and "homeland security"—the greed of corporate and banking directors, the hunger for power of politicians, crime related to drug sales, pollution and nuclear waste, and infrastructure breakdown, to name a few—are not given priority by the nation's leaders or the majority of its citizens, giving rise to the idea that all parties seem to have a stake in this state of affairs no matter how disadvantageous they seem to be for the general welfare.

Although the subject of change is perpetually brought forward, significant change seems questionable given America's historical experience. Over and over America has been governed by the same exhausted cycle—crisis, call for action, and reactive measures which then lead to further crisis. While elitism has always been disparaged in both business and politics in America, it is primarily an elite minority that has consistently benefited from policies and attitudes instituted by that same elite and, paradoxically, supported directly or indirectly by the majority of the people. For the most part, political discourse takes the form of huckstering or cheerleading, utilizing buzz words and euphemisms such as "growth," "build," "development," "expansion," "jobs," "work," "choice," "opportunity," "progress," "challenge," "freedom" "rights," and "strength"—language that only serves to obfuscate clear vision and understanding.

Although political discourse typically tends to frame issues to be addressed as uniquely contemporary, the state of affairs described here is not particular to any specific time. Issues that are central to American political dialogue, such as health care reform, have consistently been brought forward during previous decades without being acted upon in a substantial way. (In 2012 two-thirds of Americans wanted the Supreme Court to overturn part or all of President Obama's health care reform law.) To illustrate how matters are recycled through the body politic, the unlikely example of the southwestern town of Bisbee, Arizona, presents itself. In this copper mining community in the 1890s, the public's attention was brought to bear on a handful of social issues: gun control, drug use, the plight of women, violence along the border, illegal immigration, the corruption of elected officials, and war in the Balkan countries (the homeland of most of the miners in the area). One hundred years later, in the mid-1990s, all of these areas were still drawing major public attention on a nationwide scale.

One can see how deeply seeded the roots of contemporary issues are by examining the history of one predominant aspect of American culture, namely, capitalism is king and money is the bottom line. America was a country formed by the Puritans as a theocracy, but also as a stock-holding company for which repeated financial appeals to English stockholders were necessary. At the time of the Revolution, the standard of living in the colonies was higher than any European country and the Revolution itself can be seen as a "shopper's revolt" of merchants and buyers angry at the taxation policies of England.[2] Throughout the political career of Abraham Lincoln in the mid-nineteenth century, he made more speeches about economics than any other topic. In Puritan times, during the Revolution, and in the mid-nineteenth century, the statement of James Carville, Bill Clinton's campaign strategist in 1992, has been apropos: "It's the economy, stupid!"

The connection of money with democratic politics is often decried, yet one sees it at work historically. Senator Daniel Webster noted to the banker Nicholas Biddle that his retainer had not been "renewed or refreshed as usual" and that Webster needed recompense if his relationship with the bank was to be continued. Corporations were informally treated as individuals since early in the nation's development and were formally granted the rights of individuals, including the right to contribute to political campaigns as insured by the Fourteenth Amendment, by the Supreme Court in 1886. Theodore Roosevelt became a champion of the Progressive movement, but only after his campaign of 1904 was bankrolled by the very corporations he turned against in his policies. Wall Street spent $2.7 billion lobbying Congress for favorable policies in the decade leading up to the "meltdown" of 2008, brought about in large part by those very policies.[3] Finally, in 2010, the Supreme Court of the country gave corporations a blank check for influencing elections through donations.

A story: A frog and a scorpion stand at the edge of a river they both want to cross. The scorpion asks the frog for a ride, but the frog is skeptical, thinking the scorpion will bite him. The scorpion assures the frog, "Why would I do that when we both would drown?" The frog is convinced and starts out across the river with the scorpion on its back. Halfway across, sure enough, the scorpion bites the frog, and they both start to sink. "Why did you do that?" asks the frog. "Because," answers the scorpion, "it is my nature."

The nature of any psychological body is its essence, that which provides the limits of change, its soul, the "unmoved mover," its very definition. C. G. Jung referred to the essential part of the psyche in terms of its myth. By myth Jung did not mean something fallacious, but rather the fundamental reality, the bridge to consciousness revealing the unconscious truth. The word "myth" comes from the Greek *mythos,* which means literally "sound of the mouth" or the "word" in its final pronouncement. Myths are stories that describe the behavior and relationships of the archetypes, the original stamps or patterns that form the ground of our being. As James Hillman has reminded us, in its original Greek sensibility myth fulfilled three essential notions of truth: it exists as a counter to deceit, it involves memory of the fundamental patterns of the soul, and it is a stark, direct representation of things as they are—all of which are independent of human interpretation.[4] Myth stories us and renders us all fundamental.

Myths reveal images of essence or identity in relation to individuals and groups or collectives. Jung was interested in both individual and national identity in relation to myth, and in an essay entitled "The Complications of American Psychology," he wrote: "Almost every great country has its collective attitude, which one might call its genius or *spiritus loci.* Sometimes you can catch it in a formula, sometimes it is more elusive, yet nonetheless it is indescribably present as a sort of atmosphere that permeates everything."[5] Following Jung, the endeavor becomes to locate a myth that best expresses the underlying "collective attitude" or fundamental tacit assumptions of American consciousness.

We have already seen how Tocqueville considered America's fundamental life, or myth, to be lived out, as derived from Puritan influence, in service to self-interest, with the redeeming factor that the idea could be "rightly understood" to allow for connection to the world. Recent scholarship grounded in American history reveals a remarkable confluence of themes associated with biblical narrative in American discourse.[6] This underlying narrative, which can be ascertained in most aspects of the American psyche, is actually a form of sectarian religion following the Judeo-Christian heritage in its Protestant form.[7]

As an example, for Americans God has a special place for the country and its people.[8] God is referenced four times in the Declaration of Independence. America's money carries the words "in God we trust" and God "approves our undertaking." National anthems ritually sung at the beginning of public events emphasize God's blessing of America. The phrase "under God" was placed in the Pledge of Allegiance during the McCarthy era of the 1950s. During the Republican convention of 2008, the word "God" was used more often than any other word except "tax" and "business." Starting with George Washington, presidents through the years have habitually made reference to God in their inaugural address as did liberal Democrat John F. Kennedy, who asserted that the rights of Americans come from God and it is the destiny of America to carry out God's will on earth. Conservative-leaning Republican President George W. Bush made numerous quasi-fundamentalist statements which only echoed those of his Democratic predecessor nine decades earlier, Woodrow Wilson, stating or implying the sentiments that they were president as a matter of God's doing, they placed themselves in God's hands, God spoke through them, and they knew the intentions of God. Historically, biblical images have been used to promote national agendas such as the acquisition of land, the removal of Native Americans, the expansion of American influence abroad, the New Deal, the New Frontier, the Great Society, the New Federalism, the Star Wars initiative, the dropping of the atomic bomb, and the invasion of Iraq.

A close look at American consciousness, imagery, thought patterns, and behavior, both historically and in contemporary times, reveals several interrelated themes that not only have an archetypal basis, but more importantly a Judeo-Christian coloring that, when woven together, produce a fundamental tapestry in their American setting. These themes emerge in everyday life as well as in overarching national policies. Nine of these themes can be seen as core to American identity: chosen people, American righteousness, "journey," redemption through travail, privilege for the elite, ambivalence toward the law, consumerism and material well-being, the promised land, and dominance and empire building.

Chosen People

> I will make of thee a great nation, and I will bless thee, and make
> thy name great and thou shalt be a blessing. (Genesis 12:2–3)

Although many nationalities across cultures see themselves as divinely chosen, this sensibility has a particularly American version, beginning with the Puritans who explicitly identified themselves as

God's latter-day children. The consciousness of Americans leading up to and through the founding of the nation continued the Puritan identification with the notion that God has a special plan for America.[9] When Ethan Allen demanded surrender at Fort Ticonderoga, he did so "in the name of the great Jehovah and the Continental Congress."[10] Washington saw the new country as under the "smiles of Heaven" and God's "invisible hand," Adams referred to America as God's "Providence," and Jefferson, who wanted the Great Seal to depict the children of Israel crossing the Red Sea, characterized America as the "Israel of Old."

Underlying America's interaction with non-Western peoples is the notion that all cultures must be created in the political and economic image of America, an orientation that follows the mythical footsteps of the children of Israel with their special connection to God.[11] The expansion of America in the nineteenth century as well as America's leadership in global politics and globalized economy in the twentieth and twenty-first centuries has been carried out through rhetoric that emphasized America's status as a nation with a divinely inspired mandate allowing for a unilateral consciousness in regard to the rest of the world.[12] In short, Americans have historically acted as if God's messages of entitlement to the children of Israel were meant for them: "Thou art an holy people unto the Lord the God, and the Lord hath chosen thee to be a special people unto himself, above all the nations that are upon the earth."[13] "The Lord thy god will set thee on high above all nations of the earth."[14]

Self as Good / Other as Evil

> I will bless them that bless thee, and curse him that
> curseth thee. (Genesis 12:3)

Although diversity is supposed to be a central part of the American psyche, American consciousness is more often than not intolerant of difference. For Americans, vision tends to be polarized so that "other" easily becomes threatening—at best to be ignored, at worst to be conquered or obliterated. An enduring American political recipe is to cast an agent (be it a foreign country or a social evil) as problematic and outline a plan for conquering it, usually through massive force, such as the War on Poverty or the War on Terrorism. The Puritans framed their endeavor as a "bulwark" against the "Antichrist,"[15] and the colonists considered the Revolutionary War as a battle with the "beast" of England. During the Civil War each side cast the other in terms of evil. Franklin Roosevelt proclaimed the need for Americans to "march toward the clean world our hands can make."[16] Communism was depicted as evil in the mid-twentieth century, and the term carried over to terrorism in the twenty-first century. George W. Bush's fundamentalist rhetoric regarding his administration's actions in service to the good implied that anyone not in agreement with his policies was on the side of evil.[17] In early twenty-first-century America, fear of difference manifested in extreme attitudes related to gay and lesbian marriage and illegal immigration.

The nature of American partisan politics has always been severely antagonistic. Although Thomas Jefferson and John Adams eventually carried on a friendly exchange of letters, their race for election in 1800 was extremely hostile. Jefferson called Adams a "blind, bald, crippled, toothless character with neither the force and firmness of a man, nor the gentleness and sensibility of a woman." Adams responded by referring to Jefferson as a "mean-spirited, low-lived fellow, the son of a half-breed Indian squaw, sired by a Virginia mulatto farmer."[18]

In spite of its professed ideals of freedom and equality for all, America has historically been racially biased.[19] Most predominantly, white racism has worked against people of other color. Although the interface of races has contained complex dynamics, generally speaking, it was the white man who confiscated the land of the red man and built the nation on the backs of racial minorities, particularly the black man. At the start of the twenty-first century, one-third of black men were likely to spend some time in prison with the resulting stigma of second-class citizenship when they were released.[20] The Asian and Latino populations and even peoples with shades of white like the Irish and Italian have historically been treated with severe discrimination in America.[21] On the other hand, racial bias works both ways in America as evidenced by the fact that 90 percent of church congregations have at least 80 percent of their membership of one race.[22] Finally, dualistic consciousness inevitably breeds an underlying anxiety which can be played upon by political rhetoric and results in large sums being spent on homeland security as well as phenomena such as the great lengths suburban middle-class America goes to in order to create distance from impoverished groups.[23] In light of the good/evil split it is metaphorically significant that "heart dis-ease" ranks as one of America's most deadly afflictions.

The biblical narrative presents good and evil in starkly dualistic terms with God and His will on one side facing anything different as evil on the other. The Garden of Eden becomes the arena where God is "all good" and Satan "all evil," the serpent "cursed . . . above every beast of the field."[24] Satan is a dragon to be vanquished for a thousand years when the heavenly city will descend, populated by God and his people cleansed of all who are "fearful and unbelieving, and the abominable, and murderers, and whoremongers, and sorcerers, and idolaters, and all liars . . . and there shall in no wise enter into it anything that defileth, neither whatsoever worketh abomination, or maketh a lie."[25]

Journey

> [T]hey shall mount up with wings as eagles; they shall run, and
> not be weary; and they shall walk, and not faint. (Isaiah 40:31)

American consciousness is organized around movement. Historically, the journey for Americans has been: across the Atlantic to build the "New Haven," "Westward Ho" to conquer the frontier,[26] across the Pacific to civilize the Eastern world, to the Middle East to secure oil resources, to every country that America has occupied militarily in the last two centuries in the name of "making the world safe for democracy," and on to the conquest and colonization of outer space as national destiny. Even the experience of happiness is framed as a matter of pursuit by the Founding Fathers. The sentimentalized image of the journey home is a staple of Hollywood movies, and American consciousness is disdainful of conditions of stasis such as wallowing or to be mired, stuck, or held down. Instead, rise up, move on, get on with life, pick up roots, forward looking, hit the road, on the road again, get back on the trail, let's roll, come fly with me—all typify a consciousness with its eye always on the horizon, yet also forgetful of past lessons and neglectful of the complexity of conditions at hand.

America makes itself manic with its hands perpetually on the wheel, going for the fast lane, everything express, geared to the fast break. The road becomes a home and drive-through a way of life, not only in procuring fast food, but in attending wedding and funeral rituals from the seat of a car. America creates mobility as an architectural form, while the networks of its roads and highways become the often damaged blood vessels of the national body where congestion is dreaded. Upwardly mobile becomes a desirable way of life in America, creating the paradox that whereas American homes are often built to outsized proportion, their inhabitation comes about with an eye to the next move.[27]

And the move must be made in haste. Buy now, act now, or you will miss the boat or the train or the plane, any hesitancy or reflection risking missed opportunity and indicating a breach in faith. President Obama's post-election promise to "act swiftly" in regard to the economy was an echo of FDR's call for "action, and action now" in his first inaugural address. Action now, action for its own sake, governs the tone of every American sales pitch and political agenda from the war in Iraq to economic bailout to buying another product.

Yet a country that can't stand still—obsessed with upward mobility—inevitably becomes an Alzheimer's Nation, unable to remember as witnessed by the repetitive cycle of America's financial breakdowns and involvement in foreign military occupations.[28] America, where millions of dollars are paid for motivational speakers and books to spur on its business, is a country in which just under half of all adults are diagnosable as problem sleepers. In addition, the gaze to the horizon inevitably leads to a neglect of that which is at hand, its infrastructure. Every year more than $62 billion is spent on car and truck repairs necessitated by roads that are poorly maintained, and over a quarter of America's bridges are in need of structural repair.[29]

The myth makes the path. Adam and Eve take their leave of the garden, Noah casts off into the flood, and Abraham departs from the land of his father. The children of Israel hasten from Egypt following the Lord's edict, "Speak unto the children of Israel, that they go forward" and journey for forty years before entering Canaan, only to be eventually displaced into exile, necessitating another journey of return.[30] Joseph and Mary hit the road for Judea and take flight to Egypt before finally landing in Nazareth.

Suffering and Victimhood

> For as soon as Zion travailed, she brought forth her children.
> (Isaiah 66:8)

Part of what makes the chosen people special is that despite their innocence, they suffer. The Sunday magazine *Parade* carries stories of celebrities hitting on bad times before the inevitable comeback. In movies John Wayne falls off his horse, Brando is beaten up, Rocky is bloodied, and Oprah's cult of self-empowerment necessitates the public detailing of personal travail as a means to healing. At election time, politician after politician cites his or her history of overcoming adversity as certification of their ability to empathize with the hardships of the people and their eligibility for office.[31] The Puritans saw the dangers and difficulties of settling a new land as an indication of their entitlement in the eye of God, and it is this sensibility of specialness through travail that echoed through such historical sufferings as that of the Revolutionary army, the pioneer movement westward, both armies of the Civil War, the majority of the population during the Depression, and the African American freedom movement.

Americans would seem to carry an underlying identification as descendants of the fall of Adam and Eve, Abraham struggling in the unknown land, and Noah persevering on the ark. The Israelites suffered through a period of submission followed by forty years of wandering in the wilderness, the three faithful servants of God were cast into flames, the prophets persecuted, and the early Christians martyred. Job with his travails and boils became the very image of suffering, anticipating Jesus's stagger toward Golgotha and eventual bloody fixation to the cross. Old Testament torment depicts God's testing the faith of his children, while John's admonition, "In the world ye shall have tribulation," sums up the Christian notion of the inferiority of the material world relative to God's heavenly kingdom.[32] Whereas all of these mythical images of suffering can be seen as representing universal modes of transformation, new life through the experience of death in torment, change coming about by way of sacrifice, new life via the experience of death, this paradigm finds an especially predominant place in America.

Governance of, for, and by the Elite

> And I saw thrones, and they sat upon them, and judgment was given unto them . . . and they lived and reigned with Christ a thousand years. (Revelation 20:4)

In January 2010 the Supreme Court of the United States voted to guarantee that large corporations could spend unlimited funds on political advertising in any political election. This outcome echoed the Court's 2000 5–4 decision in *Bush vs. Gore,* which undermined the votes of thousands in Florida and prefigured the subsequent decision in 2011 to limit workers' rights in class action lawsuits. While these decisions are appalling to any sense of principle regarding equality of access to political power, they demonstrate a subtle yet fundamental aristocratic character in American society.

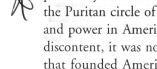

America thinks and talks of itself in the language of democracy but actually lives within a hierarchical structure. "Elitism" is a politically incorrect word in America, but from its beginnings with the Puritan circle of governing elders, an elite circle has held privilege and power in American practice and consciousness.[33] In spite of their discontent, it was not the merchants but the privileged elite of society that founded America as a nation. The wealthiest 10 percent of the population owned 50 percent of the country's assets, and Alexander Hamilton's pro-manufacturing bias informally set the precedent for the eventual advantage given to corporations. It was not the street crowds or frontier folk who put Andrew Jackson into power ultimately holding sway in the nineteenth century, rather those few who became enriched during the two industrial revolutions. In the first half of the twentieth century it was, for the most part, upper-class East Coast families and their associates that ran the nation even while focusing on the plight of the poor and disadvantaged during the Depression. C. G. Jung said, "There is no country on earth where the 'power-word,' the magic formula, the slogan or advertisement is more effective than in America."[34] Whether through a power word or a sound bite, the majority of Americans have looked to those in the hierarchical strata above for management of their living circumstances.

America sees itself as located at the pinnacle of a hegemonic international structure, but Americans also willingly subject themselves to the diminished benefits of the subordinate in favor of the elite. Forty percent of the total American income goes to the highest 10 percent of the earners, the richest 1 percent claiming almost 25 percent of the total income.[35] Eighty-four percent of the net worth of Americans is held by the top 5 percent of American households, while the top 1 percent own 40 percent of all assets and 90 percent of all stocks and bonds.[36] The average income for the highest-earning 5 percent of families is almost twenty times that of the lowest 20 percent, who earn only 4 percent of the total national income. Wall Street bonuses in 2010 totaled $20.8 billion, more than fifty times the size of the budget cap of the Consumer Financial Protection Bureau.[37] The country's six largest financial institutions account for 55 percent of all banking assets, and the SEC repeatedly grants exemptions in the cases of large financial institutions to laws meant to act as deterrents to fraud.[38] It is estimated that almost 30 percent of all jobs in America pay at the poverty level, and 15 percent of the population are defined as poor by the federal government, ranking the U.S. poverty rate the highest among all developed countries. In the years leading up to the 2008 financial crisis, most Americans actually lost spending power during the financial bubble, while America's economic growth showed itself only in gains by the upper class. To further the cycle, 50 percent of all political campaign donations come from the top 1 percent of earners and 75 percent from households with an annual income above $200,000. Most of the serious contenders for the presidency in 2012 were in the top 1 percent of earners. During the Kennedy administration tax reductions yielded 45 percent benefit to the wealthiest 12 percent of the population. In both the Reagan and Bush Jr. administrations, Americans continuously voted into office representatives who voted for tax breaks working to their disadvantage while favoring those at the top of the income ladder. Forty-two percent of Americans have said they favor tax structures that overwhelmingly help those in the upper strata income brackets, and 44 percent think that business faces either too much or the right amount of regulation.[39]

Using measures other than assets and income also reveals disparity between the elite and the rest of the population. Eighty-nine percent of burglars are sentenced to serve an average of more than four years in prison, while 63 percent of fraudsters are sentenced to an average of just sixteen months and 42 percent of tax evaders serve an average of twelve months.[40] The federal drug laws of the 1980s penalized street users of crack far more heavily than white-collar users of cocaine. In 2008, over 5,200 workers were killed on the job and 50,000 workers succumbed to diseases related to their workplace, putting the U.S. at a ranking of twenty-first among industrialized countries in rate of killed or injured workers.[41] Soldiers serving in combat are generally known to come predominantly from the lower economic strata. Finally, fifty million people in the U.S. were without health insurance and 80 percent were underinsured until the Obama health plan passed over the objections of many who stood to benefit from its provisions.

Corporate welfare rules America. Huge government subsidies go to energy and agriculture corporations making enormous profit. In the country's agricultural industry, the four largest companies control 81 percent of its beef production, 59 percent of its pork, up to 75 percent of its chicken, 61 percent of its wheat, 80 percent of its soy beans, and 57 percent of its corn. Although Barack Obama was purported to have acquired most of the record campaign donations he received from small donors, the fact is that three-quarters of his funds came from large donors. It was the opinion of historian Arthur Schlesinger Sr. that American government was of, by, and for the corporation and economist John Kenneth Galbraith stated that American socialism was socialism for the rich. The dynamics of trickle down in the pyramid structure of American socioeconomic life, in fact, work in the opposite direction—those on the bottom rungs of the economic ladder support those few on the highest rungs who call for deregulation in the name of jobs but in fact reap the benefits of regulatory relaxation.

The political structure of patriarchal elitism to which Americans subscribe is established in the Old Testament in the covenant between God and his people: God takes care of his children, and the children are faithful to God. When Moses complained to the Lord that the burden of government was too heavy for him to carry alone, God commanded him to bring seventy men, chosen by elders, and present them at the tabernacle to be given the spirit of the laws by God. Thus was formed the patriarchal elite that was given the power of governance. Jesus had his inner circle, reproduced in Revelation as the body of saints who ruled the millennial period along with Christ before the final fall of Satan.

Ambivalence toward the Law

> Now therefore hearken, O Israel, onto the statutes and unto the judgments, which I teach you, for to do them, that ye may live, and go in and possess the land which the Lord God of your fathers giveth you. (Deuteronomy 4:1)

In April 2004, five large Wall Street investment banks pressured the SEC and received an exemption from capital reserve requirements that limited investment at their brokerage units. Four years later, decisions like this one, based on a belief in relaxed law enforcement relative to regulatory policies, came back to haunt not only Wall Street but all the Main Streets of the nation. Voluntary supervision for investment banks, an atmosphere of denial of tangible consequences, winking at the law as a way of business are all part of a largely nonpartisan stance that extends back to the creation of the country's financial system. Former super-lobbyist Jack Abramoff stated, "So much that happens in Washington stretches the envelope, skirts the spirit of the law and lives in the loopholes."[42]

Ambivalence toward the law is a fundamental American attitude. Problems are considered in terms of action, which is frequently translated into making more laws, but each new law is created with loopholes inviting more opportunities for creativity in skirting the law. Americans want laws but tend to think of the law as applicable to others rather than themselves. Those who go above and around the law are often revered as antiestablishment heroes or rewarded financially for beating the system. The biblical metaphor of the difficulty of the camel going through the eye of the needle is turned on its head in America, becoming instead the ease with which the individual or corporation goes through the loophole. What is within the law, what is outside the law, and what can be gotten away with are questions reflecting the *ethos* of American business and politics. Americans take pride as individuals in avoiding taxes (the average taxpayer pays about 85 percent of what he or she actually owes), while two of every three corporations paid no income tax from 1998 through 2005.[43] Financial crises evoke cries of greed on the part of Wall Street, but greed is institutionalized throughout the body politic in laws and policies made by politicians and policy makers reflecting the underlying attitude of the population at large.

Again American consciousness follows the underlying biblical narrative. God gave his children manna from heaven "that I may prove them, whether they will walk in my law, or no."[44] Yet, God's children constantly fell away from his law, and the Old Testament can be seen as a story of the back and forth of contractual negotiations between God and his children through the mediation of their leaders. Of the first five books of the Old Testament, three—Leviticus, Numbers, and Deuteronomy—are largely taken up with the issue of the law, the formation of the law, and penalties for transgressions.[45] Moses teaches his people to obey the laws the Lord has given him, saying, "Keep therefore and do them; for this is your wisdom and your understanding in the sight of the nations, which shall hear all these statutes, and say, Surely this great nation is a wise and understanding people," yet Moses broke God's laws . . . literally, an image that gives metaphorical testimony to the ambivalence with which God's law was held by his children.[46]

In this light, American individualism can be seen as a derivative of the biblical dynamic of privileging the line of unique individuals who have a direct relationship with God—Adam, Noah, Abraham, Isaac, David—to Jesus who gives up the game of earthly rule—give unto Caesar what is Caesar's. Paul then writes that after faith is established, there is no need for earthly law as teacher because all laws are God's.[47] The self-interested American who has forgotten Tocqueville's call for right understanding through an eye to the community replaces faith in God with faith in self, feels above earthly laws, and becomes beholden only to the god of the self within.

Consumerism and Material Well-being

> And that ye may prolong your days in the land, which the Lord sware unto you to give unto them and to their seed, a land that floweth with milk and honey. (Deuteronomy 11:9)

For the Puritans, material well-being was a sign of God's beneficence. Faith in God was reflected through work on earth, which was, in turn, rewarded materially by God. The Puritans turned this idea around so that one's wealth became viewed as a sign of one's virtue and making money was seen as an extension of God's blessing—if one was wealthy, then one was pure. Adam Smith's *The Wealth of Nations* and the Declaration of Independence emerged in the same year, 1776. Shortly afterward, Capitalism took the hand of her sister Democracy and began to define America's pursuit of happiness through freedom to acquire and consume following "the inalienable right" to "the pursuit of happiness." At the time of the nation's founding, the statesmen of the north who favored manufacturing, particularly Franklin and Hamilton, furthered this idea into a political right to wealth—for the individual *and* for the individual corporation. The American mantra of the nineteenth century, manifest destiny, was not only the conquest of land but the acquisition of riches. Traveling evangelists heralded the idea that high profits were a sign of a commitment to Christian principles. The Gilded Age of the later nineteenth century was changed only moderately through trust legislation around the turn of the century. There ensued a series of political-economic cycles of world war, economic boom, depression, world war, boom, economic downturn, war in Southeast Asia, economic upturn, and recession. The massive economic meltdown of 2008/2009 merely followed a pattern—twelve recessions since World War II, all fueled by government deficit spending, followed by lowered interest rates, easy credit, and relaxed regulation—a vicious cycle of income-chasing prices and boom-chasing bust, all in the name of market well-being.

America tends to enter into crisis mode when it is not spending enough.[48] From the 1950s through the 1980s Americans spent 90 percent of what they took in, and in more recent years the figure was closer to all of what was earned. In the first half of 2008, lenders wrote off around $21 billion in bad credit card debt. Looming over the world as appetite itself, America with 5 percent of the world's population consumes about a third of the earth's natural resources, including a quarter of its oil, 8 million trees per month for mail order catalogs, and 214 billion gallons of water daily, mostly for industrial purposes. America throws away 426,000 cell phones per day and 106,000 aluminum cans every thirty seconds. Two-thirds of America's adult population is overweight while one-third is obese, and estimates of childhood obesity range from 16 to 33 percent.[49] America's spending tastes include almost $12 billion annually on bottled water, and 2 million plastic bottles are used every five seconds. Americans watch on average four and a half hours of television per day, and children are exposed to between five and six thousand ads per year for junk food. Each year $45 billion is spent on pets and $6 billion on Halloween paraphernalia.

The model for America as consumer nation, the American dream, stems from the promises of the Lord to the children of Israel in return for abiding in His ways.[50] "Behold, I will rain bread from heaven for you, and the people shall go out and gather a certain rate every day" is the promise of windfall to be had just around the corner.[51] An extension of this promise is that at the end of the road: "the Lord thy God shall have brought thee into the land . . . to give the great and goodly cities which thou buildest not, And houses full of all good things, which thou filledst not, and wells digged, which thy diggedst not, vineyards and olive trees, which thou plantedst not; when thou shalt have eaten and be full."[52] Here is the good life promised, the good things in life are there to be had without effort if one gives oneself over to the Lord. Indeed, "What hath God wrought?"[53]

Promised Land

> I saw a new heaven and a new earth: for the first heaven and the first earth were passed away; and there was no more sea. (John 21:1)

In the midst of the financial crisis which dominated the end of the 2008 presidential campaign, Barack Obama fell back upon the cardinal rule for American politicians—always be optimistic—and insisted that "better days are ahead." The days ahead turned out to be not better by much, and the crisis dragged on throughout his first term in office. Two weeks before Wachovia was forced to put itself up for sale, the CEO of the giant banking firm, Robert K. Steel, boldly stated, "We have a great future as an independent company . . . We're also focused on very exciting prospects when we get this thing right going forward."[54] Robert S. Fuld, CEO of the bankrupt Lehman Brothers investment house, apparently believed until just days before the bankruptcy that the company was in good condition despite the fact that all objective measures indicated otherwise. Here is the dominant voice of America speaking: all development, all growth, all optimism, all hope, all future, all opportunity, fueled by "the power of positive thinking." America is excess, perpetually oriented toward the promised land, the place of no limits, for which the apocalyptic cult of progress creates the most important product.

America is taken by the notion of establishing or developing the new. Throughout his term as president, Ronald Reagan alluded to religious imagery, most famously to the Puritan image of the sun rising on the city on a hill as a utopian vision. The American journey is toward the new Jerusalem, the house behind the white picket fence, the new Eden, paradise regained, the New Deal, the New Frontier, the Great Society, "I have a dream," Reagan's Star Wars defense for the America of his New Federalism, globalization. Americans are taken with the future and anything pointing toward the future—change, youth, in itself a value—and the new, a necessity.[55]

In its quest for promise America becomes enveloped in the spin of corporate media images which create a fabric of consciousness blanketing what Jean Baudrillard called "the desert of the real." In other words, America lives out an "as if" life of fabrication based on a matrix or "models of a real without origin," a virtual reality. The map is taken as the territory itself, and the replica serves to conceal a deprived community landscape.[56] The desert of the real, if revealed, would look something like this: Hunger continues to be a problem for many American children. American high schools have a graduation rate of two-thirds (one-half for minority students) and more than half of Americans aged 17–24 lack the math and English skills to qualify on a standardized military test. One of ten adults suffers from depression and one of five from hypertension, with one in five taking at least one psychiatric medication, just a portion of the hypermedicated orientation of the population at large under the influence of pharmaceutical companies.[57] Four hundred thousand Americans die annually from the effects of smoking. Water cannot be certified as safe for one in five of the population.[58] Sixteen percent of the entire gross domestic product goes to medical care expenses with only half of this actually improving health. Among industrialized nations America ranks among the last in infant mortality, overall preventable deaths, income inequality, security relative to food supply, student performance in math, and employment rate.[59] If America's mythic gaze is perpetually caught on the horizon, drawn toward a promised land of plastic images, and the spin of artificial language weaves an obfuscating veil, then the actuality of what is at hand inevitably becomes lost.

The imagination of America is derived from a myth of perpetual promise wherein Yahweh tells Abram to leave the home of his father for a new land which Abram believes will be better, and the pledge is renewed with Abram's descendants.[60] God tells Moses that the Israelites under his care in Egypt will be delivered unto this same promised land.[61] During the exile of the Jews, God restates his promise, "I will bring them again into their land that I gave unto their fathers."[62] Daniel goes further in his prophecy of a new heavenly order, a vision which anticipates that of John: "And he (God) that sat upon the throne said, Behold, I *make all things new* . . . and he carried me away in the spirit to a great and high mountain, and shewed me that great city, the holy Jerusalem, descending out of heaven from God."[63] It is this new Jerusalem which is the paradigmatic structure underlying the fantasyland of the American psyche.

Domination and Empire

> I will send my fear before thee, and will destroy all the people to whom thou shalt come, and I will make all thine enemies turn their backs unto thee. (Exodus 23:27)

Historically, a long line of popular and political figures in America have appeared as warrior/statesmen, messianic heroes stretching back to the Puritan leader William Bradford as "Nehemius Americanus" struggling against the New England wilderness, George Washington marching against the British, Ulysses Grant conquering the South, Theodore Roosevelt waving his "Big Stick," Woodrow Wilson warring against war itself, Ronald Reagan standing tall against communism, George W. Bush accomplishing his mission—Captain America ever trampling out the vintage. All are descendants of the conquering Messiah of Revelation, throwing out the evil beast.[64]

Whether it is the March of Dimes, a corporate sales campaign, the Wars on Poverty and Terror, American capitalism and neurosis globalized, or the school bully (160,000 children stay home from school daily for fear of being bullied), the American spirit warrior is ever on parade for the republic of the battle hymn, conquering new territory for the sake of the good. In a world seen as inherently competitive, America designates itself as rightfully dominant, historically co-opting outright land from Native Americans and Mexico.[65] In the twentieth century, whether launching military or economic conquests, America and its armies and corporations have taken pride in the "competitive advantage" which their zeal—a throwback to the zeal of the biblical children of Israel in their faith in God—enables them to obtain. Dante placed Empire in the Inferno, but Americans take pride in their desire for domination, even as they are dominated by the upper echelons of their own hierarchical socioeconomic structure. (The word "dominate" is associated with the root of the word "god.") For America, whether it is the ranking of an athletic team or the stock price of a company, number one is the only number.

America's Founding Fathers frequently thought in terms of empire. George Washington, a distiller and real estate agent by trade, had his own empire on the Ohio River Valley for development after his tenure as president. Jefferson's Louisiana Purchase brought the ideal of empire into fruition and gave rise to manifest destiny, the clear expression of America's violent co-option of anything foreign while in alliance with Providence. Although the beginning and the end of the century were marked by the American impulse to secure control of Canada, it was the west which was seen as the primary possibility for more territory, a new wilderness to be conquered as promised land.[66]

Eventually, the urge westward would go beyond the boundary of the West Coast, to the control of trade in the Asia, and eventual worldwide trade and globalization through American corporate capitalism of the twentieth century. The idea of globalization was prominent as early as 1916 when President Woodrow Wilson addressed the World Salesmanship Conference. He admonished the American peddlers, "Go out and sell goods that will make the world more comfortable and more happy and convert them to the principles of America."[67] The religious tone of American capitalism is clear: American commodities help convert other nations to the proper way of life, the American way. The good life is linked to consumer goods, and it is America that can provide them, with the ultimate result being the destabilization of local cultural life and American hegemony . . . Ronald McDonald become global.

The model for America's urge for empire is the Judeo-Christian conquering God. The Lord is depicted as a man of war who will do away with all the inhabitants of Canaan.[68] Joshua sacked Jericho in the name of the Lord with genocidal fury.[69] God's children are promised that they will be wholly delivered from their enemies with no holds barred and no prisoners taken.[70] Isaiah prophesies the return of the children of Israel giving voice to the Lord's words that He will feed their enemies their own flesh and have them drink their own blood.[71] The psalmist sings a song of vengeful wrath in which the enemy shall be broken by an iron rod and "dashed to pieces."[72] In Revelation, God calls upon humans to take part in the final war. Creatures like scorpions from the bottomless pit are described as torturing the godless, while a third of the men are killed by fire, smoke, and brimstone. An anonymous messianic warrior (the masked man of comic heroics), the King of Kings, emerges on a white horse, clothed in vesture dipped in blood, a sword emerging from his mouth with which he proceeds to kill the godless of the earth.[73] A final battle will take place a thousand years later in which God will send fire to kill Satan's followers, and he is thrown into a lake of fire.[74] It is within this Judeo-Christian image of domination and conquering that America finds its own identity.

Born in abundance, inspired by opportunity, nurtured in the imagination of growth and perpetual gain, spiritualized by a sense of God's blessing and call, forgetful of past, in denial of tragedy, obtuse to future consequence—this paradisiacal spell emerges as the controlling ideology of a national consciousness stemming from an underlying narrative based on biblical themes and imagery. Other nations and cultures may hold similar characteristics, and in America there have always been subdominant currents which run counter to the mainstream. If the country is to know itself, however, the material in this chapter suggests a predominant channel that would have to be navigated. An investigation of the different epochs of American history should provide a sense of the depth of this stream.

Notes

1. The Founding Fathers had already actually anticipated Tocqueville's fears: "The people . . . will forget themselves but in the sole faculty of making money"—Thomas Jefferson, quoted by Roger Kennedy in *Mr. Jefferson's Lost Cause* (London: Oxford University Press,

2008, 40). "I believe further that this is likely to be well administered for a Course of years and can only end in Despotism as other forms have done before it, when the People shall become so corrupted as to need Despotic Government, being incapable of any other," from Benjamin Franklin's closing speech at the Constitutional Convention, quoted by Edmund S. Morgan in "A Tract for the Times" (*New York Review of Books*, December 18, 2003, 28). "Oh my country, how I mourn over . . . thy contempt of Wisdom and Virtue and overweening admiration of fools and knaves! The never failing effects of democracy!"—John Adams, 1806, quoted in Steve Fraser and Gary Gerstle, eds., *Ruling America: A History of Wealth and Power in a Democracy* (Cambridge, MA: Harvard University Press, 2005, 8).

2. T. H. Breen, *The Marketplace of Revolution: How Consumer Politics Shaped American Independence* (London: Oxford University Press, 2004).

3. The meltdown itself, in which banks were buying packages of mortgages of unknowable value, was prefigured by many crises concerning buying and selling of real estate. One of the earliest was in pre-Revolutionary New England when land in Vermont was sold by an unscrupulous governor of New Hampshire who did not have title to the land he was selling, land which actually belonged to colonial New York.

4. James Hillman, *Mythic Figures* (Putnam, CT: Spring Publications, 2007), 339–40.

5. C. G. Jung, "The Complications of American Psychology," in *The Collected Works of C. G. Jung,* vol. 10, *Civilization in Transition*, trans. R. F. C. Hull (Princeton, NJ: Princeton University Press, 1964), 511.

6. See Ernest Lee Tuveson, *Redeemer Nation: The Idea of America's Millennial Role* (Chicago: University of Chicago Press, 1968); Robert Bellah, "Civil Religion in America," in *Religion in America,* ed. William C. McLoughlin and Robert Bellah (Boston: Houghton Mifflin, 1968); Conrad Cherry, ed., *God's New Israel: Religious Interpretations of American Destiny* (Englewood Cliffs, NJ: Prentice Hall, 1971); Robert Jewett and John Shelton Lawrence, *Captain America and the Crusade against Evil: The Dilemma of Zealous Nationalism* (Grand Rapids, MI: William B. Eerdmans, 2003); Christopher Collins, *Homeland*

Mythology: Biblical Narrative in American Culture (University Park: Pennsylvania State University Press, 2007).

7. In the seventeenth century Thomas Hobbes, hoping to reduce the incidence of religious warfare which had ravished Europe, proclaimed a separation between politics and the divine. Although the Founding Fathers followed this idea explicitly, America emerged as a nation more in line with its underlying Calvinist roots connecting government, economy, and religion.

8. See Nicholas Guyatt, *Providence and the Invention of the United States, 1607–1876* (Cambridge, MA: Cambridge University Press, 2007).

9. See Guyatt, *Providence and the Invention of the United States, 1607–1876*; and Jon Meachim, *American Gospel: God, the Founding Fathers, and the Making of a Nation* (New York: Random House, 2005).

10. Francis Jennings, *The Creation of America through Revolution to Empire* (Cambridge, MA: Cambridge University Press, 2000), 207.

11. Lyndon Johnson's War on Poverty actually created increased poverty in the Navajo Nation because it undermined the traditional system of barter.

12. The *New York Globe* advocated the annexation of Mexico in 1847 because "'it would seem' that its citizens 'had brought upon themselves the vengeance of the Almighty, and we ourselves had been raised up to overthrow AND UTTERLY DESTROY THEM as a separate and distinct nation.'" Joan Didion, "Mr. Bush and the Divine," *The New York Review of Books*, November 6, 2003, 84.

13. Deuteronomy 14:2.

14. Deuteronomy 28:1. Note also, "I will take you to me for a people" (Exodus 6:7) as a "light to the Gentiles, that thou mayest be my *salvation* unto the end of the earth" (Deuteronomy 7:6; italics added) and "[T]he Lord has vouched thee this day to be his peculiar people, as he promised thee" (Deuteronomy 26:18).

15. In 1629, John White wrote, in "General Considerations for Planting New England," that the undertaking was to be a "bulwark . . . against the Kingdom of the Antichrist which the Jesuits labour to rear up in all quarters of the world." Quoted in Paul Boyer, *When Time Shall Be No More: Prophecy Belief in Modern American Culture* (Cambridge, MA: Harvard University Press, 1992), 68.

16. Jewett and Lawrence, *Captain America and the Crusade against Evil*, 256.

17. See Colleen Elizabeth Kelley, *Post-9/11 American Presidential Rhetoric: A Study of Protofascist Discourse* (Lanham, MD: Lexington Books, 2007), 175–181.

18. Cal Thomas and Bob Beckel, "Must We Always Have Partisan Presidents?" *USA Today*, February 11, 2012, 9A.

19. See Scott L. Malcomson, *One Drop of Blood: The American Misadventure of Race* (New York: Farrar, Straus, Giroux, 2000).

20. Jennifer Schuessler, "Drug Policy as Race Policy," *New York Times*, March 7, 2012, C1.

21. In the 1980s, 28 percent of Americans admitted a dislike of the Japanese, who were perceived to be economic competitors. Bryan Caplan, *The Myth of the Rational Voter: Why Democracies Choose Bad Policies* (Princeton, NJ: Princeton University Press, 2007), 39.

22. Cameron McWhirter, "Southern Baptists Pick Black Leader," *Wall Street Journal*, June 20, 2012, A3.

23. See Robert M. Fogelson, *Bourgeois Nightmares: Suburbia, 1870–1930* (New Haven, CT: Yale University Press, 2007).

24. Genesis 3:14. The other is a beast to be conquered in Isaiah 30:6; Daniel 7:11, 17, 19; Acts 10:12; Revelation 4:6–9, 5:6–14, 6:1–7, 7:11, 11:7, 11:13, 14:3, 14:9, 14:11, 15:2, 16:2, 16:10–13, 16:17, 19:4, 19:11–16, 19:19–20, 20:3–4, and 20:10. Daniel dreams that four beasts, symbolizing four world kingdoms are slain by the Son of Man, prefiguring the final battle in Revelation. Revelation depicts the blasphemous force against God as a sea monster with seven heads and ten horns, opposed by the goodness and innocence of the Lamb, and his followers, "without fault before the throne of God" (Revelation 14:5). In contrast, Navajo mythology has the hero vanquish the monster, but then he learns from it the secrets of healing.

25. Revelation 21:8, 27.

26. Thomas Singer brings our attention to the American sense of journey as conquest in the 1872 painting by John Gast titled *American Progress* in which the "Star of Empire" leads the migration west conquering everything in its path. T. Singer, "A Personal Reflection on Politics and the American Soul," *Spring: A Journal of Archetype and Culture*, vol. 78, *Politics and the American Soul* (Fall 2007), 170.

27. Fourteen percent of the population relocates annually, in part due to the fact that the average American job tenure is less than any other industrialized nation, according to David Brooks, "Our Sprawling Supersize Utopia," *New York Times Magazine,* April 4, 2004, 46–51. See Travis Madsen, Benjamin Davis, and Phineas Baxandall, *Road Work Ahead: Holding Government Accountable for Fixing America's Crumbling Roads and Bridges,* U.S. Public Interest Research Group Educational Fund, April 2010; and Jim Hightower, *The Hightower Lowdown,* November 2006, 4.

28. The character played by Julie Christie, an Alzheimer's patient in the film *Far From Her,* ironically observes while watching a television news clip of the war in Iraq, "Couldn't they remember Vietnam?"

29. Bob Herbert, "Risking the Future," *New York Times,* February 3, 2009, A23.

30. Exodus 14:15.

31. The bodily suffering of John McCain as a POW in Vietnam was described in great anatomical detail prior to his confirmation as candidate for president at the 2008 Republican Convention.

32. The forty-year wandering is a test of faith: "And thou shalt remember all the ways which the Lord thy God led thee these forty years in the wilderness, to humble thee, and to prove thee, to know what was in thine heart, whither thou wouldst keep his commandments or no" (Deuteronomy 8:2), and John 16:33.

33. See Fraser and Gerstle, *Ruling America.*

34. C. G. Jung, "Mind and Earth," in *The Collected Works of C. G. Jung,* vol. 10., *Civilization in Transition*, trans. R. F. C. Hull (Princeton, NJ: Princeton University Press, 1964), 48.

35. "Income for the top 1 percent of Americans nearly tripled from 1979 to 2007, far outpacing other groups, the CBO said." "What's News," *Wall Street Journal*, October 26, 2011, 1A.

36. Jeff Madrick, "The Power of the Super-Rich," *New York Review of Books,* July 18, 2002, 25; Jim Hightower and Phillip Frazier, "Facts—Not Myths—about Our Economy," *The Hightower Lowdown*, May 2010, 1.

37. Lou Dubose, "Who's Afraid of Elizabeth Warren?" *Washington Spectator*, June 1, 2011, 1.

38. Jeff Madrick, "The Wall Street Leviathan," *New York Review of Books,* April 28, 2011, 70; and Edward Wyatt, "SEC Is Avoiding

Tough Sanctions for Large Banks," *New York Times*, February 3, 2012, A1.

39. Alex Berenson, "How Free Should a Free Market Be?" *New York Times,* October 5, 2008, B1.

40. *Public Citizen News,* May/June 2004, 2.

41. Jim Hightower and Phillip Frazer, *The Hightower Lowdown,* August 2010, 2.

42. *Public Citizen News,* September/October 2008, 2.

43. Michael H. Higley, *By the Numbers* [investment newsletter], August 13, 2012. Likewise, in 1900 Andrew Carnegie earned $23 million from stock he owned in his steel company, while the average worker in the company earned just $4,500, and Carnegie paid no income tax.

44. Exodus 16:4.

45. Obedience was the condition for the well-being of the promised land (Deuteronomy 11:28, 26:18, 28:1–2): "Behold, I set before you this day a blessing and a curse; A blessing, if ye obey the commandments of the Lord your God, which I command you this day: And a curse, if ye will not obey the commandments of the Lord your God, but turn aside out of the way" (Deuteronomy 11:26–28).

46. Deuteronomy 4:6.

47. Galatians 4:23–5.

48. Iconic inventor Thomas Edison famously stated that he didn't want to waste time inventing what wouldn't sell.

49. *Wall Street Journal*, August 14, 2012, A6.

50. "[The Lord] will give you the rain of your land in his due season . . . that thou mayest gather in thy corn, and thy wine, and thine oil. And [the Lord] will send grass in the fields for thy cattle that thou mayest eat and be full" (Deuteronomy 11:14–15). "[A]ll these blessings shall come on thee, and overtake thee if thou shalt hearken unto the voice of the Lord thy God. Blessed shalt thou be in the city, and blessed shalt thou be in the field . . . The Lord shall command the blessings upon thee in thy storehouses, and in all that thou settest thine hand unto, . . . And the Lord shall make thee plenteous in goods, in the fruit of thy body, and in the fruit of thy cattle, and in the fruit of thy ground . . . The Lord shall open unto thee his good treasure, the heaven to give the rain unto thy

land . . . and to bless all the work of thine hand . . . And the Lord shall make thee the head, and not the tail: and thou shalt be above only" (Deuteronomy 28:2, 4, 8, 11, 12, 13).

51. Exodus 16:4.

52. Deuteronomy 6:10–11.

53. Numbers 23:23.

54. Andrew Ross Sorkin, "What Goes Before a Fall: Optimism," *New York Times,* September 30, 2008, C1.

55. The issue of abortion, which involves the termination of the life of the fetus as representative of the new and the future, can be seen in this light as central to Americans.

56. Jean Baudrillard, *Simulations*, trans. Paul Foss, Paul Patton, and Philip Beitchman (New York: Semiotext(e), 1983), 2.

57. Shirley S. Wang, "Psychiatric Drug Use Spreads," *Wall Street Journal,* November 16, 2011, A3.

58. Charles Duhigg, "Millions in U.S. Drink Dirty Water, Records Say," *New York Times,* December 8, 2009, A1.

59. Charles H. Blow, "Empire at the End of Decadence," *New York Times,* February 19, 2011, A19.

60. Genesis 26:3, 28:4, 48:4, 50:24.

61. "Every place whereon the soles of your feet shall tread shall be yours: from the wilderness and Lebanon, from the river, the river Euphrates, even unto the uttermost sea shall your coast be" (Deuteronomy 11:24).

62. Jeremiah 16:15.

63. "I saw in the night visions, and, behold, one like the Son of Man came with the clouds of heaven, and came to the Ancient of Days . . . And there was given him dominion, and glory, and a kingdom, that all people, nations, and languages, should serve him" (Daniel 7:13–14); Revelation 21:1–10, italics added.

64. "[B]ehold a pale horse, and his name that sat on him was Death, and Hell followed with him. And power was given unto them over the fourth part of the earth, to kill with sword, and with huger and with death and with the beast of the earth . . . For the great day of his wrath is come: and who shall be able to stand?" (Revelation 6:8, 17).

65. "The elect are a wrathful people because they are the natural enemies of the non-elect," declared Elder Daniel Parker, Baptist Texas settler, in Roger Hodge, "Hunter-Capitalists," *London Review of Books*, December 15, 2011, 28.

66. One of the forays of the American Revolutionary army was an unsuccessful attempt to conquer Canada.

67. John Brewer, "Selling the American Way," *New York Review of Books*, November 30, 2006, 58.

68. Exodus 15:3, 15.

69. "And they utterly destroyed all that was in the city, both man and woman, young and old, and ox and sheep, and ass, with the edge of the sword" (Joshua 6:2).

70. "And when the Lord thy God shall deliver them before thee, thou shalt smite them, and utterly destroy them: thou shalt make no covenant with a them, nor shew mercy unto them" (Deuteronomy 7:2); "but for the wickedness of these nations the Lord doth drive them out from before thee" (Deuteronomy 9:4). In Canaan "shall no man be able to stand before you: for the Lord your God shall lay the fear of you and the dread of you upon all the land that ye shall tread upon" (Deuteronomy 11:25).

71. Isaiah 49:26.

72. Psalm 2:9.

73. Revelation 19:11–16.

74. Revelation 20:9.

4

Nehemius Americanus: Puritan Consciousness and American Soul

In the past I have written to you in rather ample detail about my return from those new regions . . . which can be called a new world, since our ancestors had no knowledge of them and they are entirely new matter to those who hear about them.

—Amerigo Vespucci

A mong the many striking impressions left from 9/11 was the stark contrast between the deep profundity of its images and the flatness of America's sense of meaning in relation to the event. The poverty of imagination that America brought to this epic happening might be seen as indicative of the depleted state of citizenship in America—citizen as victim, reactor, and consumer. If we see this as a matter of political psyche, then as psychotherapists of culture in the face of collective disaster, we would use history as a means of psychological investigation toward an understanding of American identity. Such an endeavor reveals that the three catch phrases that most characterized America's reaction to 9/11—"God bless America," "Let's roll!" and "Keep buying"—are in fact derived from three fundamental interrelated aspects of American character: its identification with spirit, its tendency toward domination, and the religious foundation of its economic values. These character traits can be identified as central to the core values of a group which had a central role in the founding of American culture, the Puritans.

Although America was initially settled by both plantation owners in the South and the New England Puritans, it was the Puritan legacy that has had the most profound effect in defining American character and consciousness.[1] The Puritan work ethic, economic orientation, and leaning toward technology, all intertwined with its spiritual and moral values, produced a predominant paradigm for the country as it evolved and congealed.

Puritanism was established in England in the late sixteenth century under the influence of John Calvin (1509–1564), who in turn had followed in the footsteps of Martin Luther (1483–1546), the Augustinian monk who initiated the Protestant Reformation. The English Puritans were opposed to the Church of England with its rituals and hierarchies and wanted a more direct and vital relationship with God. Calvin depicted life on earth as a fallen existence modeled by Jesus's sojourn in the wilderness. Calvinist teaching saw earthly life as "a gulf of grief in a sty of filthiness,"[2] its vastness governed by Satan, its misery a conduit to Christ, and the Puritans embraced these teachings. Two centuries later the American Puritan Jonathan Edwards would echo Calvin, saying, "Natural men are held in the hand of God, over the pit of hell . . . The devils waiting for them, hell is gaping for them, the flames gather and flash about them, and would fain lay hold on them, and swallow them up . . .You have nothing to stand upon, nor any thing to take hold of; there is nothing between you and hell but the air."[3]

The Puritan mind considered the fallen condition of man as a gift from God because it enabled humans to redeem themselves in His eyes. For the Puritans who settled in America, the physical terrain itself and the struggle to survive in it were viewed as representative of this fallen state. The first Puritan colonists on the *Mayflower* intended to settle in the Hudson River Valley but storms forced them to turn back to Massachusetts.[4] It took these settlers, now rendered "boat people" by the weather, a total of six weeks from the date of their arrival off the coast of Massachusetts to land permanently. During this time the wife of future governor William Bradford apparently committed suicide by throwing herself overboard when confronted with the harsh spectacle of winter. Bradford would later describe the land as "sharp and violent, and subject to cruel and fierce storms . . . [a] hideous and desolate wilderness, full of wild beasts and wild men . . . [with] little solace or content in respect of any outward objects . . . [while] all things stand upon them with a weather-beaten face, and the whole country, full of woods and thickets, represented a wild and savage hue."[5] For the first Puritans, this dark specter of a land which presented itself as adversarial other represented a divinely sanctioned means to redemption through suffering. Increase Mather preached, "God has covenanted with his people that sanctified afflictions shall be their portion . . . The usual method of divine Providence [is] by the greatest Miseries to prepare for the greatest Mercies . . . Without doubt, the Lord Jesus hath a peculiar respect unto this place, and for this people."[6]

The Puritans believed that redemption could be achieved not only through knowledge of the scriptures, but also through action and will. They found a mythic exemplar for their wilderness struggle in the Old as well as the New Testaments. The struggles of the Hebrew children of God were then reflected in turn by the sufferings of Christ, the ultimate model of redemption. In creating a mythic consciousness, the Pilgrims aligned themselves with the eye of God through a dual dynamic. Their experienced suffering led to redemption as modeled in scripture; travail engenders redemption. At the same time, the divinely sanctioned scheme of the scriptures, locating travail in the wilderness, pointed them toward this wild land. The suffering of the body led to a spiritual understanding, and the prophetic spiritual model for understanding was made manifest in the physical struggle to survive.

The act of settling the new land became the channel of redemption with the promise of paradise regained through the forward movement of history. John Winthrop called the quest of his followers the "accomplishment of that Prophesie concerning the coming together of . . . dry bones . . . the Holy City . . . descend[ing] upon the hill of Zion."[7] Cotton Mather exclaimed, "For the New Jerusalem there will be a seat found in wide America," and characterized "the Holy City in America [as] a city the streets whereof will be pure Gold."[8] The promised land was at hand, and it was an occasion of great triumph. Increase Mather wrote, "Jerusalem was, New England is, they were, you are God's own, God's covenant people . . . put but New England's name instead of that of Jerusalem."[9] Edward Johnson proclaimed, "This is the place where the Lord will create a new Heaven and a new Earth," and Jonathan Edwards prophesied, "The Latter Day Glory is probably to begin in America."[10] Just as God's children had sojourned across water and wilderness, so had the Pilgrim Puritans; just as God put heathen as obstacles to his children, so He placed Native Americans as obstacles to the Puritans; and just as He fed and clothed His children, so did He the Puritans. America would be the new Jerusalem.

Sainthood was fused with nationality, a federal identity with a mythical work of redemption. The Puritans found exemplars for their experience in the biblical chain of redemptive figures. Adam was expelled from the garden, Noah gathered his flock in an ark, Abraham led his people out from Ur to found a new identity, and Moses led his people across an ocean, through a wilderness to a new land. Cotton Mather wrote a biography of the great Puritan leader John Winthrop in which he placed Winthrop in this line by likening him to the Old Testament prophet, Nehemiah. Both led their people westward out of exile to form a new community in a wasteland surrounded by heathens. Both inspired their people to take up the covenant anew while tending to the practical business of founding a city.[11]

And God graced his newly found children in this endeavor by providing for their material concerns. Miraculous acts which provided for everyday needs amidst the deprivation of "the savage deserts of America" were indications to the Puritans that God was not dealing with them as he would with just any people.[12] "Some Acts of God are acts of common providence, and so he feeds us, and clothes us . . . Some acts of God are acts of special privilege . . . Some acts of God are acts of wonder."[13]

America was a divinely sanctioned, utopian New World granted as a form of salvation, and its wilderness and the struggle for survival only added to the sense of destiny that would ultimately lead to world redemption. The Puritans believed that God had been saving the New World for His grace, so that America and its process was destiny made manifest. "There are no persons in all the world unto whom God speaketh by His Providence as he doth us," declared Increase Mather.[14] The journey of the universal soul was America's journey, and in the founding of America "the light of the city on a hill [had] become the light of the world" in the words of John Winthrop.[15] Here in this utopian dream, the soul of America as redeemer nation, symbol of universal rebirth, was itself born under the gaze of both the world and Providence, the earthly and the heavenly eye on the newborn child of the Divine.

The Puritan focus on the body politic was the result of a long evolution in Western consciousness regarding the tension between notions of the soul as collective versus the soul as individual.[16] The tension between individual and collective can be traced historically to two sources, the humanist Enlightenment of the Renaissance and the Protestant revolt of the Reformation. Both placed authority within the individual, but did so in a context which contained a perspective from the standpoint of the larger world. Humanism brought an orientation toward spiritual life into a more concrete form, from the perfection of the medieval heaven to the Renaissance celebration of earthly experience. It glorified the human intellect and body and made a claim for the self-determination of the individual. Through the invention of "personality," the individual emerged bearing what Erasmus called its "natural gifts," a visible microcosm reflecting the invisible macrocosm.

In the Italian Renaissance, earth became a mirror of heaven, observable from a detached distance.[17] Brunelleschi invented linear perspective by looking at the gate of the Florentine Baptistry through an actual mirror. Linear perspective designated the center of the frame of perspective, the vanishing point, as the *logos,* the earthly derivative of the eye of God. This viewpoint, which held objectivity as in alignment with divine perspective, enabled the depiction of life as literal and ultimately gave rise to the modern sensibility of control over the earth through technology. Petrarch climbed Mont Ventoux and looked around at the earth in wonder. Petrarch's wonderment was at first with the earth as a reflection of heaven, but then he became even more awestruck at his discovery of the "inward eye" of the individual soul which he found incomparable. Likewise Dante, upon his ascent to the most sublime moment in paradise when God was to be revealed, saw an image of none other than himself. "Self" for Brunelleschi, Petrarch, and Dante was an experience of soul that occurred within a context between earth and heaven, inner and outer, self and other.

Luther's theology was based on individual faith without ecclesiastical trappings as the foundation of spiritual life. The Reformation ethic taught that the gifts of human life were God's gifts, and the individual self was subject to God. Man lived as a potential son of God with Christ as exemplar. Although he had removed the individual soul from ecclesiastical authority, Luther still preached the duty of obedience to earthly political authority. This idea was actualized by his spiritual offspring, John Calvin, who formed the government of the city of Geneva as a theocracy with civil authorities subject to the church. For the Puritans, church and state were inextricably intertwined.

Puritan consciousness held that the individual self was a self modeled after an ideal of "self nothingness" in the service of God. "None is worse than thyself" was the Puritan preaching. Self love was actually love of God made possible through the contempt of one's self. Calvin wrote that the soul on a journey to redemption "starts with holy despair in ourselves," and the way of redemption was a process of "[ridding] ourselves of self trust."[18] Christ was the true mirror of election, and the more one looked to the figure of Christ as reflection, the greater the chances of redemption. Stripping the self of its deceitful faculties meant avoiding the pleasures of the senses and the play of imagination. The certainty of God's grace was attained through faith in the spirit of reason made manifest through God's word as revealed in scripture.

The heavy emphasis on self-negation in Puritan consciousness masked its opposite, an arrogance which was made manifest in a collective hierarchical structure of cultural dominance. Liberty for the individual soul was carried paradoxically through the individual's subjection and obedience to God's will as revealed in scripture and interpreted by God's chosen representatives on earth. The individual Puritan lived with an acute awareness of the context of a collective or commonwealth of souls. John Winthrop wrote, "We must delight in each other, make the other's condition our own, always have before our eyes our community as members of the same body . . . knit together in this work as one man."[19] While the focus of Puritan doctrine was the individual, in practice the individual was subject to collective authority, government seen as an expression of God's authority.

For the Puritans, church and state (sacred and secular) were interwoven in a theocracy. Government was needed for the commonwealth of individual souls, and Puritans believed that government should be modeled after God's laws as expressed through scripture. Every experience was ratified by the infallible standard of the Word, especially the Old Testament and its clauses, which were seen as "codes of laws," to be interpreted by an elite patriarchal intelligentsia given privilege as God's spokesmen on earth.

A sensibility of domination, the desire to extend power over the other, was manifest in American character from its beginnings within the consciousness of the Puritan community. This community was structured as a hierarchy with the elect few at the top. Their laws, as reflections of God's laws, were models for redemption of the individual soul living in an earthly purgatory. Although the laws of the elders were meant to exclude the ungodly, the council recognized the value of prudence. When one lost his way, he could be redeemed through subjection to the judgment of the patriarchs. Thus interpretation of law as a reflection of scripture opened the way to hermetic social control by the elite. The seeds had been sewn for what would become the power and monetary gap in American culture between the general population and the privileged few at the top of the socioeconomic hierarchy. The Puritans had brought with them a social consciousness tending toward a rigid political system, but within this structure a mercurial element was at play that benefited an elite circle. Hierarchy, aristocracy, and theocracy merged to form a unique political identity.

Toward the end of his poem, *Paradise Lost*, the Puritan writer John Milton describes Adam and Eve departing from Eden.

> They, looking back all th' Eastern side beheld
> Of Paradise, so late thir happy seat.
> Wav'd over by that flaming Brand; the Gate
> With dreadful Faces thronged and fiery Arms:
> Some natural tears they drop'd, but wiped them soon;
> The World was all before them, where to choose
> Their place of rest, and Providence thir guide:
> They, hand in hand, with wand'ring steps and slow,
> Through Eden took thir solitary way.[20]

Here, the human soul is depicted as facing the world as fallen and making its "solitary way," the archetypal model of the "soul's journey." Shortly before this exodus, the archangel Michael says to Adam:

> Only add
> Deeds to thy knowledge answerable, add Faith,
> Add Virtue, Patience, Temperance; add Love,
> By name to come called Charity, the soul
> Of all the rest: then wilt thou not be loath
> To leave this Paradise, but shalt possess
> A paradise within thee, happier far.[21]

The world as habitat may be fallen, but a new paradise awaits within. The means to this new Jerusalem for the Puritans was to live by virtue, the uppermost being deeds. Work is invested with moral spirit and offers the way to redemption on earth. It is no longer the oppressive toil of the Middle Ages, but a vehicle for salvation. Existence in the world provides the opportunity of God's call to labor, and work puts man in the hands of God. A calling could come in secular form through vocation as regimented economic enterprise. The plain middle-class tradesman gained ethical approval in full measure from God who blessed his trade.

The Puritans imagined money itself to be enspirited.[22] The sociologist Max Weber, in his essay "The Protestant Ethic and the 'Spirit' of Capitalism," wrote that with the Protestant ethic of tireless labor as a calling, capitalism became a spiritual enterprise. Capitalism vests work with a moral spirit, economic enterprise becomes greater than those it employs, and work itself takes precedent over the worker. For Weber, there was a spirit in capitalism that called for devotion, and money making itself became a form of morality which on the one hand brings one to God and on the other indicates God's grace.

For the Puritans, wealth achieved as the fruit of labor in one's calling received the blessing of God. God's purpose was seen in the revealing to certain of His children the possibility for profit. Richard Baxter, writing as a Puritan become theological economist and capitalist of the spirit, admonished, "If God show you a way in which you may lawfully get more than in another way (without wrong to your soul or to any other), if you refuse this, and choose the less gainful way, you cross one of the ends of your calling, and you refuse to be God's steward, and to accept His gifts and use them for Him when He requireth it."[23] Man was the steward of God's gifts on earth and through perseverance at his calling and the preservation of possessions gained in His name, man achieved God's grace.

Here was a radical reversal of Jesus's assertion that earthly wealth belonged to the earthly realm, while God's wealth was spiritual— "Render unto Caesar the things that are Caesar's and unto God the things that are God's."[24] To deny the economic enhancement of God's gifts was itself a sin! Even Calvin approved of wealth for the clergy as an indication of prestige in God's eyes and permitted them to invest for profit. The Calvinist doctrine was that success reveals virtue (goodness in the Eye of God), and the Puritan ethic furthered this with the idea that the source of wealth or poverty lay in the individual. The precursor to the American self-made man and consumer society had been formed.

The Puritans did not view wealth as sinful, but rather found the temptations that sometimes accompanied wealth, including pleasure and idleness (which in turn lead to imagination!), to be unacceptable. John Cotton depicted the model Puritan as a man who would "rise early, and goe to bed late, and eate the bread of carefullnesse, not a sinful, but a provident care, and . . . avoid idelness, cannot indure to spend any idle time, takes all opportunities to be doing something, early and late and looseth no opportunity, go anyway and betstir himselfe for profit, this will he doe most diligently in his calling: And yet bee a man deadhearted to the world."[25] Here is the spiritual ancestor of an American culture that would eventually go manic— action for action's sake, growth for growth's sake. Will exerted within God's order could be used to gain profit, and a thin line was thus formed between God's will and human desire, between sanctified entrepreneurial spirit and covetousness.

Weber wrote that American culture was the beneficiary of a movement that put obedience to God ahead of obedience to state, freeing the individual of deference to traditional office, encouraging personal dynamism and initiative while at the same time engendering ambivalence to law. The shadow of this ethos is that individual initiative slides over into corporate manipulation; profit in the name of the Lord easily becomes profit for personal aggrandizement. Nevertheless, in Puritan America, material gain seen as indication of God's approval acted as a means for establishing a moral order. Hard work,

meticulousness, punctiliousness, discipline, patience—all were seen
as spiritual virtues revealed by economic success. Through economic
means a spiritual community was established, albeit one with an
emphasis on political dominance. Individual and community life
became ordered through an imperceptible authority of which
economic well-being was the visible reward.

The initial Puritan enterprise in America was a business company,
the Massachusetts Bay Company, which was founded for the purpose
of establishing a colony in the New World for Puritans seeking asylum
from political/religious persecution in England. A charter was granted
in 1629 by King Charles I. When the directors of the company came
to America, they transformed their business into a one-party
government in which religion, business, and government were all one.
When John Winthrop went back to England to plead for further capital
from the stockholders, he used the hard sell: "Consider the difficulty
of plantations, when God himself would transplant Israel into Canaan,
he was forced to feed them and clothe them by miracle."[26] What had
started as a modest fishing venture had turned into a full fledged
mercantile effort, a commonwealth based on Old Testament tradition
("Let Israel be . . . our glass to view our faces in") with a board of
directors serving in the place of Hebrew judges.[27] In this enterprise,
Cotton Mather saw clear signs of divine mandate, "the blessing of
Christ on the Labors of an American."[28] Jonathan Edwards later
prophesied both economic and spiritual globalization with his words,
"The changing of the course of trade, and the supplying of the world
with its treasures from America is a type of and forerunner of what is
approaching in spiritual things when the world shall be supplied with
spiritual treasures from America."[29] If money was directly associated
with fruits of the Divine, then the success of American commerce meant
that a prophecy had been fulfilled.

Political dominance, spiritual identification, and economic
morality are all woven together in the Puritan tapestry to form a utopian
canvas that gave America its particular national myth. Several themes
emerge from the consciousness of the American Puritans that establish
a basis for the American character. The Puritans saw their project as a
rebirth, which would later transform into an American obsession with
the new. However, with newness comes uncertainty, and a fundamental

American anxiety. As children of God, the Puritans privileged themselves over anyone other than themselves. With entitlement comes the need to dominate, which is reflected in America's narrow focus on being number one and making its will preeminent in relation to anything other. Power gleaned by the Puritan intellectual elite through their interpretations of scripture would eventually lead to the establishment of an economic elite who would maintain a canon (though one which could be manipulated) of economic law and policy. The Puritan work ethic would become a central part of American life, but "right to work" would come to mean profit for the few in a capitalistic hierarchical structure that privileges those in the upper strata. The commonwealth of Puritan souls prefigured the American corporate mindset. The Puritan tendency toward self-abnegation would come to set the paradigm for extreme in all things, but especially in its opposite, self-aggrandizement. The mythical sense of the forward movement of redemptive history would come to mark America's sense of entitlement and the dynamic that would govern its business and national enterprise. The "new world" was set to emerge into a political entity, the birth of a nation.

Notes

1. See in particular John M. Barry, *Roger Williams and the Creation of the American Soul: Church, State, and the Birth of Liberty* (New York: Viking Press, 2012); Sacvan Bercovitch, *The Puritan Origins of the American Self* (New Haven, CT: Yale University Press, 1973); Max Weber, *The Protestant Ethic and the "Spirit" of Capitalism and Other Writings*, edited, translated, and with an introduction by Peter Baehr and Gordon Wells (New York: Penguin Books, 2002); and Darren Sataloff, *The Making of an American Thinking Class: Intellectuals and Intelligentsia in Puritan Massachusetts* (London: Oxford University Press, 1998).

2. Bercovitch, *The Puritan Origins of the American Self*, 13.

3. Arthur Schlesinger, *The Cycles of American History* (New York: Houghton Mifflin, 1986), 4.

4. Ironically, given Calvin's distaste for pleasure, the *Mayflower* was originally a vessel for transporting wine.

5. William Bradford, *Of Plymouth Plantation 1620–1647: The Complete Text, with Notes and an Introduction by Samuel Eliot Morison* (New York: Alfred A. Knopf, 1959), 62. It is interesting to see the shift in America's relationship with the other as gauged by its attitude toward the land. Today it is America's inner cities that could be described as representing a "wild and savage hue," while the land that Bradford describes is what naturalists and ecologists preciously call "the beauty of nature." America's collective relationship toward the land is best exemplified in its most prominent form of landscape architecture, the golf course. In John Sayles's film *Sunshine State,* Alan King's character exalts that the golf course is "nature on a leash."

6. Schlesinger, *The Cycles of American History,* 13.

7. Bercovitch, *The Puritan Origins of the American Self,* 69–70.

8. *Ibid.,* 70 and 107. Mather called out to his congregation, "Awake, Awake, put on thy strength O New English Zion, and put on the Beautiful Garments O American Jerusalem."

9. *Ibid.,* 61.

10. Schlesinger, *The Cycles of American History,* 13.

11. Winthrop, the original personification of spiritual identity unified with secular concern, can be seen as the latter-day exemplar of what would become the wandering redemptive hero of American myth alluded to by Tocqueville as the subjectivist, individualistic, self-made man.

12. Keith Stavely, *Puritan Legacies: "Paradise Lost" and the New England Tradition, 1630–1890* (Ithaca, NY: Cornell University Press, 1987), 4.

13. Bercovitch, *The Puritan Origins of the American Self,* 40. Looking ahead in time, we can see that Puritan faith in God's miraculous ability to satisfy the material needs of His chosen people would eventually turn into America's faith in technology as miraculous grace not only taking care of life's every discomfort but, as we shall see in the case of Ronald Reagan, providing a laser shield of protection in the heavens of outer space.

14. Bercovitch, *The Puritan Origins of the American Self,* 51.

15. *Ibid.,* 69–70.

16. This tension can be seen in contemporary America, which prides itself on individualism, yet the most powerful cultural social structure is the corporate hierarchy, and there is an active readiness in the collective to conform to a singular mentality.

17. The evolution of modern individualism was reflected in the invention of the mirror during the Renaissance. Paradoxically, the mirror itself became a metaphor of the ideal of the selfless nature of psychological life for the Puritans. The mirror or glass was Christ or Israel of the Old Testament. In other words, the selfless man would not perceive a reflection of himself in the mirror, rather mirrored in himself were the ideal images of the scriptures. See Bercovitch, *The Puritan Origins of the American Self*, 14. American proclivity for individualism can be seen in the fact that when Thomas Edison invented a moving picture, he did it for an individual viewer, as opposed to the French inventors of motion pictures, the Lumiere brothers, who invented a medium for collective viewing.

18. Bercovitch, *The Puritan Origins of the American Self*, 17–18.

19. Schlesinger, *The Cycles of American History*, 28.

20. John Milton, *Complete Poems and Major Prose*, ed. Merritt Y. Hughes (Indianapolis: Bobbs-Merrill Educational Publishing, 1957), 468–69.

21. *Ibid.*, 467.

22. See James Hillman, "A Contribution to Soul and Money," in *Soul and Money*, ed. James Hillman, Arwind Vasavada, John Weir Perry, and Russell A. Lockhart (Dallas: Spring Publications, 1982), for a discussion on money as a psychological phenomenon.

23. Weber, *The Protestant Ethic and the "Spirit" of Capitalism*, 110.

24. Matthew 22:21, Mark 12:17, Luke 20:25.

25. Stavely, *Puritan Legacies*, 66.

26. Sataloff, *The Making of an American Thinking Class*, 9.

27. Bercovitch, *The Puritan Origins of the American Self*, 23.

28. *Ibid.*, 153.

29. *Ibid.*, 156.

5

From Puritan
to Yankee

In the beginning all the World was America.
　　　　　　　　　　　　　　　　—John Locke

In *Paradise Lost* Milton struggles with the same kind of conflict as
did the Puritan colonists in America—the tension between an
egalitarian orientation toward God's earthly blessings and the actual
power of government claimed by the few. The question of the
subordination of the many in favor of a few had been resolved by the
Puritans through the notion that some were closer to God through
their knowledge of Scriptural principle. The result was an "aristocracy
of grace" or a class of "saintly elite" following the model of the
privileged elders among the children of God establishing His earthly
law. For Milton, God's rays of spiritual light were ideally accessible to
everyone up and down the social ladder as it shone through openings
like "loopholes" cut in the "thickest shade of trees," but his thought
was that it was the man of reason to whom God was most available.[1]

For Milton Adam personifies reason and therefore holds the
office of superior power, and Eve, personifying will, takes the
subordinate position. Eve would embody the desire of Puritan laity
for a hand in government. She suggests to Adam a division of labor
between herself and him—will separating itself off from reason, the
human impulse pulling away from divine guidance. Separated from

Adam, Eve comes under the spell of Satan. In this configuration a connection with Satan would represent the abuse of Puritanism which held that God's grace was shown through material wealth as indication of faith. The perversion of God's benefaction would be the turn to self-interest blinding one to God's eye. Under Satan's influence, "God" becomes "profit," and labor is something enacted, not as an extension of the divine, but for the purpose of self-enhancement independent of community. Loss of connection with God would result in economic enterprise in the service of self-interest not "rightly understood" in Tocqueville's schema. In this sense, we can see that Milton's image of "loopholes" as entryways through which the spirit of God could shine on the lowest of His order would eventually become a metaphor representative of the means by which those with the most facility to manipulate capitalistic economy tend to become its "elite." Milton's poem can then be interpreted as a prophecy of the specific ways that Protestant notions of earthly well-being, promise for the future bestowed upon the faithful, and labor serving the glorification of God would serve as the foundation of American capitalism.[2]

In *Paradise Lost,* Satan can be seen as the first "self-made man," a symbol of the capitalist revolution and its license in the service of subjectivity favoring competition, aggression, and self-interest. It is Satan who inspires the formation of a civic religion based upon economic self-aggrandizement. Men "ransack'd the Center and with impious hands / Rifl'd the bowels of their mother Earth" to create a "temple" built in service to Mammon, god of money. Anything other than what would fit into a scheme of self-interest would be an obstacle to be conquered. Technology would provide "such implements of mischief as shall dash / to pieces, and o'erwhelm whatever stands / Adverse."[3] Thus the Puritan quest in the form of the American venture would become a perpetual compulsion for the apple as symbol of transcendence of the condition at hand, a consciousness oriented around escape, anything new, and a departure for the good life. Satan promises to Eve, "Taste this, and be henceforth among the Gods / thyself a Goddess, not to Earth confined . . . see / What life the Gods live . . . and such live thou."[4] Such would eventually become the American dream of utopia and the "good life" promised by a myriad of ads as "apples" for the consumer appetite.

With the coming of the Puritans to America, the seed for the eventual dominating production/consuming orientation had been planted. Action in the world in the form of economic enterprise was an extension of God's purpose for His children. What had been a form of overt religious belief with the Puritans would now become a form of underlying civic religion in America. Milton's contemporary, the political philosopher John Locke (1632–1704), would presage American values with his statement, "Political society is instituted for no other end, but only to secure every man's possession of the things of life."[5]

Like Milton, Locke translated the Puritan ethic into political terms. His more direct application of the same principles that guided Milton poetically was a guide for the revolutionary formation of the new nation. Locke wrote that the natural appetite of man for happiness, in conjunction with his resistance to pain ("a desire of happiness and an aversion to misery"), is modulated by reason in the form of laws that provide reward and punishment.[6] In his *Second Treatise on Government* Locke asserted that men are naturally equal and free "to order their actions, and dispose of their possessions and persons, as they think fit, within the bounds of the law of nature"—a law that forbids harm to other individuals and emphasizes the preservation of the whole of society.[7]

Locke believed that men in their natural state live together "according to reason, without a common superior on earth, with authority to judge between them."[8] It follows that reason allows for the formation of government as well. In order to protect their right to life, liberty, and property, individuals agree to hand over their natural powers to society. Desire necessitates the call of reason for governmental authority to ensure equal access to these rights.

The frame of government is under the control of the propertied, but again, property is something to which all have equal access. For Locke, "property" can be translated into "labor" in that it is labor "that puts the difference of value on everything."[9] "Every man has a property in his own person . . . The labour of his body, and the work of his hands, we may say, are properly his. Whatsoever then he removes out of the state that nature hath provided, and left it in, he hath mixed his labour with, and joined to it something that is his own, and thereby makes it his property."[10] Whereas for Calvin labor was a duty to God, Locke interprets labor as a God-given right.

While all men have a natural right to unlimited amounts of private property, reason, as an ability to calculate a course of action, is revealed in those who accumulate property through labor. Labor and reason go hand in hand to create power or, in Locke's words, "subduing or cultivating the earth, and having dominion, we see are joined together. The one gave title to the other. So that God, by commanding to subdue, gave authority so far to appropriate: and the condition of human life, which requires labour and materials to work on, necessarily introduces private possessions."[11]

Access to higher status is furthered by the factor of money. Money, a "lasting thing that men might keep without spoiling, and that by mutual consent men would take in exchange for the truly useful, but perishable supports of life," changes the nature of property in that it gives the individual the ability to continue to accumulate property (as money) beyond his needs.[12] The introduction of money allows for disproportionate and unequal possession among men (or the introduction of the apple by the serpent in Milton's scenario). Although every individual has a natural right to all the money he can make, it is the elite class, revealed as graced by God through its power of reason, which becomes a political necessity of the natural state. It was this orientation that lay beneath the turbulence caused by England's entitled economic policy toward its colonies in North America and which pushed the colonies toward independence.

In his *Second Treatise*, Locke created the blueprint for the structures, both overt and covert, that would take its form in the foundation of the new nation in the new world. His language regarding equality, happiness, and right to life and liberty was the basis for the overt structures of democracy. The concept of the equivalence of labor, property, money, and privilege became the backbone of a hidden aristocratic structure. Locke's background influence thus helped to form America's version of democracy, which represented a transition from an institutionalized religious theocracy to a society based overtly upon democratic values and covertly upon Judeo-Christian, capitalist, hierarchical values resulting in a new civic religion.

In the late seventeenth century, forces were at work in the New England colonies that served to transform the Puritan theocracy based on spiritual entitlement, political empowerment, and economic aggrandizement into a form of aristocracy that came to embody these essences in different forms. During the latter half of the century a revivalist movement swept through New England which emphasized the individual over community in a way that only breakaway sects had done previously. As one preacher declared, there is an "absolute Necessity for every Person to act singly . . . as if there was not another human creature upon Earth."[13] Up until this point, the "commonwealth of souls" working together for survival had held sway against the Enlightenment emphasis on the individual. As survival became less of a struggle, individual welfare came to take precedence over that of community.

In the eighteenth century, the sense of the solitary soul was framed within a context of "sensibility," originally defined as the ability to feel pain. Simultaneous with the discovery of the physiological neuron as the connecting fiber of the nerve impulse, "sensibility" became the ground for moral conscience, reflecting one's inherent connection with humanity. Through feeling, each response to moral concerns had a physiological referent. Physiological and social understanding went hand in hand. The world was understood through the receptivity of the senses, expressing the idea of inherent relationship between inner and outer. From micro and macro perspectives, man and world became intertwined.

The notion of sensibility was linked to *humanitas* (humanitarian purpose), the cultivated decency and refinement of the informed citizen who was resolved to aid society. Sensibility became tied to a felt sense of political progress. In this context, Locke had considered "conscience" to be the highest human faculty, and self-preservation could be properly achieved only through enlightenment and conscience. Conscience and consciousness came to be used interchangeably. Political rights emerged along with a sense of social responsibility. Wealth and power could rightfully only be attained within an *ethos* of social connection. Philosophers such as Anthony Ashley Cooper, Earl of Shaftsbury, wrote that society would be made strong only by including the cultivation of intimate connections among the entire span of its membership. The sensibility to others was integrally related to political and economic purpose, and the true statesman and economist needed the aid of a sympathetic imagination and an appreciation for human feeling. Physiology, philosophy, politics, and social morality all came out of the same grounding in the interconnectedness of the world.

The spirit of sensibility opens up perception of the world as something that one has the ability to alter. It follows that when one is connected with the world, one's belief system brings about the need for change according to this system. In 1776, two monumental texts were published in this spirit, each a child of their mutual "father," Locke's *Second Treatise of Government*. One gave an economic blueprint for production as a means of creating the modern world, and the other offered a guarantee that government would safeguard this structure.

The first was Adam Smith's (1723–1790) classic text on capitalism, *The Wealth of Nations* (1776), which Thomas Jefferson considered the "best" book he had read on political economics. Seventeen years earlier, in 1759, Smith had written *Theory of Moral Sentiments*, which codified a cultural sensibility in which the impulse for self-interest was overcome through reason and reflection upon "the man within." Smith believed that a man of virtuous sentiment would cultivate a sense of duty, overcoming the impulse of self-love through reason and principle. *The Wealth of Nations* outlined a science of political economy that was as much about the morality of social order as it was about the production and distribution of wealth. His central idea was that the productivity of an economy will increase and reach its maximum strength under the discipline of competition. If business owners pursue their economic self-interest competitively, the invisible influence of the market would guide them to invest their time and resources so that overall production occurs as plentifully and inexpensively as possible. "By pursuing his own interest . . . [the individual] frequently promotes that of society more effectively than when he really intends it."[14] Smith's underlying value was production/consumption, the idea that "consumption is the sole end purpose of all production," and that all the agencies of production—land, labor, capital—should be available to be worked in accordance with the free will of the individual who is guided by sympathy for his fellows.[15] For Smith, liberty of choice was moral choice.

Following the humanistic tradition, Smith's theory brought together the moral world and the economic world. In *Wealth of Nations*, he translocates the "inner man" of conscience to the market as if it were an independent psychological entity. Individuals will inevitably be led by self-interest, but since all individuals are interconnected through the market, one person's striving will inevitably benefit the whole. "Man continually standing in need of the assistance of others, must fall upon some means to procure their help."[16] It takes the production of multiple individuals to provide the coat for the laborer, and all benefit by his self-interest. The more a nation produces, the wealthier it becomes and the more the population as a whole benefits from its production.

Smith does not leave out government intervention, and in fact, deems it essential. Manufacturers and merchants will always try to sway the market in their interest, and it is the job of government to tend "to the interest of the producer . . . only so far as it may be necessary for promoting that of the consumer."[17] In turn, the individual worker is "led by an invisible hand to promote an end which was no part of his intention."[18] This image of the guiding hand of the market as the agent of morality can be understood in light of Smith's earlier image of the "inner man" of moral sentiment.[19] Smith's contribution to humanism can be seen on three levels: 1) a theory of how material commerce works; 2) a theory of how material commerce civilizes; and 3) a testament to the priority of the material world.[20] Smith believed not that "markets make men free, but that free men move toward markets."[21] It would not be long before American capitalism would pervert Smith's imagination of the market in leaving its moral component behind.

The second of the two monumental texts of 1776 was America's Declaration of Independence, authored by Thomas Jefferson (1743–1826). Influenced by Locke, Jefferson made a claim for individual rights including the pursuit of happiness. Happiness for Jefferson was linked to liberty, but also to prosperity and virtue, which were associated with moral consistency and sound reason, an idea ultimately rooted in Aristotle's notion of happiness as a quality of the "soul in accordance with virtue." For Jefferson, America's freedom to pursue happiness was a reflection of the idea that America was the "world's best hope" to restore the values of "harmony and affection," an echo of the Puritan notion that America as New Jerusalem would be the salvation of the world.[22]

The transformation within the New England colonies from Puritan to Yankee during the period of the Revolution was marked by a decrease in power held by ecclesiastical authority and an increase in claims to power by laity. The structure and values once held by the church were now passed over to the market. Merchants and businessmen gradually took the informal place of community leaders once held by the clergy. Identity once organized around spiritual values now came to be organized around economic values as psychological alignment transferred from God to the market. One achieved place in the community not so much from scriptural knowledge as from economic standing.

As economics became the dominant ground of political power, spirituality worked in everyday life in a subtler, less visible way than through religious institutions. Spirituality found its way in American life informally through the morality of the work ethic. What had been an orientation around self-preservation through alignment with God, and then with sentiment or conscience, became the rational pursuit of self-interest protected by government. Although religious institutions thrived and governmental structures were set in place, that which actually governed the values of the individual became more and more a matter of economics, resulting more and more in church/market/state becoming a unitary agency.

No individual personified the psychological merger into a new civic religion more singularly than Benjamin Franklin (1706–1790). The writings of Franklin can be seen as the perfect combination of the two strains that came together in the founding of America, Puritan virtue and the Enlightenment's prioritization of reason. Born into a Puritan family in Boston in the early eighteenth century, Franklin was actually a contemporary of Jonathan Edwards. As the youngest son of an artisan, he had little opportunity in his father's business and ultimately became a symbol of the American roving spirit, the man without a place.

Franklin was the prototype of the self-made man, rising from obscure origins to fortune and fame. He frequently told the story of how, upon his arrival in Philadelphia for the first time, he walked around the streets with three bread rolls. From his father, Franklin culled the Puritan morality that would become a central strain in his life's work. One of the virtues he most frequently referenced, diligence, can be traced to one of his father's favorite biblical passages, Proverbs 22:29: "Seest thou a man diligent in his calling, he shall stand before Kings."

As a child of the Enlightenment, Franklin displayed reasoned judgment available to compromise, a penetrating curiosity, a lively scientific intellect, a high regard for civic sensibility, and optimistic faith in reason and technology. He mediated American concerns with both England and France, helped to frame both the Declaration of Independence and the Constitution, sought ways to improve everyday life through the inventions of the stove and bifocals, organized neighborhood constabularies and lending libraries, and helped to foster a style of humor mixed with pragmatism that would mark the American character.

Franklin's writings exemplified the movement of American consciousness from obeisance to ecclesiastical authority to an orientation around a different kind of authority that was imperceptible, the reduction of everyday life into a regimentation of virtues. In his *Autobiography* he listed the qualities all people should strive for— temperance, silence, order, resolution, frugality, industry, sincerity, justice, moderation, cleanliness, tranquility, chastity, and humility. His essay "Plan for Self-examination" gave a daily checklist for each virtue. This popular book and its program exemplified a form of secular religion tying virtue to economic self-aggrandizement.

With a blend of Puritan morality of self-improvement and Enlightenment reasoning, Franklin embodied the original model of self-help and created a distinct national ideal. In his best-selling booklet, "The Way to Wealth," Franklin fashioned aphorisms about work and labor which read like edicts in religious homilies. "Time is money." "Credit is money." "Money can beget money." "The good paymaster is lord of another man's purse." "After industry and frugality, nothing contributes more to the raising of a young man in the world than punctuality and justice in all his dealings." "Never keep borrowed money an hour beyond the time you promised." "The way to wealth . . . is as plain as the way to market. It depends chiefly on two words, industry and frugality."[23] What had been God's favor for the Puritans was now individual initiative and responsibility as virtuous in and of itself.

Franklin's *Poor Richard's Almanac*, America's first self-help book, was meant as a playful guide to the would-be American man of business which Franklin, in fact, was. "Richard" wrote, "We are taxed twice as much by our Idleness, three times as much by our Pride, and four times as much by our Folly." "Lost time is never found again." "He that riseth late must trot all Day, and shall scarce overtake this Business at night: while Laziness travels so slowly, that Poverty soon overtakes him." "Industry pays Debts, while Despair encreaseth them." "Leisure, is Time for doing something useful." "Trouble springs from Idleness and grievous toil from needless Ease." "Buy what thou hast no Need of, and ere long thou shalt sell thy Necessaries." "He that goes a borrowing goes a sorrowing." "Pride is as loud a beggar as Want." "The Borrower is a Slave to the Lender, and the Debtor to the Creditor."[24] Moral spirit was now infused into economic practice, while utilitarian pragmatism became the ground for virtue.

Although Franklin tended to write in an ironic tone, his words, when taken literally, epitomized the shift in consciousness from Puritanism to a more overt orientation around economic self-interest. He wrote, "Interest will not lie,"[25] meaning that a conscious orientation toward self is a primary practical necessity and will show in the tangible achievements and rewards in one's life. His writings tended to detach Puritan industriousness and diligence from its dogmatic spiritual foundation, where these qualities were seen as a means of doing God's work, and transformed them into a mode of advancing individual pursuits. Franklin's genius was found in his ability to take the lofty abstractions of Puritan spirituality and bring them to earth in a pragmatic way, just as he was purported to have brought electricity from the heavens to earth where it could be put to use.[26]

Franklin's morality could be seen as a creature of utility. Honesty was useful; it brought credit which produced money, a sign of virtue. "Nor is Duty beneficial because it is commanded, but it is commanded because it is beneficial."[27] Thrift and frugality would bring men distinction. Through diligent work habits, men might take their rightful places in the upper echelons of the community, to "establish themselves in Business . . . and become respectable citizens."[28] In this way the religious morality of the Puritan work ethic was made into a morality of self-interest, and Franklin became the patron saint of the small businessman by bringing together faith in virtuous personal qualities of industriousness and the financial rewards that would result. Franklin saw America as the place where the project of self-aggrandizement and advancement through self-initiative could best take place, and reciprocally, enlightened self-interest of the individual would lead to the prosperity of the whole.[29]

As the colonies moved toward independence, and the solitary soul under the influence of Reason replaced the Puritan commonwealth of souls under the influence of the Holy Spirit, self-interest replaced self-preservation as the dominant American myth or core story. Although issues of religious freedom had been at stake in the founding of Massachusetts, Rhode Island, and Pennsylvania, for the most part the colonies had been established by profit-seeking corporations and proprietors. In 1606, the Virginia Company was formed to seek profit through American settlement, and in 1626, the Dutch founded Manhattan for the purpose of creating a center of trade, setting a precedent for the next generation of cities: Boston, Baltimore, and Philadelphia. Even William Penn justified his systematic purchase of land from Native Americans with the language of profit and loss: "Though I desire to extend Religious freedom, yet I want some recompense for my trouble."[30] The growing diversity of religious groups in the colonies made uniformity of religion impossible, and there was a developing sensibility which echoed Roger Williams's original inclination that a "wall of separation" was needed to insulate the state from the church. At the same time, mercantile interests saw the need to neutralize the state's power and direct government in their favor. Jefferson wanted only "useful" immigrants to be granted citizenship, and Hamilton was skeptical of Enlightenment sensibility connecting all men. The ideal of the Man of Feeling had very soon been overtaken by the Economic Man who felt at home in the aggressive world of business marked by the evolution of the competitive market in which trade and exchange replaced traditional ranks and loyalties.

By the time of the Revolution, industries such as shipbuilding and the refining of metals—steel, copper, and brass—were thriving, paralleling the success of agrarian producers, and the American colonies enjoyed a standard of living higher than any country in the world. Historian T. H. Breen notes that shops displaying goods had become sites of imagination, and desire for happiness took the form of taste for material comfort.[31] He suggests that the Revolution was not so much based on ideological principles as exemplified in the pamphlets of political ideologues like Tom Paine, but as a consumers' revolution of common people, artisans, and merchants alike. These groups desired optimal conditions for the production of goods to be consumed by local clientele free from financial ties with Great Britain.[32]

Four major legislative events constricting the economic freedom of the colonists occurred during the years leading up to 1776 which collectively tended to stir the colonists into rebellion. The Sugar Act of 1764 ensured that tax on foreign molasses was collected, thereby protecting British planters in the New World, while the Stamp Act of 1765 imposed a multitude of stamp duties on the colonists, and the subsequent Townshend Act of 1767 created taxes on an even wider variety of articles. The last straw was the Tea Act of 1773, giving a monopoly on tea sales in the colonies to the East India Company of Britain which would effectively wipe out the thriving business of colonial merchants. Both the Stamp Act and the Tea Act elicited a response of mob violence among the colonial tradesmen, artisans, and merchants and effectively galvanized a unity of revolutionary vision within the disparate colonies (although this unified fervor was shared by only about a third of the colonists).

While it is popular to think of the founding of America as predominantly from the democratic vision of Thomas Jefferson and James Madison, the nation was actually formed around an underlying aristocratic structure.[33] Even Jefferson talked about a "natural aristocracy" made up of young men with promising "virtues and talents."[34] This was in part a reflection of the upper-class orientation of most of the gentlemen Founders who attained the status of gentility either through marriage (Washington, Adams, Jefferson, and Hamilton) or on the basis of their own business accomplishments (Franklin).[35] New England had been ruled by a Puritan elite, landlords had been dominant in New Jersey and New York, and in Pennsylvania, Maryland, Virginia, and the southern colonies manor and plantation lords were in control. The platform for this hierarchical structure had been laid by John Winthrop in his shipboard sermon in 1630 in which he expressed the idea that inequality was God's will, reflecting the Puritan privileging of an elite class to govern the community according to scripture. The powerful were meant to take care of the poor in return for their loyalty. What was good for the upper crust was good for the whole of the community, and a sense of domination over anything presenting itself as other to the value of self-interest prevailed. The eventual primary architect and craftsman in the formation of a government privileging an elite, Alexander Hamilton, would never become president, but his legacy is evident in the power structure of American life based on the mutual interaction of political bodies and the economy. America became a Hamiltonian nation.

Hamilton believed that the best way for America to survive would be for it to establish itself on a strong economic foundation from which it could compete favorably with other nations. The newly born nation was bankrupt, with neither tax structure nor money supply, and yet, under Hamilton's guidance, it became a nation whose financial foundation enabled it to thrive. He devised a system of taxation, organized the monetary and banking system, paid off the debt from the Revolution—both federal and state—and devised a means that would allow the government to have a sound basis for credit in the future.[36] Further, it was under Hamilton's leadership that government became centralized, a national bank was formed, a navy was established to protect commercial trading interests, and the entrepreneurial interests of moneyed citizens who could establish and maintain dominance in private business were supported by the government.

Hamilton was born out of wedlock, grew up impoverished, and was orphaned at a young age in a port city in the Caribbean. He learned business, economics, and international trade working as a clerk in the shipping business of his adopted family. With the support of patrons, Hamilton came to New York as a young man to attend school and went on to King's College (Columbia University). The young student quickly grew sympathetic to the cause of the Revolution, dropped out of school, and very early in the war became attached to George Washington, serving as his secretary.

After the Revolutionary War, Hamilton came to see the need for the colonies to be united in order to be strong politically and economically. He served as representative to the Constitutional Convention from New York, later became a prominent spokesman for the passage of the Constitution, and then joined with James Madison and John Jay to write a collection of essays, *The Federalist*, which remains one of the most eloquent political documents ever written

favoring constitutional government. Once Washington was elected
president, Hamilton again became his right-hand man as the first
secretary of the treasury. From this position of power, he alienated
himself from the democratic thinking of Madison and Jefferson while
advocating a centralized government made up of men "who are
concerned for the security of property . . . whose principles are not of
the leveling kind."[37] Hamilton saw these men as the ones who could
best bring about a state of commercial prosperity, insuring "that there
be plenty of money in the community, and a brisk commerce to give
it circulation and activity."[38] The state would prosper politically with
a market free from government interference while being protected by
the government from foreign influence.

Hamilton's thinking was expansive. The new nation not only
needed to survive, it needed to grow and eventually come to dominate
its peers. He believed that in order for the country to be a force
internationally, especially in relation to Great Britain, government
needed to work in tandem with industry. The economic atmosphere
would be permeated with an entrepreneurial spirit engendered by a
sympathetic federal government. Those with money would benefit the
most from this arrangement, but the newly acquired wealth of the
owners of domestic industry would naturally trickle down, benefiting
the entire community.

Hamilton provided American capitalism with its foundational
programs out of which contemporary corporate culture would
eventually emerge. The concentration of capital in the hands of a select
few ensured commercial investment and economic growth. A national
bank would provide capital by printing money and facilitate providing
shares and bank services, while the government would provide tariff
protection and grant charters for corporations. The interests of the
owners and managers of domestic commerce, protected globally by
the federal government and free of interstate competition, would serve
public interests. "I do think we are and shall be great consumers," he
declared.[39] Finally, Hamilton's sensibility went beyond America's
borders. In *Federalist* No. 11, he asserts that the goal for the nation
should be to become a global power. Economic and military strength
go hand in hand. The nation with a well-established business
establishment would be formidable in the world.

Hamilton's vision is outlined most substantively in his "Report on the Subject of Manufactures," submitted to the House of Representatives in 1792. His purpose was couched in the language of humanism: "To cherish and stimulate the activity of the human mind, by multiplying the objects of enterprise, is not among the least considerable of the expedients by which the wealth of a nation may be promoted."[40] The context of the report was the conflict in political and economic circles of the time as to whether agriculture or industry was more important for a nation's well-being. Hamilton objected to the ideas of the Physiocrats, economists and politicians such as Jefferson who were influenced by the French and considered agriculture to be the preeminent means for production at the expense of manufacturing. While giving agriculture its due, Hamilton advocated that industry could contribute to a nation's productivity just as well, if not better, since manufacturing renders the production and revenues of agriculture greater than they would be alone. Further, industrialization subdivided work into simpler operations and lent itself to mechanization for optimal efficiency, both concepts that prefigured the Industrial Revolution.

If a flourishing manufacturing base was equally, if not more, important than an agricultural base, then the question existed as to how much the government should be able to intervene in private industry. Hamilton was not in doubt. He believed that the primary role of government in the economic sphere should be to enable the welfare of manufacturing interests, which would indirectly result in the common good. In this opinion he precipitated a remarkable shift in political thinking by taking the language of rights for individual agency and applying it to corporate agency. Hamilton agreed with Adam Smith regarding the goal of each individual finding "his proper element and calling into activity the whole vigor of his nature."[41] Therefore, "it is in the interest of nations to diversify the industrial pursuits of individuals."[42] Men are slow to change or see the need for change even when profits are inadequate necessitating the involvement of government in order to insure "the confidence of cautious sagacious capitalists."[43]

Ensuring the confidence of the moneyed indirectly provides for the care of the poor. Government is needed to favor those with capital in order to increase the "total mass of industry and opulence [which] benefits the totality."[44] Enriched wealthy interests supported by government would allow for a vigorous nation through providing employment for those who otherwise would not be engaged with business. This type of government would also promote emigration "furnishing greater scope for the diversity of talents and dispositions which discriminate men from each other . . . [thus] affording a more ample and various field for enterprise."[45] In sum, there would be no greater purpose to which public money could be applied "than to the acquisition of a new and useful branch of industry."[46]

Hamilton shared Franklin's value that the personal quality of industry should be rewarded, but he applied this notion to corporate interests and envisioned the government as the ultimate benefactor of corporations. Status with the government had to be earned, it was not a matter of birthright, and it needed to be based on marketplace performance by the corporate concern. Deeds and goods should be impartially valued, and industry rewarded. At the same time, the fact of wealth was itself indicative of merit, and successful entrepreneurs should be favored as a reflection of the government's valuing of enterprise. What was for the Puritans the work of the Holy Spirit had become for Hamilton the foundational spirit of a perpetually expanding economy. Whereas Franklin had established the moral virtue of self-interest, Hamilton established the political value of corporate self-willed acquisitiveness. A strong nation would emerge from the government's orientation toward corporate self-fulfillment, self-improvement, self-reliance, and self-interest. Hamilton's "Enterprise is our element" would prefigure General Electric's slogan, proclaimed by Ronald Reagan, "Progress is our most important product."[47]

Franklin and Hamilton served as cornerstones for what would become the foundation of the America's character. Both men began their careers as outsiders to the colonial establishment, and each became the epitome of the self-made man. Both brought a practical orientation to the problems presented by the burgeoning life of the newly formed country. Franklin addressed the moral power inherent in an individual's quest for wealth, while Hamilton spoke of the political power that accompanied corporate wealth. The fact that the nationalization of American political life occurred largely through industrial capitalism is a tribute to their imagination. Through each of their visions, spirit, power, and economy were molded into a single mythical form that would take on increased energy in the coming century through the actualization of the idea of manifest destiny.

Notes

1. John Milton, "Paradise Lost" (9:1110), in *Complete Poems and Major Prose*, ed. Merritt Y. Hughes (Indianapolis: Bobbs-Merrill Educational Publishing, 1957), 404.

2. See Keith Stavely, *Puritan Legacies: "Paradise Lost" and the New England Tradition, 1630–1890* (Ithaca, NY: Cornell University Press, 1987).

3. Milton, "Paradise Lost" (6:489–90), 335.

4. Milton, "Paradise Lost" (5:78–81), 304.

5. John Chamberlain, *The Roots of Capitalism* (Indianapolis: Liberty Fund, 1976), 61.

6. John Locke, *Second Treatise on Government,* ed. and with an introduction by C. B. Macpherson (Indianapolis: Hackett Publishing Company, 1980), xi.

7. Locke, *Second Treatise,* 8.

8. *Ibid.*, 15.

9. *Ibid.*, 25.

10. *Ibid.*, 19.

11. *Ibid.*, 22.

12. *Ibid.*, 28.

13. Gordon Wood, "American Religion: The Great Retreat," *New York Review of Books,* June 8, 2006, 61.

14. Quoted in Chamberlain, *The Roots of Capitalism*, 28.

15. Quoted in George Brockway, *The End of Economic Man: An Introduction to Human Economics* (New York: Norton and Co., 2001), 195.

16. Quoted in Adam Gopnik, "Market Man," *The New Yorker,* October 18, 2010, 84.

17. Quoted in Gopnik, "Market Man," 86.

18. Adam Smith, *An Inquiry into the Nature and Causes of the Wealth of Nations,* vol. 1 (New York: Random House, 1937), 456.

19. Michael Vannoy Adams, in his unpublished paper, "The Invisible Hand and the Economic Unconscious: The Most Important Image of the Last 750 Years" (delivered at the Congress of the International

Association of Analytical Psychology, Montreal, August, 2010), has very usefully seen the metaphor of the invisible hand governing the market as derived from the image of the hand of the Old Testament God, Yahweh, guiding His children.

20. See Gopnik, "Market Man."

21. *Ibid.*, 87.

22. Andrew Burstein, *The Evolution of America's Romantic Self Image* (New York: Hill and Wang, 1999), 43.

23. Benjamin Franklin, "Advice to a Young Tradesman," in *Benjamin Franklin and Jonathan Edwards: Selections from Their Writings* (New York: C. Scribner's Sons, 1950), 63–64.

24. Franklin, "The Way to Wealth," in *Benjamin Franklin and Jonathan Edwards*, 67–75.

25. Jeffrey Sklansky, *The Soul's Economy: Market Society and Selfhood in American Thought, 1820–1920* (Chapel Hill: University of North Carolina Press, 2002), 17.

26. Other psychological qualities championed by Franklin can be seen as manifest in his inventions: industry in the lightning rod, perseverance in the stove, common sense and moral vision in the bifocals.

27. Walter Isaacson, *Benjamin Franklin: An American Life* (New York: Simon & Schuster, 2004), 30.

28. Robert Bellah, Richard Madsen, William M. Sullivan, Ann Swidler, and Steven M. Tipton, *Habits of the Heart: Individualism and Commitment in American Life* (Berkeley: University of California Press, 1985), 33.

29. Jean de Crèvecouer wrote of the late-eighteenth-century American, "Here the rewards of his industry follow with equal steps the progress of his labour; his labour is founded on the basis of his nature, his self interest." Bellah et al., *Habits of the Heart*, 35.

30. John Steele Gordon, "An Empire of Wealth," *American Heritage*, October 2004, 16.

31. See T. H. Breen, *The Marketplace of Revolution: How Consumer Politics Shaped American Independence* (London: Oxford University Press, 2004).

32. At the time of the Revolution, the total debt owed by the colonists to British interests was £4 million.

33. Jefferson, however, did subtly orient his priorities toward the welfare of his fellow southern plantation owners. See Roger Kennedy, *Mr. Jefferson's Lost Cause* (London: Oxford University Press, 2003).

34. Isaacson, *Benjamin Franklin: An American Life*, 149.

35. Although Franklin bracketed work with glory, his underlying bias was toward an aristocratic social structure which placed the gentile above work. His personal ambition was to rise to the level of gentleman, and gentility can be seen as the underlying goal of his utopian vision. Being a gentleman meant being independent, free of the need for labor. "It seems certain that the hope of becoming at some time of Life free from the necessity of care and labour, together with fear of penury, are the main springs of most people's industry." Isaacson, *Benjamin Franklin: An American Life,* 39.

36. The nation's first insider buying scandal took place when Hamilton's colleague, William Duer, was found to have bought up government notes that had been thought to be worthless at reduced prices, knowing of Hamilton's intentions to pay off the notes at face value.

37. Edward Countryman, *The American Revolution* (New York: Hill and Wang, 2003), 198.

38. *Ibid.*, 198.

39. Ron Chernow, *Alexander Hamilton* (New York: Penguin, 2004), 299.

40. Alexander Hamilton, *The Papers of Alexander Hamilton*, vol. 10, ed. Harold C. Syrett (New York: Columbia University Press, 1966), 256.

41. Hamilton, *The Papers of Alexander Hamilton*, 255.

42. *Ibid.*, 260.

43. *Ibid.*, 267.

44. *Ibid.*, 294.

45. *Ibid.*, 376.

46. *Ibid.*, 301.

47. Chernow, *Alexander Hamilton*, 345.

6

Empire Builder

I will make thee ruler over many things.
—Matthew 25:21

America was established as a country by men who felt their endeavor to be an experiment in democracy and who, at the same time, often referred to the newly born country as an empire. In 1776, Timothy Dwight, Jonathan Edwards's grandson, wrote that "the empire of North America will be the last on earth."[1] For George Washington, America was a "rising Empire"[2] and the Founding Fathers were "lords of a great empire."[3] James Madison saw America as "one great, respectable and flourishing empire,"[4] and in *Federalist* No. 1, Alexander Hamilton urged the ratification of the new Constitution as the means to determine "the fate of an empire."[5] Thomas Jefferson thought of America as the divinely sanctioned "empire of liberty" and wanted the Great Seal to portray the children of Israel led by a pillar of light. Although the Founding Fathers might have used the term to indicate sovereign security, the sense of dominion as the assumption of power and authority over the fate of other peoples was ever present. They were not able to see the contradiction between this implication and the principles of democracy, a paradox that has been characteristic of America's vision of its place in the world ever since. It is clear that in addition to independence for the colonies, the Founding Fathers had a sense of the nation that stretched beyond territorial boundaries. As early as 1765, John Adams wrote, "I always consider the settlement of America with reverence and wonder, as the opening of a grand scene and design in Providence for the illumination of the ignorant, and the emancipation of the slavish part of mankind all over the earth."[6] In his passionate advocacy of revolution, Tom Paine wrote in *Common Sense*, "We have it in our power to begin the world all over again."[7]

The notion of empire, in concordance with the motif of the Promised Land, has played a dominant role in the country's psyche since the arrival of the Puritans. The Puritans exemplified the psychology of empire builders, taking on the mantle of the chosen people in a spiritual sense by spreading God's word to the heathen and materialistically through warfare against the natives for the sake of land acquisition by rights of conquest.[8] The subsequent systematic Anglo takeover of Indian lands occurred throughout the colonies during the eighteenth century as settlers pushed westward, culminating in the Royal Proclamation of 1763, which declared that Indian lands could be occupied by homesteaders. In fact, hostilities against Native Americans throughout the century, such as the war waged by Virginia governor John Murray, Lord Dunmore, against the Shawnee which made Kentucky available for open settlement, were more often than not provoked with the underlying purpose of gaining land for occupation.

The Revolutionary War was fought not just for independence, but also with a background goal of expansion. In 1775, the Continental Congress, seeking greater power against England, authorized the invasion of Canada, but the resulting siege of Quebec was a failure. The colonies had generally been desirous of greater domain for purposes of power and wealth, and several had laid claims to western territory. Dunmore, for example, seized Fort Pitt, claiming the Ohio headwaters as part of Virginia in 1774. During the Revolutionary War competition for land—the "western problem"—dominated congressional politics, taking more of the Congress's attention than anything except the war itself. After independence was won, the colonies had to cede their western territorial claims for the possibility of unification. The Northwest Ordinances of 1784–1787 defined how new states could be added from western territory "on an equal footing" with the original states. Using procedures from this ordinance, five new states were eventually added: Ohio, Indiana, Illinois, Michigan, and Wisconsin.

Expansionist values can be seen at work in the personal as well as the political lives of the founding fathers, as exemplified by George Washington. While he tried to deal fairly with Native Americans, Washington did not recognize any limit on westward expansion by white settlers, resulting in natives being deprived of their land. Washington's expansionist sensibility reflected that of the Virginia gentry, which in turn was derived from the Charter of Virginia of 1609, which established no western boundary. As a young man, Washington worked as a surveyor of western territory for the Ohio Company, which was made up of Virginia landholders. He then bought parcels of land he had surveyed from these landholders and sold them at profit, when they had originally been intended for soldiers who had fought under him in the Seven Years' War. During his lifetime he owned more than 60,000 acres in New York, Pennsylvania, Maryland, Virginia, Kentucky, and Ohio. Washington's expansionist vision was later reflected through his policies to formally organize western territory. In 1783, while awaiting the results of the peace accords being conducted with the British, Washington toured the New York frontier. He wrote, "I shall not rest contented 'till I have explored the Western Country and traversed those lines . . . which have given bounds to a New Empire."[9]

In the nineteenth century, the expansionist movement looked to the West as the primary object of the desire for more territory. In 1803, the purchase of the Louisiana Territory by Thomas Jefferson from a cash-strapped, preoccupied Napoleon Bonaparte doubled the territory of the country and provided another biblical promised land for conquest and development. Already Jefferson had future settlement in mind—he instructed Lewis and Clark to collect information regarding Native Americans and natural resources during their 1804–1806 expedition.

The new Eden emerged as the exemplar for American settlement in the West. Jonathan Edwards had already identified the West as the place where God's latter-day glory would begin, and now west became the direction of redemption as the new "Garden of the World," at once wilderness and land of renewal.[10] In 1835, Lyman Beecher wrote "A Plea for the West" in which he proclaimed:

> If this nation is, in the providence of God, destined to lead the
> way in the moral and political emancipation of the world, it is

> time she understood her high calling, and we harnessed for
> the work . . . [T]he religious and political destiny of our nation
> is to be decided in the West . . . [T]he West is destined to be
> the great central power of the nation, and under heaven,
> must affect powerfully the cause of free institutions and the
> liberty of the world.[11]

That same year, Tocqueville wrote of the passionate pursuit of fortune
by Americans in their incessant movement westward.

> It would be difficult to describe the avidity with which the
> American rushes forward to secure this immense booty that
> fortune offers. In the pursuit, he fearlessly braves the arrow of
> the Indian and the diseases of the forest; he is unimpressed by
> the silence of the woods; the approach of beasts of prey does
> not disturb him, for he is goaded onwards by a passion stronger
> than the love of life. Before him lies a boundless continent, and
> he urges onward as if time pressed and he was afraid of finding
> no room for his exertions.[12]

In 1844, Ralph Waldo Emerson wrote that the West would
bring out the national character. "The strong-nerved, rocky West
is intruding a new and continental element into the national mind,
and we shall yet have an American *ethos*."[13] Toward the end of the
century, the West still held its fascination for those such as Frederick
Jackson Turner who saw it as "another name for opportunity,"[14] and
Theodore Roosevelt who envisioned it as the place where America
would achieve its "highest destiny," a virtual Canaan for "another
chosen people."[15]

The idea of a manifest destiny had been in existence in Europe
for several years when journalist John O'Sullivan used the term in
1839 to justify American expansion into Oregon. In an article
entitled "The True Title," he addressed the argument the United
States was engaged in with England over claims to the Oregon
Territory. American rights did not have to do so much with legal
claims, he said, but rather with a "claim [which] is by the right of
our manifest destiny to overspread and to possess the whole of the
continent which Providence has given for the development of the
great experiment of liberty and federative self-government entrusted
to us."[16] Manifest destiny gave the nation a renewed moral mission.
America's people were again God's elect by His will and by virtue
of their inherent superiority. America would create another new

Jerusalem through subjugation of the continent—its natives and its geography, both barriers to progress.

The election of James Knox Polk as president in 1844 was the political enactment of manifest destiny as a spiritualized, aggressive impulse toward expansion. Polk, a Jacksonian Democrat and ardent expansionist, presided during three events that added greatly to the territorial domain of the United States. After Polk's election, Congress passed a resolution admitting Texas to the Union in 1845, which followed up on Texas's request from the previous year. Polk then worked out a compromise with the British that added the Oregon Territory (later to be the states of Washington, Oregon, Idaho, and parts of Wyoming and Montana) to the United States. Finally in 1848, as the result of a war with Mexico largely provoked by the United States, Polk ratified a treaty that added 1.2 million square miles to the country, increasing its size by a third.

Manifest destiny was the focus of a larger spirit at work in America, cast as the redeeming "Light of the World."[17] This zeitgeist fulfilled the movement of history by following a call echoing the call of the faithful in the book of Revelation. Forward motion and an orientation toward futurity became predominant ways of being in America, and any thinking that took on the aspect of halting or looking to the past was seen as a form of moral backsliding or a hindrance to progress. As New York politician Philip Howe wrote in 1837, "'Go ahead' is our maxim and our password. We go ahead with a vengeance, regardless of the consequences and indifferent about the value of human life."[18] Notions like "get ahead," "progress," "ascend," "development," "success," and "prosperity" had already become American passwords, and success was founded on the Puritan heritage of internal virtue: material success was, at the same time, the product and indicator of spiritual virtue. Harriet Beecher Stowe wrote, "God's mercies to New England foreshadowed the glorious future of the United States of America . . . commissioned to bear the light of liberty and religion through all the earth and to bring the great millennial day, when wars should cease and the whole world, released from the thralldom of evil, should rejoice in the light of the Lord."[19]

For pre–Civil War Americans, the image of the nation as another New World carried the glow of ascendant millennial splendor. In 1844, Ralph Waldo Emerson wrote, "This land is the appointed remedy for whatever is false and fantastic in our culture . . . here in America is the home of man . . . [where] the new love, new faith, new sight shall restore [creation] to more than its first splendor."[20] America was the new man. Those who would "complain of the flatness of American life have no perception of its destiny"; they were not Americans, for "here is man in the Garden of Eden; here the Genesis and the Exodus."[21] In 1850, Herman Melville wrote a novel, *White Jacket,* which attacked the practice of flogging in the United States Navy, taking the moral ground that America is a "latter-day Israel."

> We Americans are the peculiar, chosen people—the Israel of our time; we bear the ark of the liberties of the world . . . God has predestined, mankind expects, great things from our race: and great things we feel in our souls. The rest of the nations must soon be in our rear. We are the pioneers of the world; the advance-guard, sent on through the wilderness of untried things, to break a new path in the New World that is ours . . . The political Messiah [has come] in *us.* [22]

America was God's Word incarnate, destined to liberate the world through its dominance. By 1885, Josiah Strong was referring to America's amalgamation of liberty and Christianity as the "die with which to stamp the peoples of the earth."[23] America was to be the redeemer nation, God's means for worldwide redemption, the ultimate flowering of the Reformation, and the fulfillment of Daniel's prophetic vision:

> I saw in the night visions, and, behold, one like the Son of man came with the clouds of heaven, and came to the ancient of days, and they brought him near before him.
>
> And there was given him dominion, and glory, and a kingdom, that all people, nations, and languages, should serve him: his dominion is an everlasting dominion, which shall not pass away, and his kingdom that which shall not be destroyed.[24]

As Fred Anderson and Andrew Clayton have observed in their book *America and the Dominion of War,* the history of America's appropriation of land has in large part been marked by violence. In the nineteenth century, the impulse to take dominion was made manifest through spiritually toned aggression reflecting the sensibility of a chosen people. In addition to defending American interests from

British efforts to control commercial and diplomatic relations, the War of 1812 was conducted with the hope of annexing Canada, a fantasy renewed from the Revolutionary War that persisted through the imperialist movement at the end of the nineteenth century. Florida was acquired from Spain in a forced sale brought about by the preemptive aggressive tactics of President Andrew Jackson against the Creek Indians. Jackson had signed the Indian Removal Act in 1830 resulting in the reluctant and often forced displacement of tens of thousands of Native Americans from their lands to territories in the West. When the Choctaw were removed, ceding their lands to Mississippi, their chief, Nitikechi, characterized their plight as a "trail of tears and death." The tragic Trail of Tears came to be the pathway for several eastern tribes. Jackson forced the Cherokee to give up their land in Georgia, the Chickasaw followed, and the Seminole held out in a bloody war until most were removed from Florida. The Mexican-American War, provoked by the United States, resulted in the annexation of territory that became the states of California, Arizona, New Mexico, Utah, and Nevada. As early as 1851, Secretary of State Daniel Webster went so far as to declare that America would someday command all of the oceans. Even the Civil War, begun as answer to the question of how America was to expand—with or without slavery—was seen on both sides as a form of holy crusade to bring about "Liberty all over the World."[25] Finally the Spanish-American War, again provoked by the United States, resulted in the occupation of Cuba and the Philippines with intentions that were at once moralistic, militaristic, and commercial. In short, America's wars during the nineteenth century displayed a core streak of imperialistic ambition resulting in America's dominion over the lives and land of native and foreign peoples. These wars were paradoxically justified in terms of liberty and a civilizing influence, with an underlying sense of destiny through spiritual entitlement.

By the second decade of the nineteenth century, the Puritan emphasis on work had become a national ethic. Work was celebrated as the means by which the principle of equality was exercised and expansion made possible for everyone. The self-made man—who acted independently, relied upon hard work and ingenuity, and developed his own resources, while aiming his efforts toward self-gain—became a national ideal. Independent endeavor involved risk, but fortune was seen as the great equalizer, and the prospects for success were seen as available to all who worked for them. Faith in the future was contained in the notion of progress, while happiness was seen as the inevitable product of economic growth.

In the nineteenth century, the American messianic spirit not only manifested in rhetoric and military exploits, but it emerged as well in the convergence of notions of economic and spiritual well-being. In 1815 a Russian visitor remarked, "Money is the American's deity: only his piety and the wealth of the country have until now sustained his morals."[26] Not only did money become a form of god in itself, but institutional religion now embraced the making of profit as a moral value. In 1840, Tocqueville wrote, "The love of wealth is . . . at the bottom of all that the Americans do," and at the same time, "Christianity has . . . retained a strong hold on the public mind in America."[27] Tocqueville's observations reflect the fact that in eighteenth-century America, Christianity and material prosperity converged in mainstream culture. The term "economics" emerged in the 1870s on the crest of a wave of evangelical Christianity that saw the new industrial economy as a fulfillment of God's will. In 1854, Samuel Baldwin wrote *Armageddon: Or, the Existence of the United States Foretold in the Bible, Its . . . Expansion into Millennial Republic, and Its Dominion over the Whole World,* depicting the self-made man of business not only as a "secular version of a visible saint" but also as an embodiment of personal and historical ideals grounded in the belief that America was meant to carry out God's will on earth through work.[28]

Ministers advocated a form of "Christian capitalism," which preached that the Christian's duty was to prosper, and in which Christian piety was seen as an asset to material success.[29] The laissez-faire orientation of the economy assumed that the virtuous worker would prosper, while those who did not succeed were seen as lacking in moral value. Work in this view was both a right and a means of redemption. In 1870, after the decline in agricultural workers relative to industrial workers, 85 percent of the workforce worked for wages. Henry Ward Beecher: "If men have not enough, it is from want of provident care, and foresight, and industry and frugality. No man in this land suffers from poverty unless it be more than his fault—unless it be his sin."[30] Emerson echoed, "There is always a reason in the man, for his good or bad fortune."[31] Factory owners could be seen as doing God's work on earth by providing opportunity for the worker to attain God's acceptance in fulfilling his duty to increase his own material value. Emerson wrote, "We rail at trade [industrial capitalism], but the historian of the world will see that it was the principle of liberty, that it settled America."[32] Henry Ward Beecher preached, "Nothing is more remote from selfishness than general expenditure in building up a home and enriching it with all that shall make it beautiful without and lovely within."[33] Thus the secularized Protestant ethic rationalized and spiritualized capitalistic economic transformation. Christian influence was in the forefront of the spirit of forceful expansion with the purpose of subjugation through military and commercial as well as industrial and technological means.

The marriage of modern technology and capitalism is illustrated by the fact that both the steam engine and *The Wealth of Nations* emerged from the same milieu: Glasgow, Scotland, in 1769 and 1776 respectively.[34] The steam engine was the first new source of functional energy since the windmill, and it gave rise to the locomotive and the steamboat. As the nineteenth century unfolded in America, the expansionist mentality of the country was represented in these two modes of movement, which in turn fueled the steel and mining industries. The railroad, especially, was a symbol of unfettered power and aggressive expansion. Emerson wrote, "Fear haunts the building [of the] railroad but it will be American power and beauty."[35] Noninterventionist laissez-faire government policies served to enable corporations that were presented as serving public interest. The rights of the individual were gradually co-opted by the corporation, and faith in self-interest complemented faith in a self-regulated economy with self now firmly housed in the corporation. Railroads, built with government support through loans, land grants, and cavalry protection, made long-range trade possible. They also oppressed thousands of immigrant workers, undermined local businesses with goods brought from afar, and enabled a monopoly to be set upon prices the local farmers had to pay for goods received. It was not until 1887, when President Grover Cleveland created the Interstate Commerce Commission, that railroad monopolies became limited in their control over local farmers and manufacturers.

Technological advances in America were perceived as if they were blessings that Providence bestowed upon its children as extensions to their will, enabling them to battle the continental wilderness and make it into a new Eden. With the invention of the steam engine, the telegraph, and the daily press, as well as the proliferation of trade through railroads and steamboats, the Industrial Revolution came to be seen as a time in which new gifts from heaven were bestowed upon America as a sign of God's blessing. After the Union victory in the Civil War, the industrial Northeast assumed dominion economically, militarily, and spiritually. In 1871, Henry Ward Beecher wrote, "May God give us magnanimity and power and riches that we may throw the shadow of our example upon the poor, the perishing and the ready-to-be-destroyed."[36] In his lecture "Acres of Diamonds," which he delivered more than six thousand times, Russell Conwell, Baptist minister and founder of the Philadelphia Temple, put it quite simply: "You ought to get rich and it is your duty to get rich."[37] The Right Reverend William Lawrence wrote "The Relation of Wealth to Morals" in 1901, declaring, "it is only to the man of morality that wealth comes."[38] Godliness is in alignment with riches, thus "to seek for and earn wealth is a sign of a natural, vigorous, and strong character."[39] Lawrence calls for "the rekindling of the spirit, that, clothed with her material forces, the great personality of this Nation may fulfill her divine destiny."[40]

In addition to the supply side, the demand side of the economy was also spiritualized.[41] Consuming became an indication of faith and a sign of God's blessing. It was as if, through its products, American business fostered a perpetual rain of manna for God's children on earth. Consumption moved from being a matter of survival to a matter of status—white bread and sugar were higher on the social ladder than the more natural brown. The function of corporate business shifted from supply to the creation of a market for its goods, and advertising assumed an essential part of everyday life as generated desire became democratized. Walter Lippmann wrote, "The making of one general will out of a multitude of general wishes . . . consists essentially in the use of symbols which assemble emotions after they have been detached from their ideas . . . the process, therefore, by which general opinions are brought to co-operation consists of an intensification of feeling."[42]

To both instill and meet the demand for more products in service to the "cult of the new," a unique commercial aesthetic emerged— moving and selling products in volume. Large department stores appeared to take the place of local shops. Herbert Croly, a progressive who influenced Theodore Roosevelt, enthused that American life provided the "promise of comfort and prosperity for an ever-increasing majority of good Americans."[43] As if to instill a spirit of sanctified justification for the rapid growth in corporate wealth, Andrew Carnegie asserted that certain laws involved in the enterprise of corporate capitalism reflected the laws of God. These were laws that enhanced the development of civilization through the protection of the sacredness of private property, the protection of free economic competition, and the accumulation of wealth.[44]

Despite Jefferson's suspicions, the hostility of Jackson, who made the distinction between public purpose and private interest, and the efforts of the Populist movement during the latter part of the century, moneyed interests held power and influence over the government throughout the nineteenth century. America's economy went through several spirals during the nineteenth century, but each growth spurt was reflected in further empowerment of an elite group tied to the economy. After the Revolutionary War, the merchant class took over predominance from the landed gentry. The mercantile elite formed its own incestuous community through family networks, and the money of the elite from the mercantile and financial sectors was used to support elected officials. In 1835, 71 percent of Boston's wealthiest individuals were related, and in the 1850s, 37 percent of New York's wealthiest.[45] In 1860, Philadelphia's wealthiest 1 percent owned half of the city's assets, while in New York City, 1.4 percent owned 71 percent of the assets.[46]

After the Civil War, industrialism in the United States grew exponentially, stimulated by the demands of war, which allowed industrialists to become a powerful bloc. By 1890, four-fifths of the property value of the country lay in corporate assets. It was during this Gilded Age that the Senate became a millionaire's club. As if they were not powerful enough already, corporations merged into combines led by the Standard Oil of John D. Rockefeller and the U.S. Steel of Andrew Carnegie and were enabled by financing from investment bankers like J. P. Morgan. The combination of finance and industry was tied to politics through massive contributions to the campaigns of those favoring the combines. Although the Populist movement spawned legislation against trusts and big money interests, the power of corporate interests was barely limited by government. As the horizon of moneyed interests became global around the turn of the century, it was Wall Street financiers who became the natural aristocracy of the nation.[47]

In 1893, the historian Frederick Jackson Turner famously declared that while the essence of America was pushing back the frontier, the continental frontier was closed, necessitating the further expansion of imperialist sentiment. He felt that the energy that had driven America to conquer its western frontier would now be turned to the vast territories overseas. "American energy will continually demand a wider field for its exercise," Turner wrote in his book, *The Frontier in American History*.[48] "That these energies of expansion will no longer operate would be a rash prediction; and the demands for a vigorous foreign policy, for an inter-oceanic canal, for a revival of our power upon the seas, and for the extension of American influence to outlying islands and adjoining countries, are indications that the movement will continue."[49] America's eye now turned its gaze once again beyond its borders.

At a time when the Industrial Revolution had fueled national pride and the urge for expansion of national power in European countries grew stronger, the impulse to extend American political influence also increased. "Preclusive imperialism here and elsewhere, was the motive," wrote historian Arthur Schlesinger Jr.[50] Throughout the latter half of the nineteenth century, these motivations had been checked by Congress, which was under the influence of business leaders who wanted the stability of a largely domestic economic orientation. But at the end of the nineteenth century, a sense of moral superiority, the felt need for power in the international community (and, some historians would say, the push for new markets) gave new impetus to the imperialist spirit which had guided the consciousness of the nation from its beginnings.

The sense of American dominance that came into its own at the end of the nineteenth century reflected the Social Darwinism of the time, manifest destiny, and a notion of moral rectitude which considered America to be providing the world a civilizing influence. It was a consciousness that did not and could not bring itself to take into account the fact that other nations may have nationalistic inclinations also and may take an unfavorable view of being patronized by America. Senator Henry Cabot Lodge wrote in 1895, "[Americans] have a record of conquest, colonization, and territorial expansion unequalled by any people in the nineteenth century . . . From the Rio Grande to the Arctic Ocean there should be but one flag and one country."[51] Lodge again: "The great nations are rapidly absorbing for their future expansion and their present defense all the waste places of the earth . . . As one of the great nations of the world, the United States must not fall out of the line of march."[52] Theodore Roosevelt declared, "If we shrink from the hard contests where men must win at the hazard of their lives and at the risk of all they hold dear, then the bolder and stronger peoples will pass us by, and will win for themselves the domination to the world."[53] Senator Albert Beveridge stated that God "has marked the American people as His chosen nation to finally lead in the regeneration of the world. This is the divine mission of America . . . We are trustees of the world's progress, guardians of its righteous peace."[54]

Expansion was a matter of national pride, and Americans saw themselves as a "masterful people," deserving of dominion. Americans retained a sense of moral rectitude so that imperialism became a crusade for righteousness, following the millennial pattern laid out in the book of Revelation. Theodore Roosevelt declared, "Peace comes not to the coward or to the timid, but to him who will do no wrong and is too strong to allow others to wrong him."[55] Beveridge wrote that the opposition party was "resisting the onward forces which were making of the American people the master Nation of the world—the forces that . . . now in the ripeness of time fling our authority and unfurl our flag almost around the globe . . . God's hand was in it all . . . the eternal movement of the American people toward the mastery of the world . . . Westward the Star of empire takes its way!"[56] For Beveridge and other imperialists, national interests were synonymous with the "highest holy destiny" to civilize the world.[57] In supporting the American occupation of the Philippines, President William McKinley claimed that God had told him that it was America's duty to educate, civilize, and Christianize the Filipinos.[58] William Howard Taft declared it was "indubitable fact . . . the Filipinos are at present so constituted as to be utterly unfit for self government."[59] Among the results of this phase of the imperialist movement were the Spanish-American War, America's forceful prolonged occupation of the Philippines, and the rise to power of Theodore Roosevelt.

Nineteenth-century America embodied the values of its underlying mythical narrative as modeled in the Old and New Testaments. During the nineteenth century, Americans revealed their view of themselves as spiritually entitled—the chosen People of God—and therefore, revealed themselves to be intolerant of otherness as it may show itself in the land as barrier to progress and in other peoples with beliefs different from a Christian/technological/capitalist agency. At the same time, America felt the need to dominate others and to spread its base of power beyond whatever boundary presented itself. With corporate capitalism as its foundation, America maintained a hierarchical model of political structure internally and with its military power now fully developed, assumed a place of self-entitled dominance in the world of the twentieth century.

Notes

1. Christopher Collins, *Homeland Mythology: Biblical Narratives in American Culture* (University Park: Pennsylvania State University Press, 2007), 64.

2. Arthur Schlesinger, *The Cycles of American History* (New York: Houghton Mifflin, 1986), 137.

3. Edward Countryman, *The American Revolution* (New York: Hill and Wang, 2003), 207.

4. Schlesinger, *The Cycles of American History*, 137.

5. Alexander Hamilton, James Madison, and John Jay, *The Federalist Papers*, with an introduction and commentary by Gary Wills (New York: Bantam, 2003), 3.

6. Ernest Lee Tuveson, *Redeemer Nation: The Idea of America's Millennial Role* (Chicago: University of Chicago Press, 1968), 25.

7. Schlesinger, *The Cycles of American History*, 17.

8. William Penn was the exception to hostile takeover in that he purchased land from tribes, but always through deals that were to his great advantage.

9. Fred Anderson and Andrew Clayton, *The Dominion of War: Empire and Liberty in North America, 1500–2000* (New York: Viking, 2005), 177.

10. Quoted in Conrad Cherry, "Westward the Course of Destiny," in *God's New Israel: Religious Interpretations of American Destiny*, ed. Conrad Cherry (Englewood Cliffs, NJ: Prentice-Hall, 1971), 112.

11. Lyman Beecher, "A Plea for the West," in *God's New Israel: Religious Interpretations of American Destiny*, ed. Conrad Cherry (Englewood Cliffs, NJ: Prentice-Hall, 1971), 120.

12. Alexis de Tocqueville, *Democracy in America,* vol. 1 (New York: Random House, 1990), 294.

13. Ralph Waldo Emerson, "The Young American," in *Essays and Lectures* (New York: Library of America, 1983), 216–217.

14. Katherine Roberts, "A Western State of Mind," *New York Times,* September 18, 2008, A22.

15. Sarah Watts, *Rough Rider in the White House: Theodore Roosevelt and the Politics of Desire* (Chicago: University of Chicago Press, 2003), 147, 158.

16. John O'Sullivan, "The True Title," in *God's New Israel: Religious Interpretations of American Destiny,* ed. Conrad Cherry (Englewood Cliffs, NJ: Prentice-Hall, 1971), 129.

17. Sacvan Bercovitch, *The Puritan Origins of the American Self* (New Haven, CT: Yale University Press, 1973), 148.

18. Quoted in James Morone, "Good for Nothing," *London Review of Books*, May 19, 2005, 18.

19. Quoted in Bercovitch, *The Puritan Origins of the American Self,* 87–88.

20. *Ibid.*, 157.

21. Quoted in Richard Rhodes, *Arsenals of Folly: The Making of the Nuclear Arms Race* (New York: Alfred A. Knopf, 2007), 51.

22. Tuveson, *Redeemer Nation,* 156–57.

23. Quoted in Robert Jewett and John Shelton Lawrence, *Captain America and the Crusade against Evil: The Dilemma of Zealous Nationalism* (Grand Rapids, MI: William B. Eerdmans, 2003), 68.

24. Daniel 7:13–14.

25. Anderson and Clayton, *The Dominion of War,* 303.

26. Mark Noll, *God and Mammon: Protestants, Money, and the Market, 1790–1860* (London: Oxford University Press, 2002), 4.

27. Alexis de Tocqueville, *Democracy in America,* vol. 2 (New York: Random House, 2002), 229, 6.

28. Bercovitch, *The Puritan Origins of the American Self,* 145.

29. Noll, *God and Mammon,* 172.

30. Quoted in Morone, "Good for Nothing," 18.

31. *Ibid.*

32. Emerson, "The Young American," 219.

33. Keith Stavely, *Puritan Legacies: "Paradise Lost" and the New England Tradition, 1630–1890* (Ithaca, NY: Cornell University Press, 1987), 209.

34. The precursor to the steam engine had been designed in England by Thomas Newcomen, but it was transformed into the steam engine itself in 1769 in Glasgow by James Watt.

35. Emerson, "The Young American," 219.

36. Henry Ward Beecher, "The Tendencies of American Progress," in *God's New Israel: Religious Interpretations of American Destiny,* ed. Conrad Cherry (Englewood Cliffs, NJ: Prentice-Hall, 1971), 243.

37. Quoted in Conrad Cherry, "National Progress and Wealth," in *God's New Israel: Religious Interpretations of American Destiny,* ed. Conrad Cherry (Englewood Cliffs, NJ: Prentice-Hall, 1971), 215.

38. William Lawrence, in *God's New Israel: Religious Interpretations of American Destiny,* ed. Conrad Cherry (Englewood Cliffs, NJ: Prentice-Hall, 1971), 246.

39. *Ibid.,* 247.

40. *Ibid.,* 254.

41. See William Leach, *Land of Desire: Merchants, Power, and the Rise of a New American Culture* (New York: Random House, 1993), for a complete discussion of the evolution of America as a consumer nation.

42. Quoted in David M. Potter, *People of Plenty: Economics Abundance and the American Character* (Chicago: University of Chicago Press, 1954), 183.

43. *Ibid.,* 6.

44. Cherry, "National Progress and Wealth," 214.

45. Sven Beckert, "Merchants and Manufacturers in the Antebellum North," in *Ruling America: A History of Wealth and Power in a Democracy,* ed. Steve Fraser and Gary Gerstle (Cambridge, MA: Harvard University Press, 2005), 99.

46 *Ibid.,* 94.

47. See Jackson Lear, "The Managerial Revitalization of the Rich," in *Ruling America: A History of Wealth and Power in a Democracy,* ed. Steve Fraser and Gary Gerstle (Cambridge, MA: Harvard University Press, 2005), for a full discussion.

48. Cited in Michael B. Oren, *Power, Faith, and Fantasy* (New York: Norton, 2007), 306.

49. James Chace, "Tomorrow the World," *New York Review of Books,* October 10, 2002, 33.

50. Schlesinger, *The Cycles of American History,* 143.

51. Chace, "Tomorrow the World," 33.

52. Schlesinger, *The Cycles of American History,* 144.

53. *Ibid.*

54. Chace, "Tomorrow the World," 34.

55. Howard Beale, *Theodore Roosevelt and the Rise of America to World Power* (Baltimore, MD: Johns Hopkins University Press, 1956), 26.

56. Albert Beveridge, "The Star of Power," in *God's New Israel: Religious Interpretations of American Destiny,* ed. Conrad Cherry (Englewood Cliffs, NJ: Prentice-Hall, 1971), 152–53.

57. Andrew Burstein, *Sentimental Democracy: The Evolution of America's Romantic Self-Image* (New York: Hill and Wang, 1999), 117.

58. J. William Fulbright, "The Arrogance of Power," in *God's New Israel: Religious Interpretations of American Destiny,* ed. Conrad Cherry (Englewood Cliffs, NJ: Prentice-Hall, 1971), 260.

59. Alan Dawley, "The Abortive Rule of Big Money," in *Ruling America: A History of Wealth and Power in a Democracy,* ed. Steve Fraser and Gary Gerstle (Cambridge, MA: Harvard University Press, 2005), 159.

7

The Cowboy Crusader and the Americanization of the World

I simply experiment, an endless seeker, with no past at my back.

—Ralph Waldo Emerson

In 1902 the novel *The Virginian* was published. Its main character was patterned after Theodore Roosevelt, college buddy and lifelong friend of the book's author, Owen Wister. The protagonist of *The Virginian* would later become the prototype of the American western hero depicted in hundreds of novels and grade B movies during the twentieth century, representing the manly qualities of valor, strength, and honesty. Roosevelt, himself a reader and writer of western fiction, embodied this figure and its spiritual entitlement during his entire political career as when, in 1912, he bucked his own party at the Republican convention and characterized the American people itself as a form of messianic hero from Revelation: "We stand at Armageddon and we battle for the Lord."[1] Roosevelt was alluding to a spiritual mission behind the image of the warrior in its American form, a kind of "spirit/cowboy." This figure, a throwback to the early colonial messianic Puritan hero, is itself a derivative of the Old Testament hero/leader of the children of Israel and Christ, the messianic redeemer/hero of Revelation.[2]

In his effort to build a new promised land, the "American Adam" holds himself separate from the law, his eye toward the horizon, ready to defend his personal values against socially destructive forces cast as evil. He is a cool, yet reluctant killer, willing to give over love and law in his attempt to rescue his personal image of the life of the community. This characterization would become the model for America's presence in the world during a large part of the twentieth century and on into the twenty-first century and found its first full expression in the American canon through the writings of Ralph Waldo Emerson.

Fusing Puritan and Romantic models, Emerson created the figure of an "overman," an individual that was at once a universal and a national ideal. The prime feature of this hero is his "self-reliance" or "self-trust," which mirrors the sense of independence upon which America's identity is founded and echoes Jesus's authorization of himself as sole source of spiritual reference. While Jesus proclaimed, "I am the Light and the Way," Emerson believed that "[w]hoso would be a man must be a nonconformist," for whom "nothing is at last sacred but the integrity of [his] own mind."[3] Whereas Jesus came "to set a man at variance against his father, and the daughter against her mother, and the daughter in law against her mother in law," the self-reliant man shuns "father and mother and wife and brother" when called by his "genius."[4] For Emerson, the genius of the self-reliant man lay in the genuine expression that emerges from that aboriginal self which is common to all men. This core is a spark of divinity. While Jesus said, "the kingdom lies within," the self-reliant man knows, "God is here within."[5] The self-reliant man is an emanation of:

> that Unity, that Over-Soul, within which every man's particular being is contained and made one with all other; that common heart, of which all sincere conversation is the worship, to which all right action is submission; that overpowering reality which confutes our tricks and talents, and constrains everyone to pass for what he is, and to speak from his character and not from his tongue, and which evermore tends and aims to pass into one thought and hand, and become wisdom, and virtue, and power, and beauty.[6]

For the self-reliant man, society is a "conspiracy," therefore he will "obey no law less than eternal law" and only needs self-trust as his talisman.[7] As messiah, the ur-man is "born to shed healing to nations";

"towards . . . external evil, the man within the breast assumes a warlike attitude, and affirms his ability to cope single-handed with the infinite army of enemies."[8] The millennial messiah casts out Satan and all his minions. Whereas Jesus was the Word made flesh, for Emerson, "man is word made flesh."[9] The mode of the inner man is one of action, for his soul is perpetually unfolding: "Man's life is a progress, and not a station"; the soul is perpetually in a state of becoming, life always an adventure, "the way, the thought, the good shall be wholly strange and new," accessible only to the man of courage.[10] "He is again on his road, adding new powers and honors to his domain."[11] The aboriginal man, "appointed by Almighty god to stand for a fact," is impervious to circumstance.[12] He is a "reserved force which acts directly by presence and without means," so that victory is gained by way of simple demonstration of superiority.[13]

As a political prophet, the American hero *is* the nation itself, the savior for the nations of the world. "America is the country of the Future," a place in the mind where "futurity is all. It has no past: all has an onward and prospective look."[14]

> The Genius or Destiny of America is . . . a man incessantly advancing, as the shadow on the dial's face, or the heavenly body by whose light it is masked . . . Let us realize that this country, the last found, is the great charity of God to the human race.[15]

For Emerson, America was the self, and the land was destiny.

In many ways Theodore Roosevelt was a living individual embodiment of the mythic American people as the children of God— entitled by race, privileged by class, capable of overcoming personal debilitation, headstrong to the point of arrogance, aggressively dominating, prone to glorifying power, with a mandate to spread the larger-than-life values he held as sacred. As a nearsighted and asthmatic boy, Roosevelt responded to adversity "by sheer dint of practicing fearlessness," declaring, "I'll make my body."[16] Under the influence of a leonine father, his life became a personal struggle to overcome weakness in order "to do the rough work of the world."[17] He later explained, "I had to train myself painfully and laboriously not merely as regards my body but as regards my soul and spirit," and declared that he fought for "the highest form of success which comes . . . to the man who does not shrink from danger, from hardship, or from bitter toil."[18] Roosevelt created the aura of manly power in his personhood, developing himself in the contact sport of boxing, actively engaging with the outdoors, carrying a firearm, and hunting at home and abroad. He killed many bears on his North American hunts and more than three hundred wild animals on his African safaris, and he once used a knife to slay a cougar. (Ironically, his nickname "Teddy" was coined in honor of a bear he did not kill.)

The muscular orientation to which Roosevelt devoted himself informed his belief as to what it meant to be a man in modern times, which in turn determined his sense of what it took to lead a nation of mighty manhood. Men must be judged "by the fire and vigor of their passions; by their deep sense of injury; by their memory of past glory; by their eagerness for fresh fame."[19] "As it is with the individual, so it is with the nation," he declared upon his return from his military success in Cuba. "There is no place in the world for nations who have become enervated by a soft and easy life or who have lost their fibre [sic] of vigorous hardiness and manliness."[20] Near the turn of the century he wrote,

> The twentieth century looms before us big with the fate of many nations . . . If we stand idly by, if we seek merely swollen, slothful ease and ignoble peace, if we shrink from the hard contests where men must win at hazard of their lives and the risk of all they hold dear, then the bolder and stronger peoples will pass us by, and will win for themselves the domination of the world. Let us therefore boldly face the life of strife.[21]

While accepting the vice presidency in 1901, Roosevelt asked, "Is America a weakling to shrink from the world work of the great world-powers? No. The young giant of the West stands on a continent and clasps the crest of an ocean in either hand. Our nation, glorious in youth and strength, looks in the future with eager eyes and rejoices as a strong man to run a race."[22]

For Roosevelt, the individual manly body, the soul of the nation, and the integrity of the white race were interrelated. The essential qualities for all three were "work-fight-breed."[23] Men must be inspirited by the "hot life of feeling" that accrued through passionate engagement with the world of work and conflict and results in an "iron quality."[24] A nation's community of interest emerges out of the "great primal needs and primal passions that are common to all of us,"[25] and yet must be tempered by the power of reason so that civilization could advance itself. Thus Roosevelt's zealous energy was not simply a matter of hypermasculinity as a defense against a fear of vulnerability and weakness, rather it carried the spirit of a higher cause that he identified with a civilizing influence. As president, Roosevelt's most famous tenet of foreign policy came from the African proverb, "Speak softly and carry a big stick, and you will go far." He was in large part suspicious of representative government, which he felt gave rise to ineffectual leadership and a "certain softness and luxury."[26] In his last annual message as president, he made an impassioned plea for centralized power: "Concentrated power is palpable, visible, responsible, easily reached, quickly held to account."[27]

While he was a member of the powerful elite class, being "firmly resolved to belong to the governing class, not the governed," Roosevelt also came to have a close and sympathetic relationship toward those who were impoverished and underprivileged.[28] He defined "true Americanism" as the making of "a community of interest among our people" that advanced the cause of fair treatment for all.[29] (At the same time, he had little patience for strikers when he felt the strength of the nation was weakened by their actions.) Roosevelt would eventually become a leader in the Progressive movement which was opposed to big money and corporations and advocated such moderating measures as a graduated income tax, workmen's compensation, women's suffrage, federal conservation, and the regulation of labor for women and children, while anticipating most of the reforms of the New Deal.[30]

Roosevelt's obsession with physical strength carried over into a political orientation that placed the United States at the pinnacle of world hegemony, and he became an outspoken advocate of American imperialism. As an expansionist he saw it as America's right and moral obligation to acquire and democratize foreign lands and peoples wherever the opportunity presented itself. This orientation was expressed by Roosevelt in a speech in California in 1903, in which he looked beyond America's boundaries for her realm of influence. "Before I came to the Pacific Slope I was an expansionist, and after having been here I fail to understand how any man, convinced of his country's greatness . . . can be anything but an expansionist. In the century that is opening the commerce and the command of the Pacific will be factors of incalculable moment in the world's history."[31] Roosevelt's eye for history then went to a comparison of America with one of the greatest historical empires:

> Our place as a nation is and must be with the nations that
> have left indelibly their impress on the centuries . . . Those
> that did not expand passed away and left not so much as a
> memory behind them. The Roman expanded, the Roman
> passed away, but the Roman has left the print of his law, of
> his language, of his masterful ability in administration, deep
> in the world's history, deeply imprinted in the character of
> the races that came after him. I ask that this people rise level to
> the greatness of its opportunities.[32]

Although commerce was a factor in the orientation toward expansionism, for Roosevelt it served more the power and prestige that he believed America represented to the rest of the world. In keeping with a warrior-like masculinity, he preferred the country attain its prestige through military means. Roosevelt saw war as a form of spiritual renewal for the individual and the nation, a means to the "moral life," as well as a way for America to achieve her rightful place of dominance, "the position to which it is entitled among the nations of the earth."[33] A college friend wrote, "[Roosevelt] would like above all things to go to war with someone . . . He . . . wants to be killing something all the time."[34] As assistant secretary of the navy, Roosevelt prepared for and advocated war with Spain, which would justify the buildup of the navy. He said, "I should welcome almost any war, for I think this country needs one," for "no triumph of peace is quite so great as the supreme triumph of war."[35]

Roosevelt's ambitions were fueled by his experience leading an attachment of voluntary gunmen on a charge up San Juan Hill in Cuba during the Spanish-American War, creating images that launched him into the national spotlight.[36] Toward the end of his presidency, he ordered sixteen battleships to sail around the world to establish a sense of American military superiority. (It is thought by some that this gesture so aroused Japanese anxiety that it led indirectly to Japan's confrontation with the United States in World War II.) He considered World War I a "holy war" and was highly critical of Woodrow Wilson for not entering it sooner.[37] Roosevelt's desires were further frustrated when Wilson refused to allow him to command a division of volunteers he had independently gathered to fight in the war.

Roosevelt justified expansionism, both on the continent and abroad, with the Darwinian idea that democracy had justified itself by keeping "for the white race the best portions of the new world's surface."[38] He wrote a treatise, *The Winning of the West* (1889–1896), on the idea that harsh frontier conditions had made the American people into a superior race that had replaced the "scattered savage tribes, whose life was but a few degrees less meaningless, squalid, and ferocious than that of the wild beasts with whom they held joint ownership . . . The conquest and settlement by the whites of the Indian lands was necessary to the greatness of the race and to the well-being of civilized mankind," for the continent could only be a "game preserve" to the "squalid savage."[39] "[T]he man who puts the soil to use must of right dispossess the man who does not, or the world will come to a standstill."[40]

The culmination of the expansionist movement under Roosevelt was the occupation of the Philippines by the United States, which wove together both the moralistic and the militaristic threads in the American fabric. In addition to desiring power for the sake of status among other nations, Roosevelt genuinely thought of the white race as superior, and he saw the civilizing influence of a "masterful" people as a matter of pride and duty. The lesson of expansionism was that "peace must be brought in the world's waste spaces . . . Peace cannot be had until the civilized nations have expanded in some shape over the barbarous nations."[41] America's occupation of the Philippines was justified by the belief that "we can rapidly teach the people of the Philippine Islands . . . how to make good use of their freedom."[42] He wrote to his friend and colleague Elihu Root that "brutal wrongdoing, or an impotence which results in a general loosening of the ties of a civilized society, may finally require intervention by some civilized nation."[43] Ironically, in spite of the fact that he won the Nobel Peace Prize for negotiating peace between Russia and Japan, Roosevelt's imperialistic position regarding the Philippines set the tone for future American invasion of foreign lands in the Far East and Middle East in the twentieth and twenty-first centuries. All of these occupations were characterized by disdain of local culture, the use of torture, and the overall use of military force to achieve short-term ends. A less violent, but equally imperialistic mandate to save the world was carried by the next great American president, Woodrow Wilson.

At a certain point as he was entering his older years in the late 1920s, Sigmund Freud (his name means "joy") was depressed. He had cancer of the jaw, didn't think he had long to live, and believed that his death would bear little notice. He had written everything he wished to write, and his mind had no more to offer. While in this state, he was visited by a longtime friend, an American government official, William C. Bullitt. Bullitt told Freud he was working on a book about the Treaty of Versailles that would contain studies of the major players, including Woodrow Wilson. Bullitt later wrote, "Freud's eyes brightened and he became very much alive. Rapidly he asked a number of questions, which I answered. Then he astonished me by saying he would like to collaborate with me in writing the Wilson chapter of my book."[44]

What had stirred Freud—the master detective—about Wilson was the discrepancy between Wilson's arrogance and the results of his actions. Freud wrote: "When, like Wilson, a man achieves almost the exact opposite of that which he wished to accomplish, when he has shown himself to be the true antithesis of the power which 'always desires evil and always creates good,' when a pretension to free the world from evil ends only in a new proof of the danger of a fanatic to the commonweal, then it is not to be marveled at that a distrust is aroused in the observer."[45] Freud was particularly taken by Wilson's statement to William F. McCombs, chairman of the Democratic National Committee, that he had won the presidential election because "God ordained that I should be the next President of the United States. Neither you nor any other mortal or mortals could have prevented it."[46] Freud, ever the ironist and just having finished his book on religion, *The Future of an Illusion*, could only remark, "I do not know how to avoid the conclusion that a man who is capable of taking the illusions of religion so literally and is so sure of a special personal intimacy with the Almighty is unfitted for relations with ordinary children of men. As everyone knows, the hostile camp during the war also sheltered a chosen darling of Providence: the German Kaiser."[47]

Bullitt collaborated with Freud on the chapter, which ended up becoming a book in itself and was finally finished one year before Freud's death. In his study of Wilson, Freud took an approach consistent with his view of the human personality at that time, combining the Oedipus complex with his newly realized notion that life instincts were opposed by equally strong tendencies toward death. The job of the ego was now to create psychological defenses to protect itself. Freud also took an unwittingly Jungian turn by designating an archetype, represented alternatively by Christ and God the Father, as the pathological identification at the root of Wilson's condition.

In Freud and Bullitt's assessment, Wilson, the son of a powerful Presbyterian minister, raised in the post–Civil War South, was unconsciously in love with the man whom he referred to as "my incomparable father."[48] Wilson identified with his father's Presbyterian values, especially the idea of the covenant between the brotherhood of mankind and God. Repressing his hostility toward his father, Wilson developed the higher defense of sublimation through his skill in language and oratory, which he used throughout his life to express his Presbyterian values in his conflicts with authority. He longed for paternal recognition, but his accomplishments were never satisfactory to him. As a young man he wrote in a letter to his future wife, Ellen Axson, that he had a "terrible ambition, a longing to do immortal work," and complained of his feeling "that I am carrying a volcano about with me."[49] In Freud and Bullitt's opinion, Wilson's defenses of repression, identification, and sublimation were engaged to protect a fragile feminine ego from the demands of a severely masculine superego. This resulted in Wilson's idealized perception of himself and his naïve perception of the world, which led him to "ignore the facts of the real outer world, even to deny they existed if they conflicted with his hopes and wishes."[50]

Freud and Bullitt noted physiological symptoms caused by emotional conflict that plagued Wilson throughout his life. Frequently, in times of crisis, he suffered from bouts of severe indigestion and dyspepsia, nervousness and neurasthenia, headaches and strokes, all of which resulted in frequent breakdowns or minor strokes. This condition culminated in the permanently debilitating stroke that Wilson suffered in the final months of his presidency, just prior to the Senate's vote against the treaty that included his cherished proposal for a League of Nations. The authors diagnosed this repeated physical disability as stemming from Wilson's unconscious hostility toward his father.

Freud and Bullitt saw Wilson's career as an enactment of his identification with Jesus, a defense against the association of his father, and hence his superego, with God the Father. As a Jesus figure, Wilson appealed to the masses but lost track of the actualities of the political situation at hand. Instead, he saw himself as a political messiah devoted to bringing peace to the world as God's mouthpiece. The result of this psychological drama was the catastrophic psychophysical/political martyrdom of Wilson and the setup of a world political structure that ensured another cataclysmic world war.[51]

The spirit of American Presbyterianism that was inculcated into Wilson as a child expanded the Old Testament notion of covenant and held that there was a special relationship between America and Providence. The new nation, following a political theology, would prosper under God's eye as long as it remained righteous. In an early lecture, Wilson asserted that Christianity prepares the way for international law by establishing standards of morality and common principles of civilization. For the early Wilson, Christianity, as a brotherhood of man, established a universal conscience for mankind, thus presenting a model for what would later become an image of a community of nations. In 1885, in a piece entitled "The Modern Democratic State," Wilson wrote that democracy was a "sphere of moral action" and that universal emancipation would emerge from the brotherhood that was man in the Christian model.[52] Only a short step was necessary to go from this statement to a vision of America's role as a teacher to non-Christian countries. In 1909, Wilson wrote, "Every nation of the world needs to be drawn into the tutelage of America," and again in 1912, "God planted in us visions of liberty that we are chosen and prominently chosen to show the way to the nations of the world how they shall walk in the paths of liberty."[53] For Wilson, other nations were "children and we are men in these deep matters of government and justice."[54]

Wilson's rhetoric thus became the model for future notions of democracy's mandate to establish the grounds of itself for others in service to the quasi-theological notion that democracy is a preferred form of government—a mandate that was in fact in service to national interest. It was under Wilson's unilateral direction that American forces invaded Mexico, the Dominican Republic, Haiti, and Nicaragua "to teach South American republics to elect good men."[55] Wilson strove to "keep the white race strong" as the upholder of civilized values, asserting, "the white civilization and its dominion over the rest of the world rests largely on our ability to keep this country intact."[56]

Although the word "democracy" was iconic in Wilson's discourse, he took several actions that belied this notion. He supported eugenics and, in 1907, helped to make Indiana the first state to adopt legislation aimed at compulsory sterilization. As president, Wilson allowed segregation in several federal departments. He pushed through the Espionage Act of 1917 and the Sedition Act of 1918, which severely suppressed civil rights and made it a crime to express anything in language deemed disloyal to the government's policies. He sanctioned the American Protective League, an organization promoting the act of spying on fellow citizens as a check on behavior considered antithetical to American interests. Under these acts, several individuals, including the socialist Eugene Debs, were convicted and jailed for antigovernment statements, and innocent people were rounded up and deported because of their racial heritage.

As World War I broke out, Wilson strove for American neutrality with the underlying fantasy that America, with Wilson as its leader, would be the arbiter of peace under terms that embodied his sense of American values, including a commitment to the notion of the world as a community of nations. America would serve the world as "the light which shall shine unto all generations and guide the feet of mankind to the goal of justice and liberty and peace."[57] As early as 1916, Wilson spoke of a "league of nations," in the service of a "common force" bringing into existence a "common order" serving a "common justice" and a "common peace."[58] Finally in 1917, when it seemed that Germany was intent upon conducting unlimited submarine warfare and when word came out of Germany's attempt to form a secret alliance with Mexico, Wilson made the decision to intervene. His justification, again, was framed in messianic terms: "The world must be made safe for democracy . . . and we shall fight . . . for a universal dominion of right by such a concert of free peoples as shall bring peace and safety to all nations and make the world itself at last free."[59] The involvement of America as the "greatest hope and energy of the world" made the war a vessel for Wilson's need for an apocalyptic crusade.[60] Unfortunately for these fantasies, America's involvement came too late for it to wield the power it needed to influence the peace process.

After the war, Wilson saw it as his and America's mission to establish no less than a global democracy of equal and independent nations. Following in the model of an Old Testament prophet in league with God, Wilson framed his proposal as a covenant containing

Fourteen Points that would serve as the "conscience for the world."[61]
The Fourteen Points, which Wilson had begun to formulate already
in January of 1918, contained general assertions such as open
covenants, free trade, reduction of arms, self-determination of
government by individual countries, particular arrangements for
several troubled areas such as Russia, Belgium, Alsace-Lorraine,
Italy, Austria-Hungary, the Balkans, and Poland, and finally
Wilson's personal grand vision, the League of Nations. The league
would provide for peaceful settlement of disputes, reduction of arms,
improvement of labor conditions, and America's commitment to
defend any border against foreign invasion.

Seemingly oblivious to the aggressive and greedy designs of the
Allied nations, which had been made clear in secret treaties that
he knew of as early as 1917, Wilson thought he could win political
favor at the peace negotiations by appealing directly to the European
people. He gave public speeches in cities in France and Italy, where
he was hailed by ecstatic crowds as "the Savior of Humanity" and
"the Moses from across the Atlantic." Instead, the treaty process
turned Wilson into Jesus at Gethsemene, as his popular favor carried
no weight with the Allied leaders, Lloyd George and Georges
Clemenceau, who made a mockery of his ethereal rhetoric. Wilson
could have asserted America's power with the Allies but instead
backed down against Britain's and France's claims for arms, territory,
and reparations from Germany. Above all, Wilson wanted to protect
the perfection of his vision for the League of Nations, and he felt the
league would ultimately reconcile any conflicts that emerged from the
treaty. He capitulated on issues of amnesty, annexations, indemnities,
and reparations, and as a result, Germany was left impoverished, the
Middle East was carved up to the advantage of Allied powers, and
colonial peoples in countries the world over—Egypt, India, Southeast
Asia, Korea, and China—were betrayed.

Seeing himself as a cosmic hero, Wilson thought he was returning
home with the archetypal treasure—hard to obtain, an international
agreement to his blueprint for world peace which he considered to be
"ninety-nine percent insurance against war."[62] He was unable to
understand that he had capitulated on matters that might have actually
brought about that peace, or the fact that he now had to submit the
Treaty of Versailles for approval to a Senate either resistant to international

military obligations or opposed to the extravagant benefits given the Allies. Loyal progressive colleagues such as Bullitt resigned, and the liberal press slammed the treaty as "shameless."[63]

Wilson forged ahead, undaunted by political realities, including the results of an interim election in 1918 in which his party, the Democrats, had lost power in both the House and Senate. On July 10, 1919, Wilson addressed the Senate and presented the treaty. He described American soldiers as "crusaders" for "a great moral force."[64]

> The mere sight of our men, of their vigor, of the confidence that showed itself in every movement of their stalwart figures and every turn of their swinging march, in their steady comprehending eyes and easy discipline, in the indomitable air that added spirit to everything they did would astound the masses to be saved.[65]

His words resonated with the Bible: "the monster . . . must be put in chains," the "demon of war" vanquished.[66] America was the "conscience of the world," and the League of Nations was of "indispensable instrumentality for the maintenance of a new order . . . in the world of civilized men."[67] Americans, as "unaffected champions of what was right," had a new role in the world—one that came with a new responsibility.[68]

> The stage is set, the destiny disclosed. It has come about by no plan of our conceiving, but by the hand of God who led us into this way. We cannot turn back. We can only go forward, with lifted eyes and freshened spirit, to follow the vision. It was of this that we dreamed at our birth. America shall in truth show the way. The light streams upon the path ahead, and nowhere else.[69]

After his address to the Senate, Wilson set out to win the American people over to his grand scheme with a grueling national tour that took him to dozens of cities. By this time he had become completely identified with the image of the savior hero leading the march to the new age. He spoke of "this great nation marching at the fore of a great procession" with its eye on "those heights upon which there rests nothing but the pure light of the justice of God."[70] Under Wilson's leadership, America would release mankind from bondage.

> [You] will find that the hand of pitiless power has been upon
> the shoulders of the great mass of mankind since time began,
> and that only with that glimmer of light which came at Calvary
> that first dawn which came with the Christian era, did men begin
> to wake to the dignity and right of the human soul . . . and
> realize the purposes that God had meant them to realize.[71]

America now had "the infinite privilege of fulfilling her destiny and
saving the world."[72]

In the end, Wilson's body betrayed his identification with divinity.
He collapsed in breakdown from his chronic neurasthenia in April
1919, suffering from congestive heart failure, headaches, fatigue,
difficult breathing, asthma, and nausea. His speaking tour was cut short
and ultimately had no effect on the Senate. Wilson succumbed to a
stroke in October of 1919, shortly before the treaty that included the
establishment of the League of Nations was disapproved by the Senate.
While Wilson said he wanted to make America "drunk with self-
sacrifice" in order to bring about "the new age in the world," it was
ultimately Wilson who sacrificed himself.[73] H. G. Wells wrote,

> For a brief interval Wilson stood alone for mankind. Or at
> least he seemed to stand for mankind. And in that brief
> interval there was a very extraordinary and significant wave
> of response to him throughout the earth . . . He was
> transfigured in the eyes of men. He ceased to be a common
> statesman; he became a Messiah. Millions believed him as
> the bringer of untold blessings; thousands would gladly have
> died for him . . . Manifestly the World-State had been
> conceived then, and now it stirred in the womb. It was alive.
>
> And then for some anxious decades it ceased to stir.[74]

Although Wilson's values and goals were grounded in his
fundamental belief in human progress through reason and democracy,
his grand plan was ultimately a contradictory conflation of liberty
and empire. His conscious intention was to create an international
structure based on democracy, but in fact, his vision would give
rise to a global structure of American hegemony among nations
based on its advantage in capitalism. In 1907, Wilson declared in
his lectures at Columbia University,

> Since trade ignores national boundaries and the manufacturer
> insists on having the world as a market, the flag of his nation

must follow him, and the doors of the nations which are closed
must be battered down . . . Concessions obtained by financiers
must be safeguarded by ministers of state, even if the sovereignty
of unwilling nations be outraged in the process. Colonies must
be obtained or planted, in order that no useful corner of the
world may be overlooked or left unused.[75]

Wilson later wrote, "Constitutional liberty is the soil out of which
the best enterprise springs,"[76] and pronounced, in referring to
American investment abroad, "I am willing to get anything for an
American that money and enterprise can obtain." Like other presidents
and many European leaders, Wilson believed that capitalist
imperialism contributed to a higher civilization by bringing in industry
and, with it, morality and educational resources. Although he pledged
to take on money trusts and opposed dollar diplomacy, as president
Wilson was in favor of government influence to protect investment in
foreign economy and also renewed efforts in support of globalized
corporate capitalism in which America would have an advantage. "If
we are partners, let me predict we will be the senior partners. The
financial leadership will be ours. The commercial advantage will be
ours."[77] Through this rhetoric, Wilson returned to America's Puritan
and Hamiltonian roots, reestablishing the connection between
American dominance, globalized capitalism, and Christian morality
and grounding his policies in American exceptionalism.

Former national security advisor and secretary of state Henry
Kissinger has said, "Whenever America has faced the task of
constructing a new world order, it has returned in one way or another
to Woodrow Wilson's precepts."[78] Wilson also set a precedent for the
denial of the consequences of spiritualized politics, a condition repeated
by a B movie actor who showed himself to be a master in creating
illusion—Ronald Reagan.

Ronald Reagan was raised in the Midwest, the son of an alcoholic
father. He worked as a lifeguard on the Rock River near his home in
Dixon, Illinois, and claimed to have saved dozens of lives, heroically
marking each rescue with a notch in a tree. Growing up within a
troubled family, he found security in a Christian sect, the Disciples
of Christ, an experience that would later influence the fundamentalist
tone of his political rhetoric. After attending a religious college, where
he took part in theater and sports, he worked as a radio sportscaster of

baseball games, announcing from a studio by reading from a ticker tape, at times embellishing his descriptions of the action with his own imagined ideas of what was happening.

It was in his college days that Reagan learned that the content of what he was saying didn't matter as much as how he said it. A girlfriend from this time later pointed out his "inability to distinguish between fact and fancy," a characteristic that was noted about him throughout his political career.[79] Early on he mastered the knack of speaking at people, making each encounter a one-way performance on his part. Three aspects of these early years stand out as characteristic of Reagan in his later political career—his identification with the rescuing hero, resorting to simplistic, fundamentalist morality, and his confusion of fact and fantasy.

As a politician, Reagan, "the great communicator," appealed to the anxious element of the American psyche that yearns for simplicity, certainty, moral rectitude, and optimism—with a down-to-earth tone of congeniality. He played to an audience that identifies with the perpetual innocence and simplicity of youth and that is at once intolerant of complexity, impatient with uncertainty, unmindful of the past, and naïve regarding the future. In short he took on a role something like a latter-day Moses, the father/hero/guide of the American children of Israel, innocent and besieged by malevolent forces.[80]

Ironically, Reagan started his political leanings as a New Deal Democrat and became a master of Populist rhetoric of the 1930s, which was later echoed in his famous presidential debate line, "Are you better off now than you were four years ago?" In the post-war years, communism took on a satanic aspect for Reagan as he pointed to the Soviet Union as the "evil empire" and the "focus of evil in the modern world." As master of the sound bite, he would eventually boil his approach to government down to a simple statement that easily covered over the complexities of political life, "Government is not the solution; government is the problem." Reagan's rhetoric ultimately reflected a Puritan ideal of unreflective optimism and unsubstantiated promise which was overtly expressed in an image that Reagan took directly from a speech of John Winthrop, the creation of the utopian "shining city on the hill." In his farewell address in January 1989, he said, "I've spoken of the shining city all my political life . . . in my mind it was a tall, proud city built on rocks stronger than oceans, windswept, God-blessed, and teeming with people of all kinds living in harmony and peace; a city with free ports that hummed with commerce and creativity."[81]

During his tenure as a Hollywood actor, Reagan was involved in union activity with which he eventually became disillusioned. He came to be influenced away from an ideology favoring Franklin Roosevelt's reforms, which had helped his family, and moved toward a perspective that saw government as the enemy of economic opportunity. When his acting career faltered, he used his oratorical skills to excel as a spokesman in the business community, most notably by traveling the country for the General Electric Corporation and giving the same speech over and over, first to GE plant employees and later to outside groups, for the purpose of bolstering morale and inducing pro-business motivation. "The Speech," as it came to be known, was saturated with free-market ideals. It was this sensibility—in which government as incapable, "alcoholic" (in the sense of free-spending) father authority is seen as the culprit and barrier to individual well-being—that became the hallmark for Reagan's political career catering to a public mentality that yearns for rescue.

Reagan's oratorical skill, honed on the GE plant beat, served him well as a spokesman for the conservative cause at the time of Barry Goldwater's run for president in 1964, and the public response to his speeches turned him toward politics. As a politician, Reagan surrounded himself with business-oriented functionaries who had a laissez-faire orientation to the relationship of government and the market, especially in regard to government holding back its power to regulate. The guru of this movement during the second half of the twentieth century was Milton Friedman, a Nobel Prize–winning economist who introduced a tenet known as "monetarism." Monetarism asserted that a reduction of government regulation and a slow predictable growth in the money supply was the best course for the government to take in relation to the market. Essentially this was a supply-side theory descended from a conception of Adam Smith's image of the guiding hand of the market governing itself. In fact, it was not in keeping with Smith's idea that government involvement in the market was necessary to an extent in order to keep in check the desire for profit of some merchants.

Reagan's primary domestic agenda was the budget, which reflected not only his background in business, but his optimistic sense of the religious spirit which he felt economics held for Americans. The promised land of trickle-down economics was always just around the corner if government would pull back from interference. While he preached the importance of decreased government expenditures, the fact is that his administration created a deficit three times as great as when it began. His administration accomplished a considerable dismantling of government involvement in business regulation, enhancing the economic standing of the upper levels of the population to the detriment of the majority of the people. In the area of agriculture, more than 400,000 farm families lost their land between 1985 and 1989, while $25.8 billion was spent for subsidies to agribusiness in 1986 alone. Overall, the top one percent of the population saw its average net worth grow by more than 25 percent between 1983 and 1989. Reagan cut taxes, benefiting the wealthiest 20 percent of the taxpayers, and decreased corporate taxes through the creation of loopholes, while increasing military spending by $7.2 billion.

This program of tax cuts in conjunction with inflated defense spending—which came to be known as "Reaganomics," a byword for sleight-of-hand budgeting—was masterminded by a young economist, David Stockton. Stockton resorted to manipulating numbers in selling his program, deliberately doctoring them under a confusing accounting system. "We got away with that because of the novelty of all these budget reductions," Stockton later declared.[82]

> None of us really understands what's going on with all these numbers. You've got so many different budgets out and so many different baselines and such complexity now in the interactive parts of the budget between policy action and the economic environment and all the internal mysteries of the budget, and there are a lot of them. People are getting from A to B and it's not clear how they are getting there.[83]

Stockton's numbers, meant to sell rather than meet tests of reliability, were unchecked by a compliant Congress. The result of Reagan's deceptive supply-side economics in which big business was favored, was not the growth of the economy that was advertised by the administration, but the beginning of a recession. There followed a threefold jump in the deficit, the highest unemployment of any period after World War II, the worst average wage, productivity that was the slowest since World War II, and finally a stock market crash.

In the realm of foreign policy, although he did accomplish a medium-range missile treaty with the Soviet Union, Reagan mostly displayed his penchant for policy based upon self-created black-and-white fantasy rather than objective reality. A major push was to establish the Strategic Defense Initiative, commonly known as "Star Wars," a defense program in which the boundaries of the country were reenvisioned to include space and in which enemy missiles would be shot out of the sky by American missiles guided by lasers. Defense Secretary James Schlesinger referred to it as "a collection of technical experiments and distant hopes," which Reagan nevertheless treated "as if it were already a reality."[84]

In his efforts on behalf of SDI, Reagan was articulating a belief system held by many Americans. Under this worldview, science and technology become godlike agents that can solve any problem. The "shield" made up of laser rockets was imagined as a form of quasi-divine protection associated with a utopian community. In fact, this scenario, like most of Reagan's, came out of one of his B movies.[85] In the 1940 film *Murder in the Air*, Reagan plays the role of a hero assigned to protect a secret weapon, the "inertia projector." He brings down enemy planes by knocking out their electronics systems from a distance, just as Star Wars was thought to. Star Wars was the perfect image for a man and a people who tend to look to a superman who is able fix problems with a single decisive act. When negotiating with Premier Gorbachev over ways to stop nuclear proliferation and reduce nuclear weapons, Reagan could not go the final yard in giving up the Strategic Defense Initiative.

While Reagan is often given credit for bringing down the Soviet Union with his increased defense spending, a careful analysis reveals that the communist state fell due to its own incapability to maintain its economic structure as well as the continued policy of containment adhered to by several presidents. Reagan's foreign policy, in fact, was riddled with incompetency and, in some cases, corruption, most notably in the case of the Iran-Contra scandal. This involved the illegal sale of arms to Iran for money used to support the Contras during their war against the communist-leaning Sandinistas in Nicaragua. The

Nicaraguan government brought a complaint against the United States in the World Court which found the U.S. guilty of war crimes, a decision ignored by the U.S. In a subsequent vote in both the Security Council and the General Assembly of the United Nations on a measure calling for states to observe international law, the United States (along with Israel in the latter case) was the only nation to vote in opposition.

The effects of Ronald Reagan's administration did not end with the completion of his term, rather, the overtly manipulative mode of his administration set the standard for those to come. In 1992, a group of former Reagan officials then working at high levels in the Bush Sr. administration wrote a memo that depicted the United States as a kind of colossus astride the world, imposing its will and keeping world peace through military and economic power. When the memo was leaked it had to be rewritten, but it still maintained the sensibility that was deceitfully enacted in the coming years: America had the right to act unilaterally to discourage any state in areas such as the Middle East when the United States had ascertained that the possible use of weapons of mass destruction might be used to gain exclusive access to resources such as oil and to challenge American superiority in the Persian Gulf states. The authors of this memo, Paul Wolfowitz and Dick Cheney, were prominent proponents in the subsequent administration of George W. Bush for the push toward war in Iraq, as well as the undermining of involvement by the U.S. in virtually every international institution requiring a cooperative effort. Karl Rove, speaking for the second Bush administration, reflected Reagan's mindset when he declared, "We're an empire now, and when we act, we create our own reality."[86]

Reagan's administration sabotaged a number of benefits that government offered the very people who looked to him as a symbol of the goodness of the country. He increased the burden of federal government debt and shifted it downward to those least able to bear it, exacerbated economic inequality by enhancing opportunities for the wealthy and for big business, undermined environmental programs, dismantled labor protections (especially in breaking up of the air controllers' union and in the area of overall job safety), and unraveled food and drug protection measures. Reagan's war on drug usage resulted in the needless overcrowding of jails at excessive expense to the taxpayers. The deregulation of the communications industry during the Reagan administration led to mergers that in effect resulted in the homogenization of information available to the American public. Finally, Reagan's removal of regulation in the financial sector through his signing of the Garn–St. Germain Depository Institutions Act of 1982 and the pullback from regulatory activity by his appointed chair of the SEC, John Shad, resulted in the savings and loan collapses in the mid-1980s which cost the taxpayers $150 billion in bailout funds.

Frederick Turner has stated that Reaganesque intelligence "reduces the information it gets from the outside world to its own categories and accepts reality's answers only if they directly address its own set of questions . . . It insists on certainty and unambiguity and so is at war with the probabilistic and indeterminate nature of the most primitive and archaic components of the universe."[87] Indeed, Reagan's popularity in the face of the actual disasters brought to the American people by his administration was due to what he symbolized to a core aspect of American character—America will always be the hero in the white hat out to conquer the forces of evil. The illusions that Reagan fabricated—that America's citizens, inherently innocent and purposeful, will thrive only without the encumbrance of government, and only within the secure setting which the military can bring about—appealed to that strain of the American psyche that sees itself as chosen people destined to dominate its world but is at the same time perpetually fearful of difference.[88] Former House Speaker Thomas O'Neil considered Reagan to be the worst president he had worked with since the end of World War II, but added, "He would have made a hell of a king."[89] James Lake, Reagan's press secretary during his 1984 campaign, referred to him as "the ultimate presidential commodity . . . the right product."[90] In the end, Ronald Reagan was the embodiment of the American myth; he was the movie itself.

The vision of the American spirit/cowboy—a throwback to the line of biblical hero/leaders from Adam to Christ himself—ascends upward and onward in the name of progress to the future and the city on the hill. This monocular perspective, fettered by the resistance of spirit to the teachings of the past and the complexities of the present, misses the ground of untended lived life and the consequences of reckless pursuit. The national catastrophes that followed in the years after 9/11, both domestic and foreign, give evidence of how a cultural narrative based upon notions such as promised land, privilege for the elite, children of God, ambivalence toward the law, need for dominance, and incapacity for empathic connection with the other leads to dire outcomes. The flooding of New Orleans, an event reflective of a nation's neglect of its infrastructure, both technical and human, provides an initial image for reflection regarding a cultural consciousness and its dark underbelly.

Notes

1. William Roscoe Thayer, *Theodore Roosevelt: An Intimate Biography* (New York: Houghton Mifflin, 1919), 20.

2. The New Testament warrior redeemer was described by John in Revelation:

> And I saw heaven opened, and behold a white horse; and he that sat upon him was called Faithful and True, and in righteousness he doth judge and make war.
>
> His eyes were as a flame of fire, and on his head were many crowns; and he had a name written that no man knew, but he himself.
>
> And he was clothed with a vesture dipped in blood: and his name is called The Word of God. (Revelation 20:11–13)

This messiah figure is prefigured in the Old Testament announcement of the coming of the Redeemer:

> For unto us a child is born, unto us a son is given: and the government shall be upon his shoulder: and his name shall be called Wonderful, Counselor, The mighty God, The everlasting Father, The Prince of Peace. (Isaiah 9:6)

3. Ralph Waldo Emerson, *The Essays of Ralph Waldo Emerson*, introduction by Alfred Kazin (Cambridge, MA: Harvard University Press, 1987), 29–30.

4. Matthew 10:34; Emerson, *The Essays of Ralph Waldo Emerson*, 30.

5. Emerson, *The Essays of Ralph Waldo Emerson*, 41.

6. *Ibid.*, 160. There is a striking similarity here to certain of Jung's depictions of the archetypal Self.

7. *Ibid.*, 29, 42.

8. *Ibid.*, 43, 148.

9. *Ibid.*, 43.

10. *Ibid.*, 71, 39.

11. *Ibid.*, 278.

12. *Ibid.*, 272.

13. *Ibid.*, 271.

14. Ralph Waldo Emerson, *The Collected Works of Ralph Waldo Emerson*, vol. 1, *Nature, Addresses, and Lectures,* introduction and notes by Robert Spiller (Cambridge, MA: Harvard University Press, 1971), 230.

15. Sacvan Bercovitch, *The Puritan Origins of the American Self* (New Haven, CT: Yale University Press, 1973), 158.

16. Edmond Morris, *Theodore Rex* (New York: Random House, 2001), 6; Jackson Lears, "The Managerial Revitalization of the Rich," in *Ruling America: A History of Wealth and Power in a Democracy,* ed. Steve Fraser and Gary Gerstle (Cambridge, MA: Harvard University Press, 2005), 187.

17. Sarah Watts, *Rough Rider in the White House: Theodore Roosevelt and the Politics of Desire* (Chicago: University of Chicago Press, 2003), 41.

18. Watts, *Rough Rider in the White House,* 42; Morris, *Theodore Rex,* 6.

19. Watts, *Rough Rider in the White House,* 4.

20. Howard Beale, *Theodore Roosevelt and the Rise of America to World Power* (Baltimore, MD: Johns Hopkins University Press, 1956), 40.

21. *Ibid.*, 80.

22. Morris, *Theodore Rex,* 8.

23. Watts, *Rough Rider in the White House,* 86.

24. *Ibid.*, 12, 23.

25. *Ibid.* 23,

26. *Ibid.*, 64.

27. Morris, *Theodore Rex,* 541.

28. Watts, *Rough Rider in the White House,* 64.

29. Lears, "The Managerial Revitalization of the Rich," 188.

30. Ironically, Roosevelt's campaign in 1904 was financed in large part by the very corporations he later turned against.

31. Morris, *Theodore Rex,* 228.

32. *Ibid.*, 229.

33. Watts, *Rough Rider in the White House*, 205; Beale, *Theodore Roosevelt and the Rise of America to World Power*, 39.

34. Beale, *Theodore Roosevelt and the Rise of America to World Power*, 36.

35. "Theodore Roosevelt," retrieved August 16, 2012, from http://en.wikipedia.org/wiki/Theodore_Roosevelt; Beale, *Theodore Roosevelt and the Rise of America to World Power*, 38.

36. Roosevelt is usually depicted heroically on a horse, leading the charge, although in fact he was the only one of his company to have a horse, which he was forced to abandon before he reached the top of the hill.

37. Watts, *Rough Rider in the White House*, 73.

38. Beale, *Theodore Roosevelt and the Rise of America to World Power*, 26.

39. "Theodore Roosevelt," retrieved August 16, 2012, from http://en.wikipedia.org/wiki/Theodore_Roosevelt.

40. Theodore Roosevelt, *The Winning of the West: Part I. The Spread of the English-Speaking Peoples* (New York: G. P. Putnam's Sons, 1903), 121.

41. Beale, *Theodore Roosevelt and the Rise of America to World Power*, 32.

42. Morris, *Theodore Rex*, 110.

43. Watts, *Rough Rider in the White House*, 235.

44. Sigmund Freud and William C. Bullitt, *Thomas Woodrow Wilson: A Psychological Study* (Boston: Houghton Mifflin, 1967), v–vi.

45. Freud and Bullitt, *Thomas Woodrow Wilson: A Psychological Study*, xiii.

46. *Ibid.*, xi.

47. *Ibid.*

48. *Ibid.*, 58.

49. *Ibid.*, 28.

50. *Ibid.*, xii.

51. The psychoanalytic drama of father/son was further enacted by Bullitt who had worked closely with Wilson during the Paris Peace Conference but then felt betrayed by Wilson's concessions to the Allied powers and subsequently resigned. When called to testify before a Senate Committee he revealed that Wilson's own secretary of state, Robert Lansing, did not support the treaty that Wilson was pushing.

52. Thomas J. Knock, *To End All Wars: Woodrow Wilson and the Quest for a New World Order* (New York: Oxford University Press, 1992), 5.

53. John B. Judis, *The Folly of Empire* (New York: Scribner, 2004), 76; Knock, *To End All Wars*, 11.

54. Pankaj Mishra, "Ordained as a Nation," *London Review of Books*, February 21, 2008, 3.

55. Ronald Steel, "The Missionary," *New York Review of Books*, November 20, 2003, 26.

56. Mishra, "Ordained as a Nation," 5.

57. Knock, *To End All Wars*, 20.

58. *Ibid.*, 96, 77.

59. *Ibid.*, 121–22.

60. Judis, *The Folly of Empire*, 14.

61. *Ibid.*, 80.

62. Freud and Bullitt, *Thomas Woodrow Wilson: A Psychological Study*, 195.

63. Steele, "The Missionary," 28.

64. Woodrow Wilson, "Presenting the Treaty for Ratification: An Address to the Senate of the United States," in *God's New Israel: Religious Interpretations of American Destiny*, ed. Conrad Cherry (Englewood Cliffs, NJ: Prentice-Hall, 1971), 286.

65. *Ibid.*, 285

66. *Ibid.*, 291.

67. *Ibid.*, 287, 290.

68. *Ibid.*, 292.

69. *Ibid.*, 294.

70. Ernest Lee Tuveson, *Redeemer Nation: The Idea of America's Millennial Role* (Chicago: University of Chicago Press, 1968), 210.

71. *Ibid.*, 34–55.

72. Robert Jewett and John Shelton Lawrence, *Captain America and the Crusade against Evil: The Dilemma of Zealous Nationalism* (Grand Rapids, MI: William B. Eerdmans, 2003), 4.

73. Freud and Bullitt, *Thomas Woodrow Wilson: A Psychological Study*, 227–28.

74. Knock, *To End All Wars*, 1.

75. "Theodore Roosevelt," retrieved August 16, 2012, from http://en.wikipedia.org/wiki/Theodore_Roosevelt.

76. Judis, *The Folly of Empire*, 78.

77. *Ibid.*, 115.

78. Steele, "The Missionary," 27.

79. William Kleinknecht, *The Man Who Sold the World: Ronald Reagan and the Betrayal of Main Street America* (New York: Nation Books, 2004), 38.

80. In this vein it is worthy of note that black-and-white thinking and super-responsible morality is a prominent strain in children of alcoholics who are prematurely forced to take responsibility for others.

81. Ronald Reagan, "Farewell Address, January 21, 1989," in *A Shining City: The Legacy of Ronald Reagan*, ed. D. Erik Felten (New York: Simon and Schuster, 1998), 23.

82. Gary Wills, *Reagan's America: Innocence at Home* (Garden City, NY: Doubleday, 1987), 367.

83. *Ibid.*

84. Marilyn Berger, "Ronald Reagan Dies at 93," *New York Times,* June 6, 2004, A31.

85. See, for example, Anthony Lane, "The Method President: Ronald Reagan and the Movies," *New Yorker*, October 8, 2004, 190–202.

86. Mark Danner, "How, and What, Obama Won," *New York Review of Books*, December 20, 2012, 86.

87. Edmund Morris, "The Unknowable," *New York Review of Books*, June 28, 2004.

88. In 1994 Reagan announced to the country his diagnosis of Alzheimer's syndrome, and, in fact, there were those who had noticed lapses in his memory in his last several months in office when his accessibility was tightly regulated. In addition, it was well known that he had a physical disability in terms of his hearing. Reagan's mental and physical condition can be seen as a metaphorical representation of a public consciousness that can't remember the past or hear in the present because the underlying script calls for the march to go ever forward.

89. Berger, "Ronald Reagan Dies at 93," A31.

90. Kleinknecht, *The Man Who Sold the World*, 23.

8

"Katrina"

By the rivers of Babylon, there we sat down, yea, we wept, when
 we remembered Zion.
We hanged our harps upon the willows in the midst thereof.
—Psalms 137:1–2

As Dante and his guide, Virgil, descend through the outer
regions of hell wherein souls must spend eternity actively
suffering by means of the very sins they have committed
in life, they arrive at the realm of incontinent sinners and the circle
of the gluttonous.

> I am in the third circle, of eternal, accursed rain, cold and heavy,
> never changing its measure or its kind; huge hail, foul water
> and snow pour down through the gloomy air, and the ground
> that receives it stinks.[1]

Here the souls howl like dogs while lying on the putrefying ground
as rain beats upon them. Dante's classic description of the underworld
describes several watery places—streams, marshes, rivers, lakes—each
holding a dark, befouled liquid symbolizing the blood and tears,
miseries and sorrows of human existence forgetful of divine spirit.
Continuing on, the travelers come to the circle of the wrathful, created
by the marsh of the Styx where the water is "the blackest purple." They
observe the souls "all naked with looks of rage . . . smiting each other

not only with the hand but with head and breast and feet and tearing
each other piecemeal with their teeth."[2]

The companions then enter Malebolgia—literally, "evil
pouches"—the region of willful sinners. They cross over a channel
and look down upon souls sunken by their flattery such that they
are condemned to languish, covered in mud, in its dark waters amidst
foul fumes.

> [The] banks were crusted by the exhalation from below
> with a mold that sticks on them and is repugnant to eyes
> and nose . . . [and] in the moat below I saw people plunged
> in a filth which seemed to have come from human privies.[3]

Finally, Dante discovers the barraters, those who purchase and sell
office in church and state, existing in a pit where "a thick tar was
boiling . . . which stuck to the bank on every side." Devils, as if from a
cartoon, catch souls destined for this pit with hooks and fling them in.

In late August 2005, Hurricane Katrina blew in from the Gulf of
Mexico and struck land south and east of New Orleans. In the
aftermath of the storm, some of the levees protecting the city to the
north were badly breached—not from the force of the storm but due
to poor design and maintenance. This caused the worst floods in the
country's history, which temporarily wiped out the entire city, causing
untold death and destruction. Famously, President George W. Bush
claimed later that no one could have predicted the breach of the levees.[4]
And yet a year before Katrina, Joel Bourne Jr. wrote an article in
National Geographic describing a doomsday scenario that not only
predicted with astounding accuracy the events in New Orleans, but
also expressed the prevailing opinion held by scientists, engineers, and
disaster planners and conveyed in vain to authorities that the levees
were highly unstable.

> It was a broiling August afternoon in New Orleans, Louisiana,
> the Big Easy, the City That Care Forgot . . . as . . . TV "storm
> teams" warn of a hurricane coming in from the Gulf of Mexico.
> Nothing surprising there: Hurricanes in August are as much a
> part of life in this town as hangovers on Ash Wednesday.
>   But the next day the storm gathered steam and drew a bead
> on the city. As the whirling maelstrom approached the coast,
> more than a million people evacuated to higher ground. Some

200,000 remained, however—the car-less, the homeless, the
aged and infirm and those die-hard New Orleanians who look
for any excuse to throw a party.

. . . The water [of Lake Pontchartrain] crept to the top of
the massive berm that holds back the lake and then spilled over.
Nearly 80 percent of New Orleans lies below sea level—more
than eight feet in some places—so the water poured in . . . As it
reached 25 feet over parts of the city, people climbed onto roofs
to escape it.

Thousands drowned in the murky brew that was soon
contaminated by sewage and industrial waste. Thousands
more who survived the flood later perished from dehydration
and disease as they waited to be rescued . . . the Big Easy was
buried under a blanket of putrid sediment, a million people
were homeless.[5]

An equally prophetic article that had appeared in 2002 in the *New
York Times* predicted that a category 4 or 5 storm would send "[water]
cascading over the levee wall . . . Draining the city after the storm
moves away may take weeks . . . [the] city would be trapped inside
the levees, steeped in a worsening 'witches' brew' of pollutants like
sewage, landfill waste, chemicals and the bodies of drowned humans
and animals."[6]

The floods of New Orleans were actually among the most predicted
catastrophes in the nation's history. The disaster, a collapse in literal
infrastructures as well as political structures of government, police, and
emergency aid agencies representative of the inadequate quality of the
nation's infrastructure and political structures, reveals the implications
of an underlying mythic narrative that emphasizes a future promised
land to an entitled people but which actually privileges an elite few at
the literal expense of the majority of people. The consequences of this
vision were borne directly on the backs of racial minorities, the poor,
and the elderly, as well as indirectly on the population as a whole which
bore the brunt of billions of dollars of repair and rebuilding costs.

The word "levee" comes from the French *lever* "to raise."
Historically, levees have been used for more than 3,000 years,
beginning with ancient Egyptian, Mesopotamian, and Chinese
cultures. Levees require a great deal of attention and maintenance, and
for this reason some have argued that they were a catalyst for the initial
formation of government in ancient civilizations. Since a levee is only

as strong as its weakest point, construction and maintenance of levees is best accomplished by a central governing authority. The building and maintaining of levees can be seen as a watermark for the adequacy of this authority. In the last half of the twenty-first century, in contrast to the United States, the United Kingdom, the Netherlands, and Japan have spent billions of dollars building and maintaining state-of-the-art systems of flood control using a variety of technological means. This technology combines flexibility and rigidity depending on the particular environmental circumstance. Levees, dikes, floodwalls, natural barriers, pumps, computer sensors, and floodgates are all utilized. Compared to these structures, the levees of New Orleans were medieval artifacts.

The levees and canals of New Orleans, some constructed over eighty years ago, were poorly built, poorly sealed structures. Although the Army Corps of Engineers oversees flood control in the nation's waterways, the levees of New Orleans were a patchwork, maintained by a number of different agencies, each with different guidelines resulting in different heights of levees and poor linkage of sections. These agencies included local sewage and water boards and the state transportation system, as well as the Corps of Engineers, which is charged with overall responsibility.

The maintenance of levees in New Orleans has historically been affected by budgetary compromises and the triumph of cheap, short-term solutions spread out over a long period. Concrete flood walls, inserted in earthen levees to give them additional support, were built in conformity to diminished budget allocations and tested only for a low degree of severity of weather. The standards were dictated by Congress and Corps officials in Washington over several years in response to political needs rather than engineering necessities. In addition, there were external factors that determined flood control priorities. In the 1970s, a Corps plan to put in a large barrier at the narrow openings between Lake Pontchartrain and the Gulf was canceled after a court challenge by environmental groups. A subsequent proposal for floodgates at the city's drainage canals was opposed by local officials of levee, sewage, and water boards. Each subsequent backup plan over the years entailed further risk. In addition to inadequately constructed, tested, and maintained flood walls, the Corps also lacked a plan for dealing with any breach that might occur. Concrete plans for flood control did not keep pace with the growing alarm among scientists and engineers.

Katrina was like a cosmic joke on New Orleans, a city that is known to flaunt a carefree character. As millions watched the glowing, bright red spiral of the storm make its way across the television screen toward New Orleans, at times achieving unprecedented speeds, the city prepared for the worst with a forced evacuation. The highways out of town were soon clogged, but the evacuation was planned only for those with personal transportation. Over 100,000 people had no cars, and officials gave little consideration to the means by which they would evacuate. Suddenly, the storm veered to the east, allowing the city to avert yet another calamity in its long history of daring the elements.

The punch line came the next day. As New Orleans prepared to return to daily life, its streets began to fill with a black fluid. The levees on the 17th Street and Industrial Canals had given way to the waters of Lake Pontchartrain on the north side of the city. Flood Street soon lived up to its name, and Chalmette, site of the Battle of New Orleans during the War of 1812, went down. Within hours the city was 80 percent submerged in up to twenty feet of a slimy, viscous substance—the long-anticipated witches' brew of sewage, poisons and pollutants, industrial waste, oil, toxic chemicals, and corpses, both human and animal.

New Orleans became a Venice of Hades as streets turned into darkly colored canals. One hundred and fifty thousand homes and vehicles were flooded, each one a potential source of pollutants. Natural gas and accompanying acrid fumes bubbled to the surface. Smoke from chemical explosions filled the air. Cars and buildings were mushed together as if in perverse celebratory intercourse. Bridges were washed out, electricity vanished citywide, sewage disposal became nonexistent, and communication impossible. Power lines dangled as poles tilted like match sticks, and wooden houses floated off their foundations like buoys, the cheap stuff of American dwellings—foam and plastics of all varieties—floating upon the polluted water. Fires raged untouched, and lootings and carjackings were commonplace. The airport became an impromptu triage area for the dead and infirm. Rows of people on stretchers waited with those bound to wheelchairs. One terminal served as an emergency room, another as a morgue. Corpses were tied to telephone poles like rows of crucifixes. A huge root beer mug advertising Frostop Burgers was turned upside down and half submerged, as if having dumped its brew, while nearby a sign dangled advertising "Southern Comfort."

The place where poker was invented had bluffed once too often, and the city famous for its gumbo had become a deadly soup. The birthplace of jazz had become a terminal riff on lights out, a body in decomposition, and the city famous for its funerals became a floating morgue. The City That Care Forgot had forgotten to take care of itself.

The crowds that could not be evacuated from the city were directed to the Super Dome and the convention center, two public facilities that presented themselves as secure containers for the community under normal circumstances and as emergency holding grounds for those who made it to their doors in the midst of the disaster. A total of 30,000 New Orleans residents made their way to the Super Dome, which had been built over the grave site of a famous voodoo queen, Marie Laveau, and would soon be transformed itself into an underworldly arena where games of life and death took place. Twenty thousand people filled the convention center, but as events unfolded, the group soon became a dark mockery of a political gathering.

Facilities meant to be havens of protection turned out to be among the most stressful parts of the disaster. Since the power was out, there was no air conditioning or lighting. Toilets quickly became unusable, and food and water were nowhere to be found. In the Super Dome, gangs roamed, beating, robbing, and successfully driving off police officers, while guards stationed outside were charged with keeping the arena's occupants confined within. At the convention center nearby, dead bodies sat in wheelchairs with notes in their laps, corpses lay on the floor wrapped in sheets, and a dying woman assumed the fetal position on the sidewalk. Eventually, the body count grew to ten at the Super Dome and twenty-four at the convention center. When the crowds were finally allowed to exit to the Dome's parking lots to board buses, they had to wait for hours, still without water, under a broiling sun. Armed guards, mostly white, watched over the predominately black masses, and the confrontation quickly took on racial overtones.

When the evacuation finally took place, some families were separated and were not able to reunite for days to come.

The levees that were breached in New Orleans were along canals. Initially, engineers believed that water had flowed over the top of the walls, but they finally determined that both the design and inadequate consideration given to the type of soil serving as a base and the depth of the underlying pilings in the soil caused a collapse of the levee walls. The walls were shaped like an "I," a design that gives less support than the more expensive "T-wall" alternative. The pressure of the water on the upper portion of the "I" walls caused them to tilt, allowing a gap to form between the walls and the earthen part of the levees, splitting the levees in two. The unstable underlying clay soil and the shallowly driven pilings could not hold the tilting walls, which caused the levees to cave in.

An additional aspect of the flooding was the fact that the soil under the floodwalls, and under the entire city, had been sinking at an alarming rate. Manmade structures such as canals, pipelines, and building development caused erosion and prevented natural sediment from forming. Gas and oil removed from underground contributed to a lowering of the surface so that natural marshland and wetlands surrounding New Orleans quickly disappeared. Global warming, which causes the intensity of storms like Katrina to increase, also indirectly contributed to the flooding. For years, policy makers and legislators on all levels of government failed to heed these factors, instead making decisions on the basis of short-term political benefit.

As the levees gave way, the disaster that resulted gave evidence of the inadequacies of the containers of the community—government and police agencies that had been established to protect those unable to protect themselves but which seemed to dissolve in the flood as well. Foremost in the breakdown of community infrastructure was that of the police force. For years the New Orleans Police Department had been known for ineffective leadership, lack of discipline in its ranks, and outright corruption, drawing the population's general disrespect and distrust. In 1994, a federal attorney in New Orleans estimated that 15 percent of the police force was corrupt. After Hurricane Katrina approximately 200 officers abandoned their posts during the flood.

(Others, such as one female police officer who paddled on a floating door to make her way to her job, took heroic measures to report for duty.) In the aftermath of the flood, members of the New Orleans police force were charged with the murder of unarmed civilians trying to cross Danziger Bridge and a subsequent massive cover-up of the situation. (Five were eventually convicted on several counts, not including murder, and one for the cover-up.) At least eight incidents involving police officers during the days following Hurricane Katrina came under the investigation of federal law enforcement officers. Even if the police force had been functional, there was no necessary equipment, no means of transportation or communication, and no facilities to incarcerate criminals. In fact, the whole justice system was undermined by the destruction of computers and records. One officer remarked, "The hurricane plan was: 'We hope it misses us.'"[7] There was a scheme for some kind of police response to hurricane destruction, but under the leadership of Chief of Police Edwin Compass, that plan remained on the shelf.

Compass, a boyhood schoolmate of Mayor Ray Nagin, had been chosen by Nagin from within the ranks of the force. At one point during this time of crisis, Compass paradoxically found himself in competition with looters when he was forced to take office equipment from a supply store for use by civic authorities. When reinforcements finally arrived in the form of National Guard troops, the need to establish order had already given way to the necessity of finding and rescuing survivors and recovering bodies, tasks for which the troops were not adequately prepared. Photographs of that time showed images of soldiers taking breaks among pageant masks of skeletons and monsters and props of pageantry simulating death.

Critical breakdowns occurred in the hospital system where ninety-one people died. The hospitals were drastically unprepared for a flood of this magnitude, as the state legislature had repeatedly declined requests for adequate funds for hurricane preparation. As a result, hospitals became inoperable—flooded, power gone, under siege from gangs. At Memorial Medical Center, patients died while waiting in a broiling parking garage for rescue. With no body bags available, untreated, uncovered corpses were loaded for evacuation on helicopters. Some of the elderly in hospitals for the aging were simply abandoned. St. Rita's Nursing Home was a particular disaster: over half of its sixty residents died, and their bodies had still not been recovered one week later.

The crisis also catalyzed heroic efforts by hospital staff. Functions normally handled by machines, such as pumping air into lungs, had to be performed by hand. At Charity Hospital, the city's historic care facility for the poor since its founding in 1736, a painstaking evacuation project took place. Patients had to be moved down several flights of darkened stairs and then ferried across the street to a parking garage, where trucks transported them to a roof from which they could be airlifted. During each move, care needed to be taken that the proper equipment remained attached to the patient. For patients in critical care, such as cardiac patients, this could involve gingerly moving up to 500 pounds of instruments along with the patient. And yet over the course of the hurricane and its aftermath only three patients died at Charity.

Meanwhile, another section of the population, those rescued from their homes, was forming itself much like the wandering lost souls in limbo. Thousands of residents escaped the flood by making their way to rooftops, often knocking a hole in the attic ceiling. The rescue of these individuals, now homeless, was slow and haphazard. With the Super Dome and the convention center full and dysfunctional, there was no place to take them. Many were dropped off like litter along interstate highways and told that help was on the way or more directly that they were on their own. "I will never again tell people that help is on the way," said Thomas Stone, the Bernard Parish fire chief. "It's not coming."[8] No help was forthcoming and there was no place to go. Some were told to walk down a highway and cross a bridge to get buses, only to be stopped by police on the other side and told to go back. One procession, attempting to cross a bridge, found itself the target of gunfire from police resulting in the killing of civilians—the city of parades for the dead became the city of parades of death itself. Meanwhile, families were ruptured, with babies who were days old being given up by mothers desperate for help. Richard Zuschlag, president of the Acadian ambulance service, said, "They were just looking at us with fear and horror on their faces. We would put four of them in an incubator and just fly them out. They're scattered all over the country now. We couldn't keep track of where everyone was going."[9] The consequence was a shifting mass of homeless wanderers in a macabre procession under a broiling sun with no food or water.

The city that made the funeral an art form had itself become a black mockery of the ritual. The city known for Fat Tuesday (Mardi Gras) entertained a procession of bloated corpses bobbing along its streets. Among the dead bodies floating in the streets were those of individuals previously buried in cemeteries and mausoleums but now freed by the floods. The dead literally rose as ghoulish corpses turned up in swamps and fields with no immediate way to discern their identities. The overall number of deaths from Katrina was in the hundreds. People were still drowning as late as five days after the initial flooding. The elderly died at far higher rates than the general population, as more than two-thirds of those who did not evacuate were over sixty, not including those who were hospitalized.

Although the City of New Orleans's evacuation plans and the response of the state of Louisiana were grossly inadequate, the failure of the federal government to utilize its resources in a timely manner was even more jarring. Inept government was clearest in the case of the Federal Emergency Management Agency. When George W. Bush became president, FEMA funding for flood control was cut in half, and after 9/11 the agency was merged into the Department of Homeland Security. Representative Bennie Thompson noted, "FEMA went back to being treated like a political resting place for favors owed. The entire emphasis of it was demoted."[10] Bush appointed Michael Brown, a former associate and a lawyer with no experience in emergency management to head FEMA, and the agency's role was redefined to give more responsibility to local authorities. There was no provision for funds with which local agencies could carry out their new responsibilities. Crisis management was undertaken without a centralized focus. Despite warnings from the National Hurricane Center, FEMA sent only seven of twenty-eight available search-and-rescue teams and had no plan for help in evacuation or to maintain law and order. Few of the buses under federal control arrived to transport evacuees from the Super

Dome and convention center, extending the evacuation to five days. The use of available firefighters was limited by FEMA (1,000 were sent to Atlanta!), trucks with much needed water were prevented from unloading, diesel fuel was kept from being delivered, and emergency connection lines were cut off.

Brown's inadequacy was epitomized in his response to a question from television reporter Paula Zahn, in which he stated the federal government knew nothing of deteriorating conditions at the convention center days after it had been widely reported to the public. Another reporter stated that Brown just "mumbled" when asked about buses for evacuation.[11] Meanwhile, Brown's boss, the head of Homeland Security, Paul Chertoff, waited thirty-six hours after the storm to declare the flooding in New Orleans an "incident of national significance." Chertoff's isolation from the reality of the disaster was further evidenced in his statement that there were only "isolated instances of criminality" in the city.[12]

New Orleans had become a literal waste land reminiscent of T. S. Eliot's poem:

> The river's tent is broken . . .
> . . . The nymphs are departed.
> . . . .
> And their friends, the loitering heirs of city directors;
> Departed, have left no addresses.
> By the water of Leman I sat down and wept . . .
> . . . .
> But at my back in a cold blast I hear
> The rattle of the bones, and chuckle spread from ear to ear.
> A rat crept softly through the vegetation
> Dragging its slimy belly on the bank
> While I was fishing in the dull canal
> . . . .
>   Unreal City . . .
> . . . .
> O City city . . .[13]
>
>   I sat upon the shore
> Fishing, with the arid plain behind me

Shall I at least set my lands in order?
. . . .
These fragments I have shored against my ruins.[14]

The city itself was speaking through Rainer Maria Rilke's words:

I've been scattered in pieces,
torn by conflict,
mocked by laughter,
washed down in drink.
In alleyways I sweep myself up
out of garbage and broken glass . . . .
I am a city by the sea
sinking into a toxic tide.
I am strange to myself, as though someone unknown
had poisoned my mother as she carried me.
It's here in all the pieces of my shame
that now I find myself again.
I yearn to belong to something to be contained . . .[15]

Every city, like every psyche, has its own essence that in itself tends to attract the conditions with which it is faced. How can brokenness be seen as a part of the soul of New Orleans? It is a city of fronts, both physical and psychological, where sources of power as well as inferiorities are hidden in dark corners. Its streets, unlike the wide streets of square design of most American cities, are dark and narrow, as if crawling along in curious ways. In the shadows of the flood lurks a city whose spirit seems to court disaster, where disruption and reversal of order are part of the collective structure. With Katrina, the borderland mentality of the city gave rise to the ironies of a netherworld emergent.

New Orleans is a port that historically has harbored its own paradoxes. The city is famous for its cultural wealth, elegance, beauty, and grace. And yet it is also a place of rampant poverty, broken infrastructure, violence, corruption, and crime. It is a city known for its fine food and music and through its magnificent public celebrations, its attunement to the rhythms of community life. At the same time it lives on the edge of death, perpetually anticipating natural disaster and worst case scenarios.

New Orleans embodies the archetype of liminal space, betwixt and between. In the past, black and white melded into Creole. Geographically, the city exists in the place where land and water blend

God y An Instrument of
(good

into an ambiguous marsh. The city embodies an atmosphere in which chaos and law congeal into corrupt hierarchy. Fatalism and bravado merge in public expressions of gratitude and grief, public rituals and pageants overturning social decorum. As a city existing below sea level, New Orleans has traditionally courted peril, yet is also known for its carefree style, the Big Easy. As the old song goes, "You can flood this town / you can't shut the party down." Surrounded as it is by the Gulf of Mexico, the Mississippi River, and Lake Pontchartrain, New Orleans is like a bowl with an inverted function, holding water out. When the bowl broke, the pulsing of its rhythms and the flow of its life were themselves dammed up.

Vaporous marshlands and depths are classical habitats of soul, and New Orleans holds a great attraction for those seeking a transformative experience.[16] The sense of soul as interface between spirit and matter is reflected in the polytheism of the city. It keeps its faith in miracles— the missing fingers on the statue of Jesus at St. Louis Cathedral are said to have flicked away a hurricane—yet, it also freely recognizes the devil. As a former center for slave trade, where many African natives eventually found their homes, the city channels an undercurrent of African-based religious systems. Andrew Jackson's wife described it as "Great Babylon . . . come before me." "Oh the wickedness, the idolatry of this place," she exclaimed.[17]

From a polytheistic perspective, many gods are seen to come to life in New Orleans's commitment to ritual pageantry. It is a city where carnival really matters. New Orleanians, poor, rich, and in between, white, black and in between, take their cooking and eating seriously, just as they take their music seriously, and their dancing, and their masks and costumes, and their celebratory rituals, because it is not mere entertainment to them. It is all part of a ritual in which the finiteness, the specificity and fragility and durability and richness and earthiness and sadness and laughter of life, are all mixed together, honored, and given tangible form in sound, movement, and communal cuisine.[18]

The most famous celebration, of course, is Mardi Gras. Literally meaning Fat Tuesday, Mardi Gras in its ancient Christian context represents the last day of feasting before the beginning of the Lenten season marked by Ash Wednesday. Its earlier roots lay in the fertility rites of the Egyptians and Greeks, the saturnalia of the Romans, and the medieval Feast of Fools. Uncertainty of consciousness, licentious breaking of bounds, and the inversion of political and social order and values rule the day.

Circling throughout the city is a sense of soul carried by its music. New Orleans's most famous son, Louis Armstrong, described jazz, which claims New Orleans as its birthplace, as the source of other forms of American music.

> Jazz is all the same—not anything new. At one time they was calling it levee camp music, then in my day it was ragtime . . . When I play my music . . . You want to feel the smell—the color— the great "Oh, my" feeling of the jazzmen and stomp around in the smoke and musk of the joints.[19]

Carnival, procession, music—all come together in New Orleans's funerals. Funerals in New Orleans give the community the opportunity to gather around the individual, and they are often more ornate than weddings as neighborhoods give their dead a final memorial parade past familiar places. An internal punctuation mark is provided by dancers—paid professionals mixed with just anyone off the street who wants to join up and dance along. Funeral processions are both led and terminated by bands—music as the alpha and omega of life.

At the time of the Civil War, New Orleans was the wealthiest city in America and remained the wealthiest city in the South until the 1920s. Throughout its history, no city in North America has so consistently faced disaster as New Orleans. Floods, flu, fire, and hurricanes, as well as the collapse of buildings made from poor material, have all plagued the city. Although a boom or bust economic attitude became a psychological reality for the city of reckless abandonment and a devil-may-care attitude, by 2005 New Orleans had become one of the poorest cities in the country, the delicate balance already broken before the floods.

As with the country as a whole, everything in New Orleans, a city that was two-thirds African American at the time of Katrina, has to be seen in part through the lens of race. Race has historically been a part of the landscape in New Orleans since the United States took it over in 1803. The French custom of intermarriage between whites and black slaves gave rise to the Creole class, and the Spanish custom of allowing blacks to buy their freedom resulted in a large middle class of black freemen. Americans made no distinctions and treated all blacks as inferiors. The French Quarter, which was not traditionally affected by flooding, was settled by whites in the late 1700s. Black freemen built their settlement on the land nearby, establishing Treme, one of the oldest black communities in the country and the birthplace of jazz.

When the floods came, New Orleans was two-thirds black, and a quarter of the population lived below the poverty line (compared to 9 percent in the country overall). Many of New Orleans's impoverished African American residents caught by the flood water were at home because they had no car. It was the Ninth Ward, with a 98 percent African American population, that was the first to be flooded from breaches in the levee/canal systems.

The images of the floods and their aftermath as metaphors of a nation tell us that it is not only the poor, aged, infirm, and minority populations that are trapped and left behind in American culture. We would also see that it is the spirit of New Orleans as a place—embodying as it does a delicate balance of paradox and liminality, irony and imagination, as the lowlands of the American psyche threatened by submersion. These very qualities are themselves in jeopardy of being trapped and abandoned by a culture short on memory, long on utopian ambition, and intolerant of the other in all its forms, all themes of a cultural narrative based in Judeo-Christian forms.

The factors involved in the collapse of the flood walls can be seen as metaphors for looking at America's cultural life. No image is more illustrative than the photograph of President George W. Bush flying over the New Orleans floods, peering out through the plane window for a bird's-eye view of the devastation. The fall of the levees points to the fact that America's vision from on high overreaches while forgetting what is close at hand—infrastructure, both literal and governmental. The levees of community structures don't support or contain the collective with well-grounded policies, nor do their pillars of foundational imagination go deep. If levees are only as strong as the weakest link, their demise can be seen as an indication that America's collective value system collapses with its weakest links, the disenfranchised as well as its infrastructure. A top-heavy cultural orientation has created a lowland for imagination regarding collective life—a long way from the corporate towers which make up the city on the hill.

Notes

1. Dante Alighieri, "Inferno," *The Divine Comedy of Dante Alighieri*, trans. John D. Sinclair (New York: Oxford University Press, 1961), 87.

2. *Ibid.*, 103–5.

3. *Ibid.*, 233.

4. Joseph Treaster and Deborah Sontag, "Despair and Lawlessness Grip," *New York Times*, September 2, 2005, A14.

5. Joel K. Bourne Jr., "Going with the Water," *National Geographic*, October 2004, 88–103.

6. Byron Calame, "The Public Editor: Covering New Orleans, the Decade Before the Storm," *New York Times*, September 11, 2005, 14.

7. Lee Hancock, "With little backup," *Dallas Morning News*, September 5, 2005, 12.

8. Sewell Chan and Jeremy Alford, "Heavy Damage," *New York Times,* September 4, 2005, A1.

9. Felicity Barringer and Donald G. McNeil, Jr., "Grim Triage," *New York Times,* September 3, 2005, A7.

10. Eric Lipton and Scott Shane, "Leader of Federal Effort Feels the Heat," *New York Times,* September 2, 2005, A11.

11. Peter Applebome, et al., "A Delicate Balance," *New York Times,* September 4, 2005, 23.

12. Treaster and Sontag, "Despair and Lawlessness Grip," A18.

13. T. S. Eliot, "The Waste Land, III. The Fire Sermon," lines 173–259, *The Complete Poems and Plays 1909–1950* (New York: Harcourt, Brace, & World, Inc., 1952), 42-45.

14. Eliot, "The Waste Land, V. What the Thunder Said," lines 424–431, *The Complete Poems and Plays*, 50.

15. Rainer Maria Rilke, *The Book of the Hours*, trans. Anita Barrows and Joanna Macy (New York: Riverhead Books, 1996), 99.

16. See James Hillman, *The Dream and the Underworld* (New York: Harper and Row, 1979), for a complete description of the nature of the soul and its relation to the classical underworld.

17. Peter Applebome, "Where Living at Nature's Mercy," *New York Times*, August 31, 2005, A11.

18. Tom Piazza, *Why New Orleans Matters* (New York: Regan Books, 2005), 35.

19. John M. Barry, *Rising Tide* (New York: Simon and Schuster, 1997), 215.

9

The Shell Game:
Enron and Its Fall

Should two people set out on an undertaking together, they call to one another "*Koinos hermes,*" which means . . . a find and a theft done together. Fundamentally this is the motto of every business undertaking. Even the most honest business is directed toward a no man's land, a Hermetic intermediate realm that exists between the rigid boundaries of "mine and yours," where finding and thieving are still possible.

—Karl Kerényi

Within weeks of the fall of the twin towers, another collapse occurred in America that affected the nation just as dramatically, but in a very different manner—the bankruptcy of its seventh largest company, Enron.[1] The fall of Enron and the ensuing investigation, which revealed fraudulent accounting and questionable management practices, soon led to a chain of similar collapses of behemoth businesses such as WorldCom, Tyco International, and ImClone, as well as general public mistrust of the market. The ultimate consequence was catastrophic financial hardship for thousands of individuals who lost their jobs, lifetime savings, and retirement funds. While America focused its attention upon the 9/11 attack by Islamic fundamentalists, the country was in fact being subtly terrorized by its own financial and business executives.

With reported earnings in 2000 of over $100 billion, Enron was considered by many on Wall Street to be "America's most innovative company," a prime example of the "new economy" with its orientation toward "asset-lite" structuring. In the years preceding 2001, Enron had grown at a spectacular rate by combining a substantial asset base from its origins in pipelines for gas with an increasing emphasis on trade. This transformation included a turn toward energy trading using a revolutionary online marketplace and trading access to broadband communications. The word "Enron" was coined by the company from the word *enteron*, associated with the Greek root word for energy, which also held the industrial connotation of a pipeline transmitting nourishment. However, *enteron* also refers to the alimentary canal, guts, and intestines, so that in the background of the name lies the inherent paradox of the company—that which feeds also devours; that which carries nourishment also excretes.

Enron operated under the weight of the overreaching ambitions of its leaders, Kenneth Lay and Jeffrey Skilling. The two men were fanatically dedicated to the idea of growth without limits through deregulation, and their singular ambition was international dominance. To put it simply, Lay wanted Enron to be the greatest company in the world. From the perspective of a former Enron employee, "[Individuals in upper-level management] wanted to climb to the top of the mountain and pound their chest and crush anyone or anything that got in the way."[2] The predominant atmosphere within the company was hyper-competitive, cutthroat, and authoritarian to the point of being Orwellian. Mid-level manager Sherron Watkins described the company as arrogant and intimidating. Employees like her feared for their jobs if they voiced dissent to the ambitions of the top managers, and rules were commonly pushed to the limits. The holy grail for the company was high numbers, and those who didn't produce numbers were immediately fired.

The power held by Enron's top-level managers carried over into the economic and political world. Enron made substantial contributions to politicians even as the company lobbied those same politicians for both federal and state deregulation, a policy that enabled the company to take advantage of its clients. Enron took part in the manipulation of electricity prices in California subsequent to the enactment of deregulation policies it helped to bring about. The result was record energy prices for consumers and windfall profits for Enron that it then hid from public record. In the ensuing energy crisis, President George W. Bush failed to rein in Enron, his number one campaign contributor.[3]

Enron also systematically created relationships of conflicting interest with major financial service institutions. The well-respected accounting firm Arthur Andersen acted as both auditor and consultant to Enron, and its accountants would consistently sign off on accounting records that they knew to be questionable for fear of losing Enron's business. The stock brokerage house Merrill Lynch continued to recommend Enron as a strong investment, despite evidence to the contrary. Merrill Lynch and large banks such as Citigroup and JPMorgan Chase participated in Enron's elaborate manipulation of its accounts in exchange for Enron's business.

In all of these relationships, it was the will of Enron's highest management that held sway due to their power, backed by the company's seemingly overwhelming financial resources. In August 2001, Watkins, vice president of corporate development and an accountant by training, risked her position by writing a letter to Lay outlining her concerns regarding Enron's aggressive accounting methods. The communication had no effect, just as previously she had been rebuffed in her attempt to discuss these issues with one of Lay's senior subordinates. Analysts from companies that provided consulting services and ratings who did not please Enron, such as John Olson of Merrill Lynch, were fired for going against Enron's wishes.[4] In psychological terms, the atmosphere that permeated Enron did not tolerate the influence of an other in the form of voices of dissent both within and outside of the company. This intolerance would bring about the company's ultimate demise when its own excess became the counterweight that pulled it down.

In congressional testimony Federal Reserve Board Chair Alan Greenspan remarked, "It is not that humans have become any greedier than in generations past. It is that the avenues to express greed have grown so enormously."[5] For Enron, these avenues led through several legal loopholes that bypassed the checks and balances that sound legislative guidelines and business principles are supposed to provide. Like 60 percent of all American companies, Enron did not pay income taxes for the year 2000, largely because it hid its profits by assigning them to offshore partnerships. Under the national tax code Enron was also able to take sizable tax deductions.

Historically, the most common method of accounting has been the double entry method invented during the Renaissance by Frater Luca Pacioli. Under the influence of the Neoplatonic ideal of harmony in all things, every transaction was marked in each of two columns, credit and debit. It was imperative for the two sides to be in balance at all times, and any discrepancy had to immediately be corrected "with the industry and intelligence God gave you."[6] A business was then able to assess its value at all times based on the actual original cost of an asset, and this system has been maintained by and large through the succeeding centuries to the present.

One of Enron's primary loopholes was an accounting practice called "mark to marketing" or fair value accounting which, unlike traditional accounting, used speculation to determine a fair value. Accounting according to fair value allows a business to assess the value of its assets based on an objective assessment of present market value or a subjective assessment of future market value. In the latter case, a transaction is placed on the books with an asset value based on an estimate of its value at a certain time in the future. For example, the projected revenue from Enron's agreement with the New York Power Authority to deliver natural gas at a fixed price over a ten-year period and adjustable prices for thirteen years could be marked in the quarter the deal was made using figures estimated from future earnings. The seemingly increased revenue would keep Enron's stock price high. Fair value can be useful in valuing some aspects of a business, but under Skilling's direction, Enron abused the method by using it indiscriminately in order to keep its stock price elevated. The result was a vicious cycle of a perpetual focus on new deals that involved questionable accounting to cover projections that hadn't materialized in the old deals.

Enron's most gaping loophole emerged through the practice of setting up quasi-incestuous partnership companies called SPEs, or special purpose entities. Under Security and Exchange Commission (SEC) and Financial Accounting Standards Board (FASB) rules, these entities could be established to allow companies to meet the specific needs of a given situation without disrupting the mainstream of its business flow. In this way, a company might hedge a portion of its investments against the possibility of future losses. For example, a company that wanted to sell off certain debt-ridden assets or fund a construction project could set up an SPE by obtaining only 3 percent capitalization from outside interests and then borrowing the remainder. The advantage to the host company was that it could remove the asset and its related debt (or the debt related to the construction project) from its balance sheet and therefore appear stronger to stock analysts or prospective investors. Although the practice was controversial—primarily because a company owning 50 percent or more of a partnership company was traditionally considered to be publicly accountable and thus had to consolidate its balance sheets—it was still in use forty-four years after the inception of the policy. In effect, the SPE loophole gave companies the opportunity to legally avoid the appearance of debt and stay relatively free of outside influence or—psychologically speaking—free of the influence of the other.

While SPEs were commonplace in corporate America in the 1990s, Enron's reliance on them as a fundamental mode of its business operation went beyond what even the most skeptical observer could ever imagine. Enron created a maze of hundreds of SPEs to hide its considerable debts for a number of reasons, the most significant being Enron's constant need for more capital to fund its transformation from an energy provider to an exclusively "asset lite" energy trading agency.[7] Enron's online trading marketplace required the company to have a constant flow of cash on hand in order to fund its purchases and maintain them prior to their sale. The shift from provider to middle man occurred at Enron in the face of growing public mistrust of the technology sector. This was problematic in that Enron's dealings depended upon public faith in the online trading market.

During the company's transformation, Enron's top managers needed to keep the price of the company stock as high as possible. The corporate climate of the company encouraged this orientation, as Enron employees were greeted each day by a giant scoreboard that hung over the entrance to the building giving the current value of company stock. In order to keep its stock elevated, Enron's managers financed key partnership arrangements with other companies using Enron's own stock as collateral. The more Enron's stock value fell, the more its debt to its own partnerships increased, and the more the company was forced to rely on additional partnership arrangements. Furthermore, Enron's top executives were compensated in part with company stocks, which led to an emphasis on short-term profit and partially eliminated the need for accountability to an outside group of shareholders.[8] Both Lay and Skilling secretly and legally cashed in several million dollars of stock in the year prior to Enron's collapse, while Enron's employees, who had been encouraged to take retirement funds in stocks, were unable to cash them in because the retirement fund had been frozen before it later disappeared.

The most notorious aspect of this self-enclosed system was that in an arrangement known to Lay, Skilling, and the Enron board, Enron's chief financial officer, Andrew Fastow, also served as the director of some of the key partnerships through which Enron hid its debt and had placed friends and family in important positions. In 2001, Fastow personally made $30 million at Enron's expense through a complex shell game that involved moving company debt around in partnerships of which he was essentially in control. This arrangement, known as related-party transaction, involving an obvious conflict of interest, is actually in common usage in American business. In 2003, the *Wall Street Journal* found that three-quarters of the nation's largest public companies relied on related-party transactions.[9]

By 2001, Enron had become not only asset lite, but also capital poor. The company was a top-heavy tower of cards in which the governing fantasy of dominance, generated from its own high-rise "window on the world," had caused the company to lose touch with practical ground and became a virtual reality. It all imploded when Fastow could not play his shell game quickly enough. Once the value of the Enron stock that had been used as collateral plummeted, the partnerships that Fastow controlled both directly and indirectly lost their legal independence even by extremely lax SEC standards. A pancaking collapse touched off by Enron's massive debt now become its own ball and chain, causing the stock price to hit bottom. Instead of being the greatest company in the world, Enron declared what was at the time the largest bankruptcy in history. Most noteworthy is the fact that the attitudes, assumptions, and actions that eventually brought Enron down were shared by the mainstream American business community—and were also the same as those that allowed Enron to rise to the top in the first place.

Enron and its fall mirrored that of the World Trade Center a few months earlier. Both institutions were ultimately created in the service of unlimited ambition and will to dominate, and their construction and operation occurred in association with a spiritual orientation toward unlimited ascendance. Their heights were founded upon "lightness of being"—the World Trade Center literally in its lightweight construction and Enron metaphorically in its asset-lite business orientation founded upon loopholes. In both cases, the all-important connectors that held the whole assembly together couldn't stand the heat, and the structure collapsed.

The example of Enron indicates how American culture connects power with money. A vision that sees through the phenomenon to an underlying cultural paradigm reveals the biblical examples of the privilege mythically given to the elders of children of Israel following Moses and the circle of disciples gathered around the throne of Christ in heaven. America's derived enactment of this image shows a privileged elite manipulating its way through established rules to gain power with the direct or indirect support of associated agencies and the community as a whole.

A further exploration of the collective unconscious temporarily leaves the Judeo-Christian paradigm and focuses upon that of the ancient Greek and Roman cultures, which also have a bearing upon their descendent in the Western world, specifically in regard to ancient practices, gods, and mythic stories that prefigure American attitudes toward money. Even though the Christian orientation holds that money is entirely separate from the spiritual "kingdom of God," America's worship of the dollar as almighty can be seen to have its roots in the religious origins of money.[10] The word "capital" is etymologically connected to the word "cattle." In ancient Greek family rites, bulls were sacrificed to the gods and the meat was cooked for a sacred meal during which ancestors were worshipped. The roasting spit was called the *obelos,* the root of the English word "obligation," as well as an ancient Greek term for coin. The original coins were metal tokens given to individuals outside of the family to gain entrance to the feast. In essence, what is now known as money was originally a meal ticket for the first bull market. Coins (a term from the Latin *cuneus* or "wedge") came to be imprinted with the images of gods, animals associated with gods, or other symbolic derivatives of the gods—matter and spirit integrated into a single entity. Money links humans to divinity through a covenant connecting individuals with community and the community with the gods, while it contains the community in its function of exchange.

The site of the exchange of money, the marketplace, originated as a religious festival. The word "fair" comes from the Latin *feria* which means both holy day and feast. The German word *messe* means both "mass" and "fair." Jesus overturned the tables of the money changers, but markets have always been associated with temples. A city's economy was traditionally controlled by temple authorities in the Middle Ages. Banks originated in temples in order to give loans for overseas trading. In medieval times, the crusades were conducted for purposes both sacred and secular such as opening up trade routes with the Far East— the merchant and the pilgrim were often the same.

Likewise, etymology provides an opening to the soul of money. The word "money" comes from the Latin name for the goddess of memory, Moneta. The Latin *moneo* means to "to remind," to "put in mind," to "warn," or to "admonish." The Greek word for money, *chrimatos*, means oracular response or divine warning. Money remembers and also gives warning, perhaps of the larger forces at work in commerce to which humans are subject. The Latin *mens,* which is related to the root word for money, means "mind," "heart," and "soul." The ancient Greeks considered one without money to be sick, whereas, one living in well-being was associated with *kalos* or the quality or beauty of life. *Kalos* was represented through gold, a glittering metal impervious to corrosion. Gold, in turn, gave expression to the sun, the source of life. In its root meanings, money not only connects the human with the divine and takes consciousness back to origins, but also gives expression to the beauty and health of community and individual life.

Disassociated from biblical roots, money has a soul or life of its own. For the modern Western psyche this can be difficult to grasp. Money is considered only as a lifeless medium of exchange, not as an entity in itself with its particular way of being in the world. In fact, everyday language usage gives money life in the phrases, "Let money work for you," "Money never sleeps," "Cash is king." From this perspective money, as an agent in itself, affects the psyche in a transformative way. Thoughts and fantasies become tangible, physical realities through money. Money makes the world real, giving things of the world a value held in common by the community. As such money enlivens the world, makes things happen, and brings one into the world.

The example of Enron indicates how the spirit of the American approach to the economy, a word that means "the proper ordering of the household," is driven by the need to dominate, as opposed to other countries which are more oriented toward social egalitarianism. One way of understanding the underlying significance of both the World Trade Center and Enron would be through temporarily stepping away from Judeo-Christian mythology and imagining the Greek god, Hermes, to be at work in the unconscious of American business. Hermes was the deity of trade and marketplace, windfalls (originally food left at wayside altars), and catastrophic losses, as well as stealth and deception. He was the god of holes—loop, key, and ass—always capable of finding the right threshold through which to make a way.[11] Behind American "business as usual," there is a god served by both shysters and respectable businessmen. Within a senexed, top-heavy, rules-based ethos, one can also see a divine boy at play.

Hermes is introduced in the Homeric hymns as the son of the nymph Maia, "the very crafty, / the super-subtle / Hermes: / thief, / cattle-rustler, carrier of dreams, / secret agent, / prowler."[12] On the day he was born, he left his cradle and went searching for adventure. He found a turtle, killed it, and transformed the shell into a lyre. Then, when he came upon Apollo's cattle, he separated fifty head from the herd and reversed their tracks, turning their front hooves backward and the back frontward, and outfitted his own feet with branches so as to hide his footprints. An old man saw him with the cattle, and Hermes instructed him, "you didn't see / what you just saw / okay? / You didn't hear / what you just heard."[13] When Apollo finally came to suspect him of the theft, Hermes played innocent, "faking sweet sleep, / looking like a baby" while knowing himself as "thief number one."[14] When Apollo accused him, Hermes asked how a mere baby could do such things. "Sleep is what I care about, / and the milk of my mother. I care about blankets / around my shoulders. / And having hot baths! . . . I was just born yesterday!"[15] And likewise when he is brought before his father, Zeus, for judgment, he proclaimed his innocence and winked.[16]

Within this depiction of Hermes lurks a prominent spirit in American business. Both are committed to finding loopholes, covering tracks, pushing rules to the limits, taking refuge in innocence, while at times resorting to thieving and lying. Furthermore, their activities are conducted in an atmosphere in which the community engages in tolerance, looking the other way. American capitalism is not merely a system, but also a kind of scheme in which rules are continuously manufactured and where the tilt is toward those on the inside track who know how to avoid them. A mythic structure emerging from this paradigm is a pyramid—or pyramid game—ascending toward a monocular pinnacle, representing a dominance of singular vision, a likeness of which is on the back of the American dollar bill.

This archetypal background sheds light on corporate life and its importance to American soul. Former employees of Enron who left without jobs, retirement plans, or their life savings took to creating hostile puns using the names of Enron's top managers. Putting some of these wordplays together would produce a bit of doggerel something like this—

> They took us on an end run,
> Andy pulled a fast one,
> Jeffrey made a killing,
> and we all got Lay'd.

It is comforting to indict criminals, but an ancient adage goes, "The society sets up the crime; the criminal commits it." The fact is that the cooking of Enron's books was aided and abetted directly and indirectly by a kitchen staff that greased the entire spectrum of the nation's business and political worlds. Board members, auditors, regulatory agencies, brokerage houses, banks, journalists, and legislators—nearly all of whom had an interest in the profitability of the company—contributed to the Enron debacle, which reflected the predominant attitudes in the American collective itself. In actuality, many of the practices used by Enron that presented conflicts of interest were and continue to be common and legal practices in America's business world. Auditing firms serve as both consultants to and auditors for companies, and brokerage firms provide services to companies whose stock ratings they also evaluate. Executives are paid in stock options that are not counted as expenses except as tax deductions, and shareholders have no real say in the rewarding of lavish salaries and bonuses to executives. Legislators whose campaigns have been heavily financed by accounting firms pass legislation conducive to the interests of these firms. Enron's fall was devastating because its practices involved a number of sectors of the general community.

The tendency of Enron executives to view ethics as rule-based, rather than principle-based, reflects the American business ethos, in which rules stand as other to the standpoint of principle which provides an outside eye or a balance to self-interest. The philosopher Ludwig Wittgenstein noted the hidden complexity that lies in the notion of following a rule, in that all rules are open to interpretation, and interpretation is subject to various motives. If the ethics of a capitalist economy are approached as rules, then inevitably the motive for profit will lead to interpreting rules in the service of self-interest. The principle behind fair value accounting and the 3 percent rule on SPEs is that it was meant to be an exception, but Enron managers made it their common practice.

Since the tenure of America's first secretary of the Treasury, Alexander Hamilton, business in America has never been laissez-faire. Instead, business has held hands with government. Furthermore, lawmakers and policy boards have historically created economic legislation and business policy in cycles. For the sake of perpetual economic growth, economic laws and policies frequently center around loopholes. These cracks then become targets for business executives in a mercurial atmosphere that is permeated by what has been called a kind of generalized winking at the rules.[17] Crisis ensues as well as calls for legislative reform—cleaning out the stables, plugging up the holes, raking up the muck—by creating more legislation and more rules. These rules are, in turn, loosened over time, and the cycle starts all over again.[18]

Government privileging of business inevitably extends, directly and indirectly, to corporations in America. Corporations are formed through the granting of a charter by a state government and receive a long list of benefits according to state and federal law—including a shield from all liability for directors and shareholders. From their beginnings, corporations have been the subject of the question of whether or not they should receive the rights of individuals. While the original purpose of corporations was to provide profit for shareholders, the first corporations also had to serve the public good by building public works. The sense of obligation to community was gradually diminished until 1886, when the Supreme Court granted corporations rights under the Fourteenth Amendment that had originally been intended to provide equal protection to slaves. In essence, the court's decision granted personhood to corporations. Their rights have been expanded ever since, right up to the Supreme Court's 2010 decision to grant corporations and unions unlimited powers to contribute to political campaigns. The court's decision was based upon the First Amendment's guarantee of the right of free speech to individuals and illuminated the reality that in America, money talks—any substantial power that comes from free speech is available to be purchased.

In addition to being able to make contributions to political campaigns, corporations have also gained access to politicians, and thereby political power, through lobbyists. Lobbyists are paid by single interest groups to inform or influence lawmakers (depending on one's perspective). The role of a lobbyist is subject to relatively little regulation, even while many lobbyists have established contacts with lawmakers through previous employment in the federal government. In 2009, more than two thousand lobbyists were employed by financial institutions to contact the forty-three congressional members involved in the hearings on financial regulation. Of these, more than fourteen hundred had been congressional staffers or worked in the executive branch, while seventy-three were former members of Congress. In 2011 Public Campaign, a bipartisan agency, analyzed thirty large corporations and found that during the period 2008–2010 the companies spent over $400,000 per day to lobby Congress.

Over the two decades previous to 2009, the above-mentioned forty-three committee members received a total of $112 million from donors associated with finance, insurance, and real estate industries. In return, politicians are able to reward their campaign donors in a number of ways, including sneaking tax breaks into legislation and funneling government funds to pet projects. Much of this funding is in the form of earmarks, or no-bid contracts. The Halliburton corporation, which had strong ties to Dick Cheney and the second Bush administration, received over $15 billion, largely through no-bid government contracts between 2001 and 2006, increasing Halliburton's profits by almost 400 percent.

Just as politicians use their authority to increase the power of corporations, corporations themselves are frequently governed by those individuals who reap the benefits of these policies. Boards, which are expected to oversee management, are often made up of directors' friends and associates who simply rubber-stamp the desires of the directors, as was the case with Enron.[19] Corporate executives hold great privilege relative to shareholders and enjoy a disproportionate compensation gap over the median worker.[20] Compensation for CEOs is often determined by a consultant hired by those very directors whose pay is being evaluated to find loopholes in regulations as well as other considerations favorable to the director. Additionally, CEOs are given a great many benefits such as tax reimbursements for perks such as complimentary life insurance premiums, the personal use of corporate aircraft, liberal bonus payments not connected to a company's performance, and retirement compensation and benefits awarded when retirement is not actually taken.[21]

A group of reporters covering government probes into securities firms in February 2004 stated that "[it] was no big secret that corporate boards rubber-stamped management decisions, stomping shareholders in the process . . . . One reason it has been so difficult to determine what top management and directors knew about—and did to cause—the business disasters of the late 1990s is the distortion of corporate-board minutes."[22] Under current law corporations are able to keep multiple sets of accounts—one for public disclosure, one for tax purposes, and one for managers themselves.[23] In this way it is continually those on top of the corporate hierarchy who maintain the most benefit from corporate rules.

In recent years, the payment of CEOs in stock options has led to abuse on the part of CEOs. Stock options enable a CEO to buy company stock at a certain time and price. The company supposedly benefits, as it doesn't have to account for the stock options as an expense and since a manager is thought to have a greater incentive to perform if his or her payment is made in stocks. In reality, an incentive exists for the manager to make shortsighted decisions aimed exclusively at keeping the worth of a company's stock as high as possible. The incentive for available cash from the sale of inflated stocks often involves extraordinary practices and risks, as it did with Enron. Like the top executives at Enron, the insiders in twenty-five companies that went bankrupt in the 1990s took home enormous sums ($3.3 billion) in stock sales immediately prior to the fall in their companies' stock value.[24]

In 1831, Alexis de Tocqueville wrote about America: "Nothing is greater or more brilliant than commerce; it attracts the attention of the public, and fills the imagination of the multitude; all energetic passions are directed towards it."[25] Henry David Thoreau commented in his 1863 essay, "Life without Principle," regarding the cultural atmosphere in America: "This world is a place of business. What an infinite bustle! There is no sabbath. It is nothing but work, work, work. I cannot easily buy a blank book to write thoughts in. They are commonly ruled for dollars and cents."[26] If the core of American soul is business, the essence of business in America is profit for the sake of power.[27] Sheldon Wolin has written that America is a nation whose central story deals not with freedom, but rather with economic opportunity that continually works to the advantage of those at the top of a socio-political hierarchy. In this vision, democracy comes to be not the subject of a free people, but instead an object of the powerful elite, and a tool for promoting political and economic interests.

> Democracy is touted not as self-government by an involved
> citizenry but as economic opportunity. Opportunity serves as
> the means of implicating the populace in anti-democracy, in a
> politico-economic system characterized by the dominating
> power of hierarchical organizations.[28]

In other words, the predominant yet underlying image of America, which has been supported by the majority of its citizens in a search for immediate security, is not that of a democracy working for public good, but rather that of an aristocracy working in the guise of engineering a promised land. This structure is said to serve the common good, but in fact tends to work for private interest while ensuring that those on the top of the hierarchy are best served. The ultimate result is that the figure of empowered citizen is replaced by that of somnambulant consumer.[29]

A national wake-up call occurred again in 2008 in the form of a general economic meltdown. A biblical mythical underpinning relative to this financial fall is revealed in American culture, especially in relation to the culture of the other, Islam, relative to its banking practices and the cultural myth underlying them. One way to understand the underlying interface of the two cultures is to see the interface between cultural practice (banking), predominant religion (capitalism/Islam), and foundational myth (Judeo-Christian/Sufism).

Notes

1. Enron was also housed in a double-tower building structure.

2. Alan Sloan, "Who Killed Enron," *Newsweek*, January 21, 2002, 21.

3. The interconnections between Enron and the Bush administration were legion: Kenneth Lay was a longtime friend of George W. Bush; Dick Cheney met with Lay six times to formulate a plan for the nation's energy policy; Attorney General John Ashcroft took $60,000 in contributions from Enron during his failed 2000 Senate campaign; Chief White House Advisor Karl Rove held major stock in Enron; Secretary of the Army Thomas White spent ten years as an Enron executive; Senator Phil Gramm, a key advisor to the Bush administration on economic issues (whose wife Wendy was a member of Enron's board and knew of its questionable practices), pushed through legislation shielding Enron from public scrutiny; Bush named Patrick Wood III, Ken Lay's personal choice, to chair the Federal Energy Commission; and White House Counsel Alberto Gonzalez was a former employee of Vinson and Elkins, the Houston law firm that represented Enron and signed off on its questionable accounting practices.

4. Richard A. Oppel Jr., "Merrill Replaced Research Analyst Who Upset Enron," *New York Times,* July 30, 2002, A1.

5. Floyd Norris, "Yes, He Can Top That," *New York Times*, July 17, 2002, A1.

6. Robert Bryce, *Pipe Dreams: Greed, Ego and the Death of Enron* (New York: Public Affairs, 2002), 61.

7. Although Skilling had advocated heavily for an exclusive company focus on trade, his archrival within the company, Rebecca Marks, was pushing for substantial investments in concrete assets such as the Dabhol power project in India and the Wessex Water Services in the United Kingdom. Ultimately, Ms. Marks's management of these assets proved to be quite poor, and millions of dollars were lost. In addition, the overall expenditures by upper management, time and again, outran its income, so that ultimately the company simply did not have the capital to fulfill its inflated ambitions.

8. The "Lay loophole," subsequently abolished by Congress, allowed an executive to sell stocks without disclosing the transaction until the following year.

9. John R. Emshwiller, "Many Companies Report Transactions with Top Officers," *Wall Street Journal*, December 29, 2003, A1.

10. For a thorough discussion of the influence of Christianity on money, see James Hillman, "A Contribution to Soul and Money," in *Soul and Money*, ed. James Hillman, Arwind Vasavada, John Weir Perry, and Russell A. Lockhart (Dallas: Spring Publications, 1982).

11. One of the many names for Hermes was *terminus ani.*

12. *The Homeric Hymns*, trans. Charles Boer (Dallas: Spring Publications, 1970), 18–19.

13. *Ibid.*, 24.

14. *Ibid.*, 30.

15. *Ibid.*, 37.

16. *Ibid.*, 45.

17. Alan Ryan, "Visions of Politics," *New York Review of Books*, June 27, 2002, 35.

18. As of 2003, there were more than 100,000 pages in the accounting bible known as the *Generally Accepted Accounting Principles.*

19. David Owen ("The Pay Problem," *New Yorker*, October 12, 2009, 61) states there are "too many [such] companies to list." His article cites Nell Minow, cofounder of The Corporate Library, for her work in attempting to reform the imperial practices of CEOs.

20. *Ibid.*, 58. Owen reports that in 2007 the average CEO received about 275 times as much as the average worker. In January 1911, the SEC enacted new rules that gave shareholders a voice in determining executive compensation; however, the shareholders' vote is nonbinding.

21. Cari Tuna, "Firms End Key Benefit for Executives," *Wall Street Journal*, April 21, 2009, B1.

22. Susan Pulliam, Susanne Craig, Aaron Lucchetti, and Randall Smith, "How Hazards for Investors Get Tolerated Year after Year," *Wall Street Journal*, February 6, 2004, A1.

23. William D. Nordhaus, "The Story of a Bubble," *New York Review of Books*, January 15, 2004, 28. See also Joseph Stiglitz, *The Roaring Nineties: A New History of the World's Most Prosperous Decade* (New York: Norton, 2003).

24. Nordhaus, "The Story of a Bubble," 28.

25. Quoted in Angus Gillespie, *Twin Towers: The Life of New York City's Trade Center* (New Brunswick, NJ: Rutgers University Press, 1999), 3.

26. *Ibid.*, 210.

27. See Kevin Phillips, *Wealth and Democracy: A Political History of the American Rich* (New York: Broadway Books, 2002); Charles Lewis and the Center for Public Integrity, *The Buying of the Congress: How Special Interests Have Stolen Your Right to Life, Liberty, and the Pursuit of Happiness* (New York: Avon, 1998); and Thomas Fleming, "The Long Stormy Marriage of Money and Politics," *American Heritage*, November 1998.

28. Sheldon S. Wolin, *Tocqueville, Between Two Worlds: The Making of a Political and Theoretical Life* (Princeton, NJ: Princeton University Press, 2001), 571–72.

29. Years after Enron, legislation enacted to regulate accounting procedures and eliminate abuse of accounting principles, such as the Sarbanes-Oxley Act, continued to show little effect in the corporate world. See Stephen Labaton, "Crime and Consequences Still Weigh on Corporate World," *New York Times,* January 5, 2006.

10

The Tower of Mirrors: Mythic Foundations of Capitalist and Islamic Finance

Those who expend their wealth night and day, secretly and in public, their wage awaits them with their Lord.
—Qur'an 2:275

Render therefore unto Caesar the things which are Caesar's; and unto God the things that are God's.
—Matthew 22:21

On the morning of Friday, September 12, 2008, Secretary of the Treasury Henry Paulson had a problem. He was meeting at his office in Washington, DC, with Ben Bernanke, chairman of the Federal Reserve System, to discuss a critical situation that had developed in relation to Lehman Brothers Holdings, Inc., a global financial services firm that faced bankruptcy. Paulson, "tall, excitable, garrulous . . . supremely self-confident," and self-described as lacking "the charm gene," was the former chairman of the powerful investment bank Goldman Sachs, where he had earned $37 million the year before he was appointed to George W. Bush's cabinet.[1] Paulson had been one of the Wall Street players who had designed and packaged what would become the notorious financial product, the "derivative," a package of debts whose value was based on the value of the assets involved which, in reality, could become very difficult to determine. The failure of the derivative would be a primary cause of the subsequent national financial meltdown, which ironically Paulson was then called upon to repair.

On that particular morning, Paulson was attempting to solve an impossible dilemma presented by one of his former rivals, Lehman Brothers, headed by Robert S. Fuld. For years, Lehman Brothers had been selling subprime mortgages to clients who had little means to pay and then packaging the mortgages for sale to other institutions. One observer writes of Lehman's activities,

> The salesmen were stuffing mortgages down the throats of people who had no chance of paying them back, and these mortgages were being turned into financial instruments which were spread everywhere through the economic system.[2]

Under Fuld's direction, Lehman Brothers' leverage, the ratio of bank debt versus bank equity, had become unsustainable. A reasonable ratio of leverage is considered to be $10 million of debt to $1 million of equity—and Lehman Brothers' leverage had reached 44–1. This had occurred while Fuld had personally received more than $400 million over the past eight years and while the bank had paid out more than $8 billion in bonuses in the two-year period beforehand.

At the same time, Lehman Brothers' accounting firm, Ernst and Young, had engineered a highly questionable accounting practice known as "Repo 105." Using this maneuver, large amounts of money would be temporarily shifted off the books at the end of a quarter in order to make the company look healthier. In return, Ernst and Young would receive over $150 million in fees over a seven-year period. Absent were the federal regulations that would traditionally scrutinize such operations and arrangements. These regulations had disappeared as part of a more general lax attitude toward regulation that had persisted in the Securities and Exchange Commission (SEC) for years under both parties, but especially under the Republican administration of George W. Bush.

Paulson and Bernanke were desperately attempting to avoid what they knew would be a very difficult situation resulting from a Lehman bankruptcy—without using federal funds. Although Paulson was a proponent of free-market capitalism, he could also take a pragmatic view about the need for government involvement, having presided over two previous federal interventions for which he and Bernanke had endured a great deal of criticism. In March 2008, he had engineered the merger of the failing investment bank, Bear Stearns, also overextended in subprime mortgages, with JPMorgan Chase. The action was made possible by the federal government financing $29 billion in troubled Bear Stern assets. Earlier in the month of September 2008, the Treasury had rescued the federal government-backed private mortgage agencies Fannie Mae and Freddie Mac with $200 billion in capital. Theses interventions had severally compromised the notion of "moral hazard," a capitalist principle that holds that financial actors must bear the consequences of their actions.

On this occasion, along with Timothy Geithner, president of the New York Federal Reserve, Paulson and Bernanke decided to try to find buyers of Lehman Brothers from the private sector. There were two main candidates, Bank of America and Barclays, but additional funding would have to be found in the private sector to cover Lehman's troubled assets. After several hastily convened meetings over the ensuing weekend, the vast extent of Lehman's debt was finally made clear. Bank of America moved on, setting its eye on the next troubled bank in line, Merrill Lynch, and other banks refused to become involved without government backing, which was not forthcoming due to Lehman's insolvency. Barclays also backed off, and Lehman Brothers, under the direction of Fuld, was forced to fold.

A similar situation presents itself in the mythic time and space of another culture. In the Sufi myth, "The Conference of the Birds," a throng of birds is called to make a mystical journey to a vision of God or Simorgh. It is the task of the hoopoe, the wisest of the flock, to guide the other birds along the journey with its many obstacles. In the rendition of the myth by the ancient Persian poet Farid ud-Din Attar, the hoopoe has a problem. He must respond to various protests from different birds regarding the necessity of sacrificing coveted assets in order to make the journey. The homa bird wants to remain tied to such qualities as lofty aspiration, vanity, and self-importance, while the hawk boasts of grand connections with kings and worldly power. The hoopoe, following strict spiritual guidelines, doesn't bend and instead corrects the focus of perceptions of the birds that are oriented toward earthly gratification so that they might develop the capacity for a vision of God within their own heart.

Your heart is not a mirror bright and clear
If there the Simorgh's form does not appear;
No one can bear His beauty face to face,
And for this reason, of His perfect grace,
He makes a *mirror* in our hearts—look there
To see Him, search your hearts with anxious care.[3]

While Paulson was aware of the danger that the fall of Lehman Brothers presented, he did not anticipate the unbearable pressure it would place on the market. A run on money market funds ensued, interbank lending came to a standstill, and stocks crashed. By the end of September, Merrill Lynch had lost $50 billion on subprime mortgages and was forced to sell itself to Bank of America (while billions in bonuses and its overall financial condition were kept secret from the public, including Bank of America investors). Citigroup lost $30 billion and secured $250 billion in federal loans, Morgan Stanley lost $9 billion, and Goldman Sachs required a bailout of $22.9 billion (after paying bonuses of $16.7 billion in the first three quarters of the fiscal year). All of these banks had overextended themselves by purchasing subprime mortgages. Morgan Stanley and Goldman Sachs were converted to holding banks, restricting their investing activities, while placing themselves under government supervision. A few days after the Lehman bankruptcy, AIG, a giant insurance company which operated largely outside the purview of the Federal Reserve and the SEC, would require a bailout from the government of $185 billion, also due to speculation in subprime mortgages, extending the government's involvement into yet another arena. In short, a total of over $700 billion in government bailout funds were made immediately available when large financial institutions, "too big to fail," had driven themselves to the verge of collapse. Most of the bailouts were in the form of one-way bets with government guaranteeing payments on toxic assets. By March 2009, the U.S. government had committed almost $10 trillion in toxic asset guarantees, loans, and direct investments.

One way of understanding this response to the meltdown is to see how, in the nation's psyche, the market itself is in the position of a godlike power, albeit a god with failings similar to those of Yahweh in his relationship with the children of Israel. This religious sensibility toward the market is reflected in utterances by economic priests of the politico/economic temple. Lloyd Blankfein, the CEO of Goldman Sachs, characterized his company as "doing God's work," while Phil

Gramm spoke of Wall Street with reverence: "When I am on Wall Street and I realize that that's the very nerve center of American capitalism and I realize what capitalism has done for the working people of America, to me that's a holy place."[4] The productive functioning of the market is considered essential to keep the nation's soul, its capitalist economy, actively engaged. When the temple of Wall Street was teetering on the point of collapse, every extreme measure was deemed necessary in order to keep it erect. An attitude toward the market as spiritual could be seen in the superhuman bailout effort as religious sacrifice. This idea of the spiritual and religious being alive in the American approach toward money and the market is one that goes beyond the confines of conventional religious thinking to a more psychological imagination of divinity much like that expressed by Jung: "God is the name by which I designate all things which cross my willful path violently and recklessly, all things which upset my subjective views, plans, intentions and change the course of my life for better or worse."[5] Transposing this attitude onto culture, the meltdown and subsequent bailout become a religious event in its total effect.

The uncertainty of the mood of the market, analogous to the moods of Yahweh in the Old Testament, finds its Sufi parallel in "The Conference of the Birds." As with all souls, the birds in the myth must wake up to their alien, bodily condition on earth, the crypt of the cosmos. Their focus on material well-being has kept them from recognizing their spiritual origin. The awakening occurs through a call from without offered by an agent of the divine, in this case, the hoopoe. The call to the soul is a summons to recognize the mistake of fallen life on earth and to return to the true homeland in the spiritual realm. As a stranger in a strange land, the soul undertakes a journey of revelation or learning about its essential nature. The course of the journey for the birds runs through the Seven Valleys of the Way, each one providing a unique initiatory experience as a mode of annihilating selfhood. One such valley is that of Detachment, where "All claims, all lust for meaning disappear. / A wintry tempest blows with boisterous haste; / It scours the land and lays the valley waste."[6] Another is the Valley of Bewilderment, "A place of pain and gnawing discontent— / Each second you will sigh, and every breath / Will be a sword to make you long for death . . . [Until] the pilgrim will confess: 'I cannot say; I have no certain knowledge any more; / I doubt my doubt, doubt itself is unsure.'[7]

By the end of 2007, mortgage debt in the United States had reached the astronomical, ultimately unsustainable figure of $11 trillion. There were several reasons why this happened having to do with a reckless stacking of the deck in favor of speculation. In 2004, the SEC had acted to allow banks to go beyond a 10–1 ratio in their leveraging activity. This meant that even a small amount of demand on the borrowed money would put the bank in a precarious position. Agencies such as Moody's and Standard and Poor's, which rated financial instruments used by banks, were paid by those very banks that were being rated for the purpose of structuring and then grading the same instruments the agencies themselves had created.[8] Likewise, Wall Street analysts continued to urge consumers to buy stock rather than selling it, even during the worst part of recessions. The administration of George W. Bush had pushed growth in private home ownership, providing an atmosphere in which mortgage regulation decreased and lending habits became lax. In conjunction with this loosened atmosphere, Martin Greenspan, the director of the Federal Reserve, persisted in keeping interest rates low, resulting in a false sense of security and a subsequent artificial housing bubble.

Another major factor from the legislative side was the 1999 repeal of the Glass-Steagall Act of 1933. In the face of the Great Depression when banks ran out of money due to unwise investments, Glass-Steagall prohibited banks, investment houses, and insurance companies from combining into single units. In this way regulatory laws could distinguish between banks that primarily invested money and banks that primarily held money. The repeal of the Glass-Steagall legislation, which was championed by institutions such as Citibank, came about as a bipartisan movement led by free-market economist Senator Phil Gramm of Texas. In addition to creating a form of "supermarket banking," the bill split the regulation of banks among several government agencies so that there was no central authority over an entire banking operation, making it easier to find areas of operation which would not be regulated. In December 2000, Gramm congratulated the deregulation movement he led—"the work of this Congress will be seen as a watershed, where we turned away from the outmoded, Depression-era approach to financial regulation and adopted a framework that will position our financial services industries to be world leaders into the new century."[9] By the end of 2006, 80 percent of all lending in the United States was conducted in unregulated sectors.[10]

The financial-political structure that creates the economy is also dominated by a web of personal connections between those on Wall Street and those in Washington. Henry Paulson, one of the chief architects of the bailout of AIG, was the former CEO of Goldman Sachs, which was AIG's largest trading partner. Bill Clinton's Treasury secretary, Robert Rubin, was the former CEO of Goldman Sachs and returned to Wall Street from the cabinet as a senior executive in Citigroup (whose decline he helped to bring about by tying its fortunes to the derivative market). Rubin's deputy and Clinton's subsequent Treasury secretary, Lawrence Summers, who personally made $5.2 million in 2008 on hedge fund profits, later became the head of Obama's National Economic Council. Obama's economic team of Tim Geithner, Ben Bernanke, and Henry Paulson were integral members of George W. Bush's economic team and in that capacity oversaw the collapse they were charged with repairing. Despite shifts in individual and administrative leadership, a perspective dominated by partiality toward big business has consistently run the country's economic structure.

American neo-capitalism already hedges its bet in its working of the system through the very narrow focus of the few who have access to its management, with the ready connection to powerful seats of government and via the incestuous interplay between business and politics as well as that between business and private agencies of accountability. The meltdown of the American economic edifice revealed that the major recipient of socialistic tendencies in America was the wealthy elite and the major recipients of government welfare were large financial institutions deemed too big to fail. The underlying structure of capitalism in America, tilted as it is toward big business, requires an underlying energy, base of support, and faith from across the spectrum of the community such that it emerges as a civic religion. The crash had exposed this system as a tower of mirrors built too far above the ground of monetary reality to sustain itself.

Middle Eastern religious systems emerged out of a mythical rhizome of themes that have been categorized as gnostisic, or having to do with realization of knowledge of the divine. The Sufi tradition embodies many of these themes, particularly an emergence of imagination as a means of experiencing—a story of transformation of mind as opposed to the Judeo-Christian quest for promised land. The initial experience of the soul is that the world is a sort of pit. Until one recognizes through the powers of imagination that the world is itself ensouled, a unified reflection of God and one's self, it remains a form of prison, a presence of absence of persons and things rendered as lifeless objects existing in public space.

The soul begins its transformation with a realization that its exile can only be redeemed through a return to knowledge of original kinship with divinity. The necessity of separation from the old way of being is supplanted by an even greater sadness of yearning for the original connection with divinity. This connection can be made through a process of transformation, an exodus, leading upward and onward through a series of realizations or epiphanies. The soul is the medium through which each epiphanic stage takes place, often through a change in perception, and particularly the perception of self. More and more, the soul includes a sensibility of otherness that is paradoxically familiar: what appears as other is also part of self. In "The Conference of the Birds," those who survive the journey gain a vision of God paradoxically through a mirrored image of themselves.

A realization of God from a Sufi perspective can be understood as the transformation that takes place when one's consciousness moves away from a split between materialistic reckoning and spiritualized abstracting to a "thought of the heart" or imagination. Imagination includes both the concrete form of the material world and the dynamic of spirituality. The journey or flight of the soul in this process is one of balancing—as if with a pair of wings—the effort and will of the soul living in a purely materialistic world with a surrender to a higher spiritual power. The ultimate integration of material and spiritual realms, *ta wil*, is imaged as the "place of no place," or the meeting point of two oceans. *Ta wil* is a leading back or restoring of original affinity with the divine experienced as a paradoxical reimagining of self in the presence of self, a revisioning of self through image as being at once of, and not of, the world, a mirroring contemplation of contemplation.

The mirror that served as the primary building block of the glass tower of the American financial structure was the instrument known as the derivative, a word signifying that the value of the instrument is derived from its underlying asset value. A mortgage is valued according to the actual property, whereas a package of mortgages is valued based on the mortgages, rather than on the properties. The value of a group of packages is based on the original packages, and so on, until the actual material value of the instrument, the accumulated value of the properties themselves, has been lost in its complexity. The assumption is that the mortgages will be paid, and in fact, as long as everyone is paying off their debt, everything is fine. Trouble occurs when someone can't meet their obligations.

Derivatives were invented in 1973 when Fischer Black and Myron Scholes developed an equation enabling the calculation of a price for a package of loans based on the value of the underlying assets. This equation allowed for the creation of investment vehicles, such as derivatives and credit default swaps (bilateral contracts that, for a fee, allow investors to pass the risk of default on to another party), for banks and other investors to buy and sell with little capital under no federal regulation. The instrument amounted to a kind of insurance for lenders, so much so that they eventually became indifferent as to whether or not the original loan was paid. Their investment was already secured by the hedge on the loan provided by the derivative and the credit default swap.

Deregulation was formalized by the Commodity Futures Modernization Act of 2000, a bipartisan piece of legislation pushed by Phil Gramm and backed by Clinton Treasury Secretary Lawrence Summers, Alan Greenspan, chair of the Federal Reserve, and Arthur Levitt, head of the SEC, which exempted over-the-counter derivatives from regulation. As Greenspan told Congress in 2003, "What we have found over the years in the marketplace is that derivatives have been an extraordinarily useful vehicle to transfer risk from those who shouldn't be taking it to those who are willing to and are capable of doing so."[11] By 2007, $62 trillion in loans had been made in an unregulated format through the use of derivatives. (Meanwhile, the famously successful investor Warren Buffett denigrated derivatives due to the impossibility of knowing the risks involved in the investment, alluding to their destructive nature with the term "weapons of mass destruction.") American financial institutions eventually began buying and selling products of completely unknowable value. The entire financial structure of any one institution became a maze of signifiers connected to other signifiers in ever expanding chains, while "true" value vaporized into a perpetual state of deferral. The market for derivatives eventually became vaster than the market for actual things themselves, and the financial structure became a tower of mirrors.

Islam is a religion derived to an extent from the gnostic mythic tradition which includes Sufism. It emphasizes liberation through knowledge of God. Muhammed was fully human and the last in a line of prophets that included Old Testament figures as well as Christ, to whom the word of God was revealed for the purpose of revelation to humanity. For Islam, the Qur'an, a word that means "to recite" or "gather together," is a text that is the direct word of God. The Qur'an prescribes precisely the Way of achieving perfection of soul through 1) action, *islam,* submission to God's will, 2) understanding, *iman,* faith in God, and 3) intention, *ihsan,* the doing of that which is beautiful in bringing the soul into harmony with action and understanding. The pillars of Islam are *shahadah* (mantra recitation), *salat* (ritual prayer), *zakat* (the donation of money to the needy), observance of restraint during Ramadan, *haji* (the pilgrimage to Mecca), and *jihad* (the struggle for justice, "toward the light").

Just as the Qur'an prescribes the precise concrete actions necessary for spiritual renewal, so Islam is rooted in the world itself. The world is God's creation, and everything in the world is accomplished by the will of God. There is no Caesar/God split when it comes to money which, like all concrete worldly reality, belongs to God. God is found in the things of the world, as well as one's experience of the world. All human attributes and possessions are as if on loan from God. God, as source or prime lender, is certainty itself. It is up to the individual to strive to the best of his or her individual capacity to act properly as if on loan from God or ultimately as God's mirror, life on earth being a derivative or reflection of God.

The Qur'an provides the path of practical means whereby one can repay to God that which has been granted by him. In this way the Qur'an can be seen as the map for the gnostic journey of transformation.

However, Islam embodies an entirely different consciousness than that of the Western world, in that since the world is God's creation, not man's, space is not quantitative, time is nonlinear, and cause and effect are nonexistent. The past is not a matter of "cause" as source from which movement imagined as development, growth, or progress emanates, nor is the future a matter of promise or payoff. Rather, Islam is an ahistorical consciousness, organized through a vertical vectoring where past is that which is "beneath our feet," the future is "above our head," and the present receives primary focus as an emanation of God's will.

Although it is tempting to analyze the meltdown of the American financial system as due, at best, to the unjustified expectations regarding market workings and the techniques of modern finance, and at worst, to the reckless, self-interested behavior of bankers, regulators, and politicians, depth psychology is able to offer an analysis that takes into account the ground from which the entire culture operates. Seen through a mythic lens, the meltdown of capitalist culture in America reveals an underlying set of themes particular to the Judeo-Christian narrative that informs American character. In terms of the meltdown, the sense of crisis followed by seemingly radical action that turns out to have only a temporary effect is not only a historical pattern for America but is biblically based in the crises of faith or falls of God's children, God's radical solution, and the eventual failing of the children yet again.

The sense of entitlement that comes from America's identity as the latter-day children of Israel carries over into American globalized capitalism. The belief that the market itself, as God, the all-seeing Father, can do no wrong and faith in its guiding hand of self-regulation and adjustment toward moderation and order results in a laissez-faire attitude, which further enhances the market's power. The emphasis on risk, speculation, and hedging (in a country that spends billions each year at the gaming tables and slot machines) might be seen as being at the heart of the Judeo-Christian interface with God—his demand for faith in Him, an enormous gamble in itself.[12] The emergence of home mortgages as the ultimate downfall of the American economy indicates the precarious condition of America's idealization of the individualized home as a central aspect of God's promise to his wandering children. What was, in its original Old Testament form, "Please God and receive a promissory note for land," becomes "the payoff is at hand, a mortgage for all is here, the future is now, the city on the hill arrived."

The greed of Wall Street can also be interpreted as a hunger for profit reflected in the lives of all Americans as an extension of God's promise of paradise on earth. Yet, the hedging of the bet on God's promise inevitably privileges the elite—salaries of upper-level corporate managers, bonuses paid to Wall Street money managers and banking directors, freedoms from regulation given to banks and corporations—all following the Judeo-Christian tradition from the elders of the tribes, to the ruling circle of Puritan scholars, to the present-day privileging of the upper class through tax breaks. In summary, the mythic basis of contemporary American culture holds God's promise at the heart of the global capitalist enterprise of perpetual growth and progress that emerges from the fall, but which also renders the world expendable with yearning consciousness focused on the horizon.

Islamic culture follows the Qur'an as the guide for proper behavior in all areas of life which will, in turn, allow for the eventual recognition of the individual by God. Islamic finance is a reflection of Muslim culture; 1,400 of the Qur'an's 6,226 verses deal with economic issues. In traditional Islam, money is simply a useful tool in God's world, since there is no self outside of God to strive for financial gain. Money exists to allow trade to flow freely throughout the world. The rules of finance are concretely laid out according to the laws of living called *shari'a*, "the path to the headwater" of alignment with God. Any financial operation that involves risk or uncertainty is typically avoided, and insurance is shunned as much as possible. Likewise, earning interest is frowned upon as a matter of *riba* or excess. "Those who devour usury shall not rise again except as he rises, whom Satan of the touch prostrates . . . God has permitted trafficking [trade], and forbidden usury."[13] All interest is God's interest. "God blots out usury, but freewill offerings / He augments with interest."[14] Whereas the Old Testament God allows for usury for strangers, in the traditional Muslim world usury interferes with God's plan.

This order is reflected in human relations, as in the practice of *zakat,* or the giving of money to the needy by those with excess, *riba*. Since lending that involves interest is frowned upon (all humanity is technically on loan from Allah), all risk is proportionately shared by the bank and the lendee alike. When a house is mortgaged, the property is put in joint trust, with any loss shared by both parties. Mortgages would never be packaged into derivatives, because all contracts must deal with the item itself. Any speculative financial instrument such as a derivative, where commercial imagination is running ahead of itself, would create *gharar,* or a state of uncertainty where the liability is opaque or unknown. In Islamic consciousness such uncertainty is to be avoided. It follows that traditional Islamic finance follows the Qur'an and its underlying mythology of pursuing the journey by emphasizing the need for tangible certainty on the way to God.

A year and a half after the meltdown of 2008, very little had changed about the way that large banks operated in America. Risking the money of others for the sake of profits for a few in conjunction with large bonuses was still the order of the day. Finally, in July of 2010, Congress passed and President Obama approved legislation purporting to overhaul finance rules—the Dodd-Frank law. That legislation had four primary components. It brought more companies under the oversight of federal regulation, imposed regulation upon the market of trade in derivatives, formed a federal oversight panel to detect risks in the financial system, and created a consumer protection regulator housed in the Federal Reserve. Nevertheless, detractors pointed out deep flaws in the legislation such as the fact that derivative trade would continue and consumer protection would be housed within the Federal Reserve whose policies had led to the meltdown in the first place. In addition, banks had already taken great strides to find loopholes and otherwise counter the effects of the legislation to ensure the opportunity for large profits.

A development occurred in May 2012 which illustrated both the need for regulatory reform and the tremendous effort to undo it. At this time JPMorgan Chase announced that it had lost $2 billion in trading involving derivatives (the ultimate figure for the loss was estimated to be upward of $9 billion). The derivative trades were part of a hedge to offset the bank's potential losses on holdings of bonds and loans. These credit derivatives would increase in value if the underlying creditworthiness of the loans is perceived to have deteriorated. Unfortunately, JPMorgan tried to hedge the hedge by making the opposite bet as well, resulting in its downfall. As it turned out, a portion of Dodd-Frank known as the Volcker Rule, which was in the process of being finalized, was meant to avoid such banking practices as making bets with the bank's own money. As it turned out, large banks including JPMorgan had been lobbying Washington rule-makers to write a loophole into the law known as portfolio hedging, which would allow the banks great latitude in hedging by taking into account the entire portfolio as opposed to just the individual trade, a move backed by the Treasury Department and the Federal Reserve. This loophole would have allowed JPMorgan to act exactly as it did.

In fact, the meltdown took its place in a historical cycle of market failures and ensuing reactive legislation of questionable effectiveness that extends all the way back through the Great Depression to the early decades of the nineteenth century. The most recent examples include the implosion of Enron in 2001, the collapse of technical stocks in 2000, the failure of Long-Term Capital Management in 1998, the junk bond collapse of 1989, and the savings and loan bankruptcies in the mid-1980s, which were also based on an overinvestment in mortgages. Such evidence of resistance to fundamental change would indicate a deeper, mythical basis to the underlying structure that allows for such cycles.

Even as the rules of Islamic banking are clear, since 2001 Islamic bankers increasingly look to loosen *shari'a* compliant interpretations of policy in order to move their operations in a more capitalistic direction. (In 2001 the first Islamic corporate bond was issued, and in 2002 the first Islamic sovereign bond.) An example would be *murabaha,* in which a bank, rather than lend directly, agrees to buy a commodity and then sell it to the borrower with a fee that takes the place of interest, so that the borrower can sell the commodity immediately but repay the bank in deferred payments. Investment in derivatives are accomplished in a *shari'a* compliant way by buying into a fund of shares of *shari'a* compliant companies. The fund then swaps the returns on the shares for returns on a conventional fund—a form of Islamic money laundering based on the rationalization that no portfolio can ever be pure. In this case, *gharar,* or uncertainty, is interpreted in terms of a certain degree of permissible risk. The British government has begun a practice of *sukuyk*, a form of sales of *shari'a* compliant bonds. The government creates a special purpose company and sells it as a piece of state-owned property. The company issues certificates to investors, leases the property back to the government, and uses the rental return to pay dividends to the investors. The fact that the arrangement is so concretely tied to a tangible asset makes it a tradable form of debt in Islamic finance. Finally, certain money flowing between banks is now considered funding that depends on performance of underlying assets with an accompanying Islamic interbank benchmark rate as opposed to being considered interest on loans as it has been in the past.

These practices have become more popular with some traditional Muslims due to a growing sense that competing with the Western world financially is itself a form of jihad. In sum, it is clear that the consciousness of globalized capitalism, with its underlying myth of God's promise on earth, is having an effect on Islamic finance—a fact that holds little consolation for the 40 percent of the world's population existing in absolute poverty while living in Islam-dominated countries.

While American globalized capitalism blankets the world on the one hand, it is important to see, as the next chapter shows, how its use of military force, particularly from the air, follows a parallel process of domination from above, each phenomenon derived from a mythic narrative centered upon God as an all-powerful, invisible divinity of the heavens.

Notes

1. James B. Stewart, "Eight Days," *New Yorker,* September 21, 2009, 59.

2. John Lancaster, "Bankocracy," *London Review of Books,* November 5, 2009, 36.

3. Farid ud-Din Attar, *The Conference of the Birds*, translated and with an introduction by Afkham Darbandi and Dick Davis (New York: Penguin Books, 1984), 53, italics added.

4. Graham Bowley, "$500 Million and Apology from a Bank," *New York Times,* November 18, 2009, A1; Eric Lipton and Stephen Labaton, "A Deregulator Looks Back, Unswayed," *New York Times,* November 17, 2008, A12.

5. Quoted in Edwin F. Edinger, *Ego and Archetype* (Baltimore: Penguin, 1973), 101.

6. Attar, *The Conference of the Birds*, 184.

7. *Ibid.*, 196.

8. The reader may recall this kind of dual relationship as precisely the problem with the rating of corporations such as Enron.

9. Lipton and Labaton, "A Deregulator Looks Back, Unswayed," A12.

10. The repeal of Glass-Steagall is reflective of the fact that in American politics, legislators are heavily influenced by big money concerns, which themselves have a vested interest in decreasing regulation. Senator Gramm, in fact, was the top congressional recipient of campaign contributions from financial institutions from 1989 to 2002. In the first half of 2009, finance, insurance, and real estate industries spent $223 million on lobbying activities, second only to the health-care industry.

11 Jeff Madrick, "At the Heart of the Crash," *New York Review of Books*, June 10, 2010, 37.

12. "Hedging" is the strategy used to lock in or guarantee a price at which an asset may be bought or sold in the future. During the five years from 2012 to 2017 the hedge fund industry in the United States is expected to grow to over $5 trillion in assets. See Juliet Chung, "Hedges Assets: $5 Trillion," *Wall Street Journal*, June 12, 2012, C2.

13. A. J. Arberry, trans., *The Koran Interpreted* (New York: Simon and Schuster, 1955), 69.

14. *Ibid.*

11

Captain America and His Zealous Blast: A Foray into American Foreign Policy

So the people shouted when the priests blew with the trumpets; and it came to pass, when the people heard the sound of the trumpet, and the people shouted with a great shout, the wall fell down flat, so that the people went up into the city, every man straight before him, and they took the city.

—Joshua 6:20–21

Twice during his first year as president in 2009, shortly after taking office in January and again in December after a prolonged review of the situation, President Obama publicly addressed America's military involvement in Afghanistan, which generally represented the center of the American political spectrum. This policy was based on a view of Afghanistan as a deeply unstable country where the government had been undermined by corruption and the people's basic needs largely ignored. The Afghan government, established and supported by the American government, was being threatened by the former ruling faction, the Taliban, a fundamentalist Islamic movement which had hosted al-Qaeda because of its leaders' personal relationships to Osama bin Laden. This relationship, in turn, was based on bin Laden's efforts on Afghanistan's behalf in its struggle with Soviet occupation, an effort that was also supported by the United States. American policy had historically assumed that a return to Taliban rule would inevitably result in Afghanistan again becoming a major base of al-Qaeda operations. In order to prevent this occurrence and ultimately gain victory over al-Qaeda in its war on terrorism, America would need to bring to bear a dominating military force in conjunction with a focus on economic development, in order to build a stable central government which would ensure security for the United States through the ultimate defeat of terrorism . . .

Then the Lord rained upon Sodom and upon Gomorrah brimstone and fire from the Lord out of heaven.[1]

The Lord is a man of war . . . thy right hand O Lord, hath dashed in pieces the enemy . . . thou sentest forth thy wrath, which consumed them as stubble . . . all the inhabitants of Canaan shall melt away.[2]

For the Lord thy God is a consuming fire.[3]

Though one typically thinks of Japan's greatest sites of devastation in World War II in terms of Hiroshima and Nagasaki, America's firebombing of Japanese civilian populations actually brought about far more destruction. Major General Curtis LeMay was the one who first shaped the policy of targeting industrial areas within cities, and then exploding "stray bombs," which would bring about "bonus damage," namely the incineration of civilians. LeMay described the results of the bombing of Tokyo and more than sixty other cities as over 200,000 people being "scorched and boiled and baked to death"[4] while eight million were made homeless. General Bonner Fellers described the bombing in Japan as "one of the most ruthless and barbaric killings of non-combatants in all of history."[5]

The Japanese firebombings had been preceded by the firebombing of German cities in which over 300,000 civilians were killed and almost two million made homeless. None of the incendiary bombing in World War II produced military advantage.

. . . Obama's policy toward Afghanistan revealed several interrelated assumptions which, in fact, are questionable. The first is that America had a moral obligation toward Afghanistan when actually America was one in a long line of uninvited occupying forces and had, at best, ambivalent support from the Afghan public. Arguments have been made that it was precisely American military presence in places like Afghanistan and Iraq that gave insurrectionist forces their reason for operation. The second assumption was that American efforts would be able to solve the issues it defined as problematic, whereas history had shown that America's fix-what-it-defines-as-broken thinking had failed in many similar situations such as Iraq, Vietnam, and the Philippines. Third, the "failed state" condition in Afghanistan was perceived to be of recent origin, when to the contrary, every Afghan ruler in the twentieth century had been assassinated, lynched, or deposed. Fourth, it was thought possible to establish a strong central government in Afghanistan, despite the fact that it is a country divided by formidable geographic boundaries (mountain ranges) and strong local tribal and ethnic allegiances, the police force was notoriously undermanned and underfunded with a very high rate of casualties and dropouts, the loyalty and ability of the army was in doubt, and Afghan leadership was known more for its corruption than its ability to govern. . . .

The Lord will roar from Zion, and utter his voice from Jerusalem . . .
    . . . I will send a fire into the house of Haza'el . . .
    . . . I will send a fire on the wall of Ga'za . . .
    . . . I will send a fire upon Te'man . . .
    . . . I will kindle a fire in the wall of Rab'bah . . .
    . . . I will send a fire upon Mo'ab . . .
    . . . I will send a fire upon Judah . . . [6]

*And he rode upon a cherub, and did fly: and he was seen upon
the wings of the wind. And he made darkness pavilions round
about him, dark waters, and thick clouds of the skies. Through the
brightness before him were coals of fire kindled. The Lord thundered from
heaven and the most High uttered his voice . . . And the channels of the sea
appeared, the foundations of the world were discovered, at the rebuking of
the Lord, at the blast of the breath of his nostrils.*[7]

Under the policies of two presidents of different parties, the
United States conducted three main bombing campaigns in
North Vietnam over the course of eight years. The United States
dropped close to eight million tons of bombs, the equivalent
of 640 atomic bombs on a country of eighteen million people,
all of which provided no essential, long-term military advantage.
Robert McNamara, secretary of defense during the first years
of the Vietnam War was later to admit a gross "failure of
imagination" in the U.S. approach to a war that could not be
won. In the years following the Vietnam War over 100,000
Vietnamese were killed or wounded by previously unexploded
bombs and other abandoned explosives.

. . . The fifth assumption regarding Afghanistan was that stable
economic development was possible, when the reality was that in the
years after liberation from the Soviet Union the main economic resource
had been poppy plants for heroin use. The Afghan insurgency's second-
largest funding source after the liberation from the Taliban was the
diversion of money from U.S.-backed construction projects,
transportation contracts, and agriculture development programs into
corrupt hands.[8] Sixth, it was thought that a stable government
could only come about through the complete suppression of
counterinsurgency, while in fact an established major country like
India had been battling insurrection throughout its history. Seventh,
victory for the insurrection forces would lead to the establishment of
a government hostile to American interests, whereas the Afghan Taliban
was mainly focused upon internal issues concerning Afghanistan.
Eighth, victory for the Taliban would mean the establishment of
terrorist bases in Afghanistan, while instead the situation was very

different from when the original ties had been made between the Taliban and al-Qaeda. The two groups had become more differentiated and their goals had taken them in different directions. Al-Qaeda had found a more secure home in places like Pakistan, Iraq, Manila, and certain African countries.

Each of these assumptions was intertwined into a single worldview so that if one failed, the implication was that the others would fail as well.[9] This monolithic perspective, which was generally embraced by both of America's political parties, was founded upon several questionable larger underlying assumptions and factors, including America's right to power, its worldwide moral obligation, its belief in the cultural uniformity of all foreign cultures, and a void in long-term perspective. What can explain adherence to this kind of thinking, based on misleading assumptions, which has been enacted worldwide in its basic form decade after decade?[10] . . .

And the angel took the censer, and filled it with fire of the altar, and cast it into the earth . . . And the seven angels which had the seven trumpets prepared themselves to sound. The first angel sounded, and there followed hail and fire mingled with blood, and they were cast upon the earth; and the third part of trees was burnt up, and all green grass was burnt up.[11]

Throughout the Vietnam War, America secretly bombed the small neighboring country of Laos, which was seen as a conduit for North Vietnamese forces, but which contained a largely impoverished, agrarian population of about three million people. In 1971 alone 440,000 tons of bombs were dropped by the United States on Laos, twenty-five times the power of the atomic bomb dropped on Hiroshima. In all, a total of two million tons of bombs were dropped, more than all of the bombs dropped by all countries during World War II and equivalent to almost two tons of bombs for every three people in Laos, killing 10 to 20 percent of the population and leaving two million homeless. Only two-thirds of the bombs actually exploded, in fact, making the entire country a veritable minefield for years to come.

. . . One approach to the question of a foreign and defense policy which seems to come from an elevated, out-of-touch place "on high" would be to look more deeply into one of the aspects that literalizes this position, the use of air power and bombing. As a nation, America has a particular affinity for the bomb as a form of superweapon. The first bomb-carrying submarine was pioneered by Robert Fulton, who imagined he would "secure perpetual peace between nations."[12] One of the first uses of bombs in warfare took place in the Civil War. One of the first terrorist bombs exploded in Haymarket Square in Chicago during the late-nineteenth century labor disputes. The United States conducted the first multicity aerial firestorm raids and invented the first atomic bomb, the first intercontinental bomber, the first thermonuclear bomb, the first laser-guided bomb, and the first automated system for launching thermonuclear warheads. Even the delivery of food to Afghanistan after 9/11 was accomplished by dropping pallets from the air, causing destruction underneath. . . .

And the fourth angel poured out his vial upon the sun; and power was given unto him to scorch men with fire. And men were scorched with great heat . . .[13]

. . . and fire came down from God out of heaven; and devoured them.[14]

In the decade after 9/11, thousands of civilians were killed by American bombs in Afghanistan, as well as 100,000 in Iraq, and yet military victory remained elusive.[15] The level of violence in Afghanistan in July 2011 was 15 percent higher than at the same time the previous year. Any illusion that the war in Iraq had produced a stable nation was dispelled by a coordinated attack involving forty-two separate strikes by insurgents on August 15, 2011. The *New York Times* reported, "After hundreds of billions of dollars spent since the United States invasion in 2003, and tens of thousands of lives lost, insurgents remain a potent and perhaps resurging threat to Iraqis and the American troops still in the country."[16]

. . . America glorifies the bomb in its national anthem, which features "the bombs bursting in air," as well as in its literature. Captain Ahab "piled upon the whale's white hump the sum of all the general rage and hate felt by his whole race from Adam down; and then, as if his chest had been a mortar, he burst his hot heart's shell upon it."[17] America's dark side harbors the cult of the "mad bomber." In the film *Speed*, a bus in Los Angeles is wired with a bomb so that if it goes under 50 mph, the bomb will go off—a dramatization of American character as manic: slowing down brings explosion. The bomber, played by Dennis Hopper, justifies his actions in a particularly American existential way: "The being of the bomb is unfulfilled unless it goes off!" One of the most exciting plays in football, America's most popular game, is called the bomb, and bombing is a casual staple of fascination in American entertainment media.[18]

America created a god-image in the atomic bomb, prefigured in the description in the New Testament in 2 Peter of the "melting" of the world. "The day of the Lord will come as a thief in the night; in which the heavens shall pass away with a great noise, and the elements shall melt with fervent heat, the earth also and the works that are therein shall be burned up."[19] At the time of the atom bomb's explosion in Japan, Harry Truman framed its existence in American hands in a particularly messianic way: "We thank God that it has come to us instead of to our enemies, and we pray that He may guide us to use it in His ways and for His purpose."[20] Secretary of War Henry Stinson justified its use as "the only way to awaken the world to the necessity of abolishing war altogether."[21]

The conventional rationalization for the bomb's use—that it was necessary to bring the war to an end—is historically questionable. Several times before the attacks on Hiroshima and Nagasaki, the Japanese had expressed a desire to negotiate terms of surrender. Their only condition was that they be allowed to retain the emperor as a symbol in their political structure. Most Japanese cities were already devastated, and Russia's army was ready for an assault on Japanese forces. The U.S. Strategic Bombing Survey subsequently stated unequivocally, "Japan would have surrendered if the atomic bombs had not been dropped."[22] Chief of staff to President Truman, Fleet Admiral William Leahy, declared, "the use of this barbarous weapon at Hiroshima and Nagasaki was of no material assistance in our war against Japan. The Japanese were already defeated and ready to surrender."[23] Weeks before the atomic explosions, Truman had mentioned in his diary a "telegram from Jap emperor asking for peace," and he received reports regularly on the terms of Japanese peace inquiries.[24] Recent scholarship points to the idea that President Truman, Secretary of State Byrnes, and Secretary of War Stinson felt it was necessary to use the atomic bomb in Japan as a way of keeping an advantage over Russia in the postwar world.[25] Far from bringing about the end of World War II, dropping atomic bombs on Japan was the first act in the ensuing Cold War between America and the Soviet Union.

After the war, America embarked on a forty-year nuclear arms buildup justified both as a necessity and means of progress for the defense of America and de facto of civilization, despite the warnings of its inventors. Robert Oppenheimer, chair of the scientific advisory committee to the Atomic Energy Commission in 1949, admonished, "The notion that the thermonuclear arms race was something that was in the interests of the country to avoid if it could was very clear to us."[26] Enrico Fermi and I. I. Rabi, Nobel laureate physicists on the committee, noted that the hydrogen bomb "goes far beyond any military objective and enters the range of very great natural catastrophes. By its very nature it cannot be confined to a military objective but becomes a weapon which in practical effect is almost one of genocide . . . It is necessarily an evil thing considered in any light."[27] These scientists were proclaiming, in effect, that nuclear arms went beyond the category of military weapon, and the term "nuclear war" was a contradiction in terms. Niels Bohr said flatly, "We are in an entirely new situation that cannot be resolved by war."[28]

Nor was there need on the part of the United States to regard the Soviet Union as an imminent threat. The Soviet Union had lost twenty-five million people and half its industry in World War II. Former Secretary of Defense James Schlesinger described the Soviet forces as "paltry . . . hardly enough to stage an attack on the United States."[29] Jerome Wiesner, president of MIT, suggested that fifty nuclear bombs were enough to put a society out of commission and three hundred would destroy an entire civilization—but at the height of the nuclear arms race in 1966 America had 32,200 bombs. Robert McNamara later wrote that "each of the decisions taken by itself, appeared rational or inescapable. But the fact is that they were made without reference to any overall master plan or long-term objective."[30] In fact, the effort and expense of the United States in the nuclear arms race was based on wildly exaggerated reports of the armaments and delivery capacity of the Soviet Union, perpetrated by American officials deliberately playing on the fears of the public, reports which turned out to be completely false.[31] Reduction in armaments finally was brought about during the Reagan administration, but not before five trillion dollars had been spent for involvement in an effort that turned out to be morally reprehensible to many involved and militarily unnecessary.[32] In 1946, at the dawning of what he saw as the insanity of the nuclear age, Louis Mumford, in a piece called "Gentlemen: You Are Mad," wrote: "We are madmen, too. We view the madness of our leaders as if it expressed a traditional wisdom and a common sense."[33]

We are left with an unsettling realization regarding American bombing. The extensive bombing of civilians resulting in the deaths of almost a million people in various wars from World War II to the post-9/11 wars in Afghanistan and Iraq, while intricately tied to an ethic of dominance and to American economic interests, did not produce ultimate military advantage. Mere months after Franklin Roosevelt's 1939 call to the world to cease the bombing of civilians, America, in its bombing of German-held North African countries, began an approach to warfare in which the bombing of civilians became an integral part of its aggressive tactics. This propensity culminated in 2001 in the bizarre imagery of America's most technologically sophisticated bombers attacking men, women, and children who lived in caves in Afghanistan. One is left looking toward an underlying narrative for an understanding of this cultural endeavor.

In their book *Captain America and the Crusade against Evil*, Robert Jewett and John Shelton Lawrence make note of the affinity of the American character for bombing and trace its roots to America's identification with the Old Testament Israelites and the zeal which God demands from his children.[34] The authors focus on the story of Phinehas as told in Numbers. In the story, the Lord holds Phinehas up to Moses as an example of a worthy son because of his boldness in entering the tent of an Israeli man and his Midianite wife and killing them with a spear, thus protecting the purity of the Israelites. The Lord said, "He was zealous for my sake."[35] Jewett and Lawrence note that the word "zeal" has its roots in the Hebrew *gana,* which in turn is derived from its Semitic root, meaning "to be dyed dark-red or black"—the color of rage. In several passages in the Old Testament, a "consuming" zeal on the part of individual Israelites mirrors that of the Lord or the Lord is depicted with the "burning heat" of zeal.[36] Showing zeal indicates a willingness to go beyond the established law to identification with God's righteousness, making the division of good and evil absolute.

The purity of the Israelite nation was upheld in the practice of *herem* or, in English, "the ban." After every battle the priests would order the booty and prisoners be destroyed or dedicated to God, as after the battle of Jericho when the entire city was destroyed.[37] The destruction of property and community thus accomplishes the utter destruction of the other, through a fiery form indicative of the zeal required by God to stay in His grace. The complete and utter destruction of the other also maintains a sensibility of purity and innocence central to the psyche of the Israelites—and Americans—as the chosen ones. After the Pequod Massacre of 1637 in which an entire community was slaughtered, Captain John Underhill declared, "It may be demanded, 'Why should you be so furious?' But I would refer you to David's War. When a people is grown to such a height of blood, and sin against God and man . . . then he hath no respect to persons . . . sometimes the Scriptures declareth women and children must perish with their parents . . . We had sufficient light from the word of God for our proceedings."[38] Almost three hundred and thirty years later, President Richard Nixon would say, "Our beliefs must be combined with a crusading zeal, not just to hold our own but to change the world . . . and to win the battle for freedom."[39]

America can kill in God's name so as to "march toward the clean world our hands can make," in the words of FDR, and also retain its innocence, dissociated from the effects of its bombing.[40] Joseph Biden, chair of the Senate Foreign Relations Committee at the time of 9/11 and one of the framers of the resolution that allowed the president to use unlimited force for retaliation, said, "There is zero need for declaration of war," and further that "no one should think that what we did here was less than a declaration of war."[41] For Donald Rumsfeld, 9/11 was a time to "go massive . . . Sweep it all up, things related and not."[42] Innocence and aggression working in parallel—explosion cleansing with its radiance. As the sons of Levi are purified in the refiner's fire of the Lord and as God's servants Shadrach, Meshach, and Abednego emerged from the fire even purer than they had been previously, so America would seem to make the world pure with the terrorizing "shock and awe" that comes with its mission of ridding the world of evil.

The biblical motif of the purifying effect of explosion holds a larger, universally symbolic sense as well. Ezekiel envisions that with a "noise" and a "shaking" the Lord will "open your graves . . . and bring you into the land of Israel."[43] The Greek root for the word "apocalypse" means an "unveiling of that which is hidden," so that the bomb serves the Lord's revelatory purpose. The bomb represents, as its first use in ancient China would indicate, the ushering in of a period of fertility. When asked about the explosive hostilities between Hezbollah and Israel, Condoleezza Rice responded, "What we're seeing here is the growing—the birth pangs—of a new Middle East, and . . . we have to be certain that we're pushing forward to the new Middle East."[44] In the American imagination, the bomb, the etymology of which refers to a loud popping sound, would seem to be the enactment of a pushing toward something new, a loosening, an opening up, a birthing of opportunity.

In a letter to the Thessalonians, Paul describes the rapture: "Then we which are alive and remain shall be caught up together with them in the clouds, to meet the Lord in the air: and so shall we ever be with the Lord."[45] Explosion in the Christian tradition can ultimately be seen as the occasion for the final ascendance into the sky and meeting with Christ. "Top of the world, Ma," cries James Cagney in the last scene of *White Heat,* standing on top of a refinery tank which is about to explode, while Slim Pickens, whooping, hollering, and waving his cowboy hat, rides a bucking atomic bomb as it falls from an American bomber in the film *Dr. Strangelove.* Serving a redemptive and regenerative symbolic function, fiery explosion, ritually enacted in annual Fourth of July fireworks, can be seen as the self-created image of America's myth par excellence.[46]

The American perspective, set up by a Judeo-Christian identification with God on high, plays out in the policies of defense and foreign affairs, specifically in relation to the use of bombing as a form of "fire from the heavens." A historical exploration of America's cultural biases in relation to a specific culture, the Middle East, will give further indication of how it creates antipathy in the world.

Notes

1. Genesis 19:24.

2. Exodus 15:3, 7, 15.

3. Deuteronomy 4:24.

4. John W. Dower, *War without Mercy: Race and Power in the Pacific War* (New York: Pantheon Books, 1986), 40–41.

5. *Ibid.*, 41.

6. Amos 1:2–14, 2:2–5.

7. 2 Samuel 22:11–16.

8. The Commission on Wartime Contracting estimated that as much as $60 billion had been lost to waste and fraud in Iraq and Afghanistan in the decade after 9/11. However, during that time vast, previously undetected deposits of mineral resources were discovered in Afghanistan as well.

9. For more on American military presence in Afghanistan, see Mark Mazzetti and Eric Schmidt, "U.S. Study Is Said to Warn of Peril in Afghanistan," *New York Times*, October 9, 2008, A1, A13; Rory Stewart, "The Irresistible Illusion," *London Review of Books*, July 9, 2009, 3–6; Ahmed Rashid, "The Afghanistan Impasse," *New York Review of Books*, October 8, 2009, 42–45; "The Afghan Struggle: A Secret Archive," *New York Times,* July 26, 2010, A1, A8.

10. Obama did shift some of the expectations for American troops, but his policy still required large numbers of American forces, wrongly assumed a "successful conclusion" through the reversal of Taliban gains, and overestimated the ability of Afghans to take responsibility for the government and safety of their country. After the killing of Osama bin Laden in 2011 in Pakistan, Obama turned the focus of America's intervention even farther away from occupational forces to the use of special operations and drone missile attacks. America's involvement in the liberation of Libya was marked by an entirely different attitude of "leadership from behind." In this situation American policy was to engage only when genocide was feared and as a part of a coalition of NATO forces.

11. Revelation 8:5–8.

12. H. Bruce Franklin, *War Stars: The Superweapon and the American Imagination* (New York: Oxford University Press, 1988), 15.

13. Revelation 16:8–9.

14. Revelation 20:9.

15. Drone missiles became the air weapon of choice during the Obama administration, and the collateral deaths of civilians remained a predominant issue in Afghanistan and Pakistan. Prior to the election of 2012, it was revealed that President Obama was personally involved in the choices of targets for drones. In September 2011, the United States went so far as to use a drone to kill an American citizen residing in Yemen, Anwar al-Awaki, a leader of al-Qaeda in the Arabian Peninsula. The strike brought up legal issues regarding the killing of a citizen without his being charged with a crime or tried in court. See David Cole, "Killing Our Citizens without Trial," *New York Review of Books*, November 24, 2011, 27–28. Significantly, the use of drone missiles was ruled out in the planning for the raid by American forces on the compound of Osama bin Laden at the time he was killed, precisely due to the danger of civilian casualties.

16. Michael S. Schmidt, "Threat Resurges in Deadliest Day of Year for Iraq," August 16, 2011, A1.

17. Herman Melville, *Moby Dick or The White Whale* (New York: New American Library, 1980), 186.

18. One context in which the image of a bomb is undesirable is when a theatrical production is poorly received.

19. 2 Peter 3:10.

20. Robert Jewett and John Shelton Lawrence, *Captain America and the Crusade against Evil: The Dilemma of Zealous Nationalism* (Grand Rapids, MI: William B. Eerdmans, 2003), 259.

21. *Ibid.*, 153.

22. Franklin, *War Stars*, 150.

23. *Ibid.*, 150.

24. *Ibid.*, 151.

25. See Franklin, *War Stars*, 223, note 5, and Gus Alperovitz, *Atomic Diplomacy: Hiroshima and Potsdam* (New York: Penguin, 1985).

26. *Ibid.*, 76.

27. Richard Rhodes, *Arsenals of Folly: The Making of the Nuclear Arms Race* (New York: Alfred A. Knopf, 2007), 76.

28. *Ibid.*, 101.

29. *Ibid.*, 86.

30. *Ibid.*, 99.

31. Dick Cheney and Donald Rumsfeld were in fact involved in one of these reports in 1976.

32. On May 3, 2010, President Obama revealed that America had a nuclear stockpile of 5,113 nuclear weapons.

33. Franklin, *War Stars*, 4.

34. By contrast James Hillman has differentiated between the archetypal styles of warfare of the Greek god Ares, with his hand-to-hand ground attacks, and his counterpart Apollo, with his attacks "from afar" via bow and arrow. James Hillman, *Mythic Figures* (Putnam, CT: Spring Publications, 2007).

35. Numbers 25:11.

36. Joshua 7:26, Psalms 69:9, 119:139; and Psalms 18:13–15, 79:5, Isaiah 66:15, Ezekiel 36:5, 38:19, 39:6, Zephaniah 1:18, respectively.

37. Joshua 6:17–21.

38. Jewett and Lawrence, *Captain America and the Crusade against Evil*, 253.

39. *Ibid.*, 4.

40. Jewett and Lawrence, *Captain America and the Crusade against Evil*, 256.

41. Biden was also an initial supporter of the invasion of Iraq. Jewett and Lawrence, *Captain America and the Crusade against Evil*, 16.

42. David Bromwich, "Euphemism and American Violence," *New York Review of Books*, April 3, 2008, 28.

43. Ezekiel 37:7, 12.

44. Bromwich, "Euphemism and American Violence," 28.

45. 1 Thessalonians 4:17.

46. Historically, Americans have treated fireworks on July 4th as a unique national tradition when in fact they can be found in celebrations worldwide and throughout history.

12

What Ishmael Saw: An Overview of American Involvement in the Middle East

> . . . and the angel of God called to Hagar out of heaven, and said unto her, What aileth thee, Hagar? Fear not . . .
> . . . Arise, lift up the lad, and hold him in thine hand; for I will make him a great nation.
>
> —Genesis 16:15–21:18

After 9/11, Americans asked why they were the target of militant Islamic Middle Eastern terrorists. In accordance with their sense of innocence, many Americans gave the answer in terms of pathology—Islamic cultures were jealous or envious of America's materialistic way of life, as well as their freedoms. Americans could not consider that over years, decades, and centuries their nation had behaved toward the Middle East in such a way as to be seen as a barrier to peace and prosperity by Islamic cultures.

A historical overview is required in beginning an exploration into the manner in which America's underlying cultural narrative dictates its attitudes and behavior toward the Middle East.[1] Such a perspective reveals that while a portion of America's engagement with the Middle East has been humanitarian in nature, especially in the arenas of education and medicine, the major emphasis of America's involvement has been marked by self-serving policies and actions which have created distance and hostility. American engagement in the Middle East has been characterized by a dismissive cultural bias together with an economically based dependency resulting in ambivalence, a Christian missionary zeal, an orientation toward economic advantage exclusive of its impact on local culture, and a tendency toward the use of military force for the sake of economic and political dominance. This approach can be seen as a reflection of America's underlying identification with the Israelites resulting in a condescension toward cultures of differing values, specifically Islamic culture, and sympathy with modern-day Jews and their conflict with the Arab community.

In the years leading up to the American Revolution, the colonies had become quite prosperous through trade with various parts of the world. By the 1770s, 20 percent of the colonies' exports were bound for Mediterranean countries.[2] When the colonies went to war with England, they no longer had naval protection from pirates along the Barbary Coast based in the Ottoman regencies of Tunis, Algiers, and Tripoli. During the next thirty years, a pattern of engagements ensued in which pirates would attack and hijack American merchant ships, take hostages, and then demand a ransom. The American government would respond with threatening language, but in the end would make payoffs that took up a fair portion of the new government's expenditures. This pattern revealed American ambivalence, in that while holding the possibility of a military superiority, the government refused to act decisively, fearful of the cost of protracted engagement and its effect on trade with the Middle East. It is a pattern that would come to characterize America's involvement in the Middle East in future decades.

In the months leading up to the Constitutional Convention in 1787, the colonies' statesmen held mixed opinions about the appropriate policy toward the Barbary pirates. George Washington confided to Lafayette, "Would to Heaven we had a navy to reform those enemies to mankind, or crush them into non-existence."[3] Thomas Jefferson, hoping that America would develop a strong, independent approach to foreign policy, thought that the people would support raising a military force rather than succumbing to paying ransom. The practically minded John Adams analyzed the costs and determined that continuing to pay off the pirates would be less expensive than undergoing the long-term military cost of maintaining security in the area. "We ought not to fight them [the Barbary states] at all unless we determine to fight them forever," he declared.[4]

Finally, with sailors imprisoned in North Africa and American ships imperiled, delegates gathered in Philadelphia for the sake of considering a more centralized government, including one that could respond to the Barbary states in an effective way. This gathering became the Constitutional Convention. When the Constitution came up for ratification, Alexander Hamilton took advantage of the colonies' need for a navy as one of his main arguments for accepting unification. In *Federalist* No. 24 he wrote, "If we mean to be a commercial people . . . we must endeavor as soon as possible to have a navy," and referred specifically to the threat from the "rapacious demands of pirates and barbarians" in *Federalist* No. 41.[5] Still, after the Constitution was ratified, the newly born country had no navy, and the Barbary states continued their harassment of American merchant ships. Finally, in 1794, Congress had had enough of the persecution and authorized the construction of six frigates to serve as protection for American commerce.

Even after Washington signed the measure into law, doubt remained as to the use of force and the people's readiness for armed conflict. As the government vacillated, 20 percent of its yearly revenues went as ransom to the Barbary states. President John Adams stuck to a policy of appeasement through tributes and appointed representatives to each of the Barbary regencies. In contrast, Thomas Jefferson consistently maintained that force would be necessary to remove the threat of the Barbary states. "There is no end to the demand of these powers, nor any security in their promises," he insisted in spite of his more general tendency toward isolationism. He argued that military force would be "more economical and more honorable" as a solution to the conflict as opposed to continued payment of ransom.[6] As president, Jefferson first tried unsuccessfully to arrange a multinational security system with European nations. He then bypassed an uncertain Congress, authorized military action in the Middle East, and ordered the navy to "chastise" any hostile pirates by "sinking, burning, or destroying their ships."[7] When Tripoli declared war on the United States in May of 1801 for a delay in payment, America sent three frigates to blockade the state, a mission that ultimately failed due to the relatively small size of the American force, the loss of the ship *Philadelphia,* and the capture of its crew. The result was, for Jefferson, a "national stain." The nation was continuing a pattern of ambivalence emanating from conflict between its leaders and doubt amongst its citizenry regarding use of force, followed by an unsuccessful military action allowing for the moral compromise of continued payments to the perpetrators—all, a prefiguration of conditions to come in future centuries relating to U.S.-Middle East relations.

The Barbary situation continued to be a thorn in the side of the young country up until the War of 1812. An America that was not fully invested in a definitive military action continued to respond to taunts from the Barbary Coast with half measures. Finally, having been given congressional approval for war, President James Madison sent Stephen Decatur to win reparations, compensations, and the release of any remaining hostages. "The United States, while they wish for war with no nations, will buy peace with none," Madison declared.[8] With overwhelming strength at his disposal, Decatur won a peace agreement with Algiers and then Tunis and Tripoli in quick succession.

After thirty years, the Barbary conflicts were finally over. Barbary pirates had captured thirty-five American ships and more than seven hundred sailors, and in addition, America had paid millions in bribes. And yet the Barbary conflicts had also helped to unify the colonies, spurred America to establish a navy, and for better and for worse, served as a stimulus for Jefferson's foreign policy ideal of an "erect and independent attitude" in the Middle East. Unfortunately, this ideal would, over the years, embody America's arrogance, its intolerance of cultural difference, and its need to perpetrate its own values.

The attitude of the American community at large toward Middle Eastern culture has been imbued historically with both an underlying and an overt sense of superiority. Throughout the nineteenth and early twentieth centuries, when Americans encountered Middle Eastern culture, the rhetoric within their informal communications reveals a fantasy of "civilization" as rooted in Western languages, capitalism, and Western technological practices, whereas the local culture was seen as fraught with cruelty, thieving, and murder. William Shaler, American consul to Algiers in 1815, couldn't believe that so "worthless a power [as Algiers] should have been so long permitted to vex the commercial world and extort ransom."[9] While touring the Middle East in 1825 for the American Board of Commissioners for Foreign Missions, Eli Smith reported a "land of darkness, and of the shadow of death . . . (of) ignorance, indifference and wickedness."[10] William Francis Lynch, American soldier and adventurer, wrote of the Arab, "[H]is ruling passion . . . is greediness of gold, which he will clutch from the unarmed stranger, or filch from an unsuspecting friend."[11] William Dye, an American consultant to the Egyptian army, thought of his clients as vulnerable to "lying, baksheesh, blackmail, bribery, forgery, theft and corruption . . . and murder!"[12] Theodore Roosevelt implied his Arab audiences' inferiority from a patriarchal, imperialist standpoint when he lectured Egyptians on the need to be "patient" in their desire for freedom from British rule and of the need for a "slow, steady, resolute development of . . . substantial qualities."[13]

The architecture and geography of the Middle East itself—as well as the very physical appearances of Middle Easterners—were also targets of contempt for Americans. Sarah Haight wrote, while touring Istanbul in 1839, "I only saw a mass of irregular buildings, thrown together without any architectural rule, and in defiance of all good taste."[14] David Bliss, a missionary in Beirut in 1855 observed of Middle Easterners, "Their faces are so entirely devoid of expression. It is hard to realize that some of them have souls."[15] Mark Twain denigrated Palestine as a "hopeless, dreary, heart-broken land," and its villages as "frescoed . . . with disks of camel dung."[16] In 1913, Assistant Secretary of State Francis Huntington Wilson dismissed Persia as "no place for us to waste ammunition."[17]

For Americans, the religion of Islam carried associations with "violence" and "brutal sensuality," as compared to Christianity which held the fantasy of "civilization." Shaler testified that Islam "seems peculiarly adapted to the conceptions of barbarous people."[18] John Quincy Adams considered Islam as "fanatic and fraudulent," founded upon "the natural hatred of Mussulmen toward the infidel" as well as the subjugation of others by the sword following a "doctrine of violence and lust."[19] Haight, declared that Islam "pulls down . . . every country in which it predominates."[20] William Loring, post–Civil War American consultant to the Egyptian army, considered Islam "born of the sword" and "opposed to enlightenment," while it "crushes out all independence of thought and action."[21] While on a visit to the Holy

Land, the usually progressive Mark Twain characterized Muslims as a "filthy, brutish, ignorant, unprogressive, superstitious, people."[22] Theodore Roosevelt referred to "the mass of . . . bigoted Moslems" who were committed to "driving out the foreigner, plundering and slaying the local Christian, and return[ing] to all the violence and corruption which festered under the old-style Moslem rule."[23] Toward the end of Woodrow Wilson's administration, Henry Morgenthau, America's Jewish ambassador to Turkey railed, "So long as the Qur'an makes murder a part of the Mohammedan religion, the Moslem must not be permitted to rule over Christians or Jews."[24]

A condescending attitude on the part of a Judeo-Christian culture acting out of a biblical mythology of entitlement and superiority in conjunction with a will to empire inevitably led to a zealous missionary enterprise in place of an attempt to understand the local culture and religion. Such was the predictable attitude of American Christians toward the Middle East, home of the Holy Land, on the crest of the Second Awakening. "The Christian . . . ought to cultivate patriotism to a high degree," wrote the missionary Pliny Fisk. "What could be more suitable than the glowing fire and burning zeal of political enthusiasm *consecrated* to Christ?"[25] Missionary William Goodell informed the Lebanese, "We have come to raise your . . . population from that state of ignorance, degradation and death [into] which you are fallen."[26] Every eye had turned toward Jerusalem and the Holy Land, and the American missionary movement was determined to bring what it thought of as salvation to the non-Christian world through biblical teaching and the American political agenda.

The reality of the enterprise was quite different from the rosy-cheeked ideals with which the missionaries departed. Between 1821 and 1846, one-third of American missionaries had died, and in 1834 the American Board of Commissioners for Foreign Missions admitted that "not a single soul" had been converted in the Holy Land. Author Hendry Field concluded that Christian missions "make no more impression upon Islam than the winds of the desert upon the cliffs of Mount Sinai . . . more converts are . . . made from the Gospel to the Qur'an in a day, than all our missionaries have made from the Qur'an to the Gospel in a century."[27] Thus, the cross of Christianity did not triumph over the crescent of Islam, nor was the Middle East remade in the image of America. Instead, Americans met with the counter-contempt of Muslims. "You Americans think that you can do everything . . . that money can buy or that strength can accomplish. But you cannot conquer Almighty God," declared a nineteenth-century Arab guide, reflecting the predominant reaction of the Arabic population toward American economic and missionary endeavors in the Middle East.[28]

What did not work as religious conversion did succeed to an extent in the arena of education. Here again, however, American influence in the Middle East was tinged with Christian values intermixed with American ideals of patriotism, republicanism, and individuality—all of which did not work in an Islamic culture that was largely tribal based, hierarchical, and family oriented. Missionary schools in Syria, freed by European powers from occupation by Egyptian troops and inspired by the precepts of manifest destiny, gained a foothold for Christian-based education. By the end of the American Civil War, thirty-three mission schools were in operation there. Once the war ended, the Egyptian government invited forty-eight officers from both Union and Confederate armies to train their army and build schools.[29] Officer William Dye wrote of this effort: "They were men of established reputation . . . educators anxious to assist in the great work of civilizing . . . the classic land of the Nile."[30] Between 1885 and 1895, the budget of the American Board had increased by a multiple of seven, which enabled the construction of more than four hundred schools, nine colleges, and nine hospitals in the Middle East. Ultimately, while American schools succeeded in meeting a need for Western-style education in the Middle East, the attempt to instill political ideals of democracy had little success.

In addition to missionary and educative endeavors, another leg in the platform from which American involvement in the Middle East has historically launched itself has been economic. From the days of the Barbary Coast conflicts through the years of America's dependence on oil in the twentieth and twenty-first centuries, America has looked to the Middle East first for trade and then for oil. No one understood the importance of trading relations with the Middle East better than the first American ambassador in the Middle East, David Porter, a veteran of the Barbary wars, who set a precedent for America's future role as a primary provider of technology and arms for Middle Eastern countries. Porter was so intent on staying in the good graces of the

Ottoman authorities that in 1841 he provoked the ire of American politicians by reproving the overly aggressive behavior of American missionaries in Syria, which had been offensive to the Turks.

America's nonintervention with the Ottoman Empire during the Armenian genocide in the late nineteenth and early twentieth centuries was a throwback to the American policy of appeasing Barbary pirates for the sake of trade. William Westermann, a history professor, was among the scholars enlisted by the Wilson administration for advice on the Middle Eastern situation at the time of World War I. His resulting statement could be seen as a lament for American policies— during the era of Armenian genocide as well as throughout the history of America's interactions with the Middle East—wherein economic advantage took precedent over moral considerations.

> When boldness, confidence in the strength of our own political integrity, and active support of a new political ideal might have saved Armenia and with it the Near East, we held back. Where we might have led at the zero hour of political opportunity, we faltered and refused to go over.[31]

Trade with the Middle East was especially important with the emergence of the Second Industrial Revolution and America's role as a world power. American products such as the camera, the sewing machine, and the telegraph were in heavy demand in the Middle East. General William T. Sherman took pride in America's involvement in the new technological awakening of Egypt bringing "steam engines to help poor laborers . . . railroads that skim over the dry deserts and telegraphs that carry messages from Cairo to Suez in a minute."[32] Although Americans cast their efforts to bring technology to the Middle East in terms of beneficence, those efforts were also highly profitable. In 1877, exports to Turkey were over $4.5 million, prompting Cyrus Hamlin to report that the Turkish army "now gets its . . . Martini-Henry rifles from Providence, Rhode Island, and its ammunition from New Haven, Connecticut!"[33] By 1900, American exports to the Middle East exceeded imports by fourteen to one.

The factor in American attitudes and policies that has alienated contemporary Middle Eastern Islamic peoples the most has been America's role in supporting the movement to restore a national homeland for Jews in Israel and the subsequent displacement, oppression, and, in some cases, genocide of the millions of Arabs who have called Palestine a homeland for centuries. America's support of an Israeli state in Palestine to the exclusion of any consideration for Palestinian rights, its overwhelming subsequent military aid to Israel, as well as its implicit support of Israel's continued growth through the illegal settlement of occupied territories, can be attributed to several sources: America's inherited identification with the Jews as the children of God; the fundamentalist Christian notion that the Second Coming of Christ can only occur if the Jews are securely settled in the Holy Land; America's imperialistic motivation as an entitled people; America's Cold War political need for a power base in the Middle East; America's dependence on Middle Eastern oil; America's guilt over the Jewish oppression during the Holocaust; and the strength of the Jewish vote in American politics.[34] A historical march through many decades encounters similar dynamics repeated over and over in various forms and the unfortunate consequences that have resulted from their having been played out.

The American fantasy of restoring Palestine as a homeland for Jews dates back to the Puritan colonies and John Cotton and Increase Mather's calls for the return of the Jews, which, in turn, echoed John Milton and Protestant thinking going back to the early seventeenth century. Zionism in America in the early nineteenth century was not so much a fantasy of American Jews, nor a response to anti-Semitism, but rather a means by which Christians could bring about Christ's return and usher in a new millennium.[35] Asa McFarland, during the Second Great Awakening in 1808, voiced the notion that the fall of the Ottoman Empire would open the door for the return of the Jews to Palestine. In 1844, the Reverend George Bush claimed that the creation of a Jewish state in Palestine would form a "link of communication" between God and humanity. It would "blaze in notoriety . . . [and] flash a splendid demonstration upon all kindreds and tongues of the truth."[36] Abraham Lincoln regarded the restoration of Jews to their "national home" in Palestine as "a noble dream."[37] The persecution of Jews in Russia around the turn of the century stimulated further American interest in Zionism.

The onset of World War I brought about even more Zionist fervor. President Woodrow Wilson, who held a passionately Judeo-Christian orientation and was also strongly attuned to the Jewish vote, declared during his 1912 campaign: "If ever I have the occasion to help in the restoration of the Jewish people to Palestine I shall surely do so," and his administration worked hard to ensure that emergency money and supplies were given to Jews in Palestine.[38] Theodore Roosevelt wrote: "It seems to me that it is entirely proper to start a Zionist State around Jerusalem," and asserted that "there can be no peace worth having [until] the Jews [are] given control of Palestine."[39] In 1917, with Wilson's implicit consent, the British cabinet published the Balfour Declaration, which stated that the British government "viewed with favor" the establishment of a national Jewish home in Palestine that would not interfere with the "civil and religious rights of existing non-Jewish communities in Palestine." The fact that the declaration had the backing of America was worrisome for many American diplomats, however, including William Yale, who accurately predicted that support for Zionism from the United States would provoke Muslim retaliation. Yale prophetically foresaw "fierce antagonisms" as the consequence of a Jewish state in Palestine and the need for "force of arms amid an overwhelmingly hostile population."[40] Louis Brandeis, the father of American Zionism, disagreed, stating: "The Arabs in Palestine . . . do not present a serious obstacle."[41] In September 1918, President Wilson officially identified Zionism with American policy when he expressed "satisfaction" with the progress of the Zionist Movement and with Great Britain's approval of the establishment in Palestine of a national home for the Jewish people.[42]

The Inter-Allied Commission, headed by two Americans, was created in March 1919 with the express purpose of ascertaining the desire of Arab peoples in service to the principle of self-determination contained in Wilson's fourteen recommendations for postwar peace. The commission found that the vast majority of the peoples of Syria, Lebanon, and Palestine craved independence, and Palestinians demanded the end of Zionist settlements in their country. The commission wrote:

> The Peace Conference should not shut its eyes to the fact that anti-Zionist feeling in Palestine and Syria is intense and not lightly to be flouted. No British officer, consulted by the Commissioners, believed that the Zionist program could be carried out except by force of arms. The officers generally thought that a force of not less than 50,000 soldiers would be

> required even to initiate the program. That of itself is evidence
> of a strong sense of the injustice of the Zionist program, on the
> part of the non-Jewish population of Palestine and Syria.[43]

Though ultimately accurate in its predictions, the voice of the commission held little power at the time, and the colonizing powers of England and France held sway. They carved up the Middle East for their own benefit, and America failed to use what leverage it had to push for a different outcome.

World War II and its aftermath brought the question of a Jewish homeland to a head once more, and far more poignantly this time, given the atrocities and displacement suffered by Jews at the hands of the Nazis. The Holocaust itself can be seen as a source of guilt in the American psyche resulting in a subsequent renewed identification with the notion of a Jewish homeland and extending America's denial of a meaningful presence of Palestinian Arabs. In 1946, President Truman repeated his call for the entry of one hundred thousand Jews into Palestine, and by 1947, Americans favored a Jewish homeland in Palestine at a rate of two to one. Truman's administration was divided on the issue, but nevertheless, Truman advocated the creation of "a viable Jewish state in an adequate area of Palestine," which drew further enmity from the Arab states.[44] In 1948, the continued settling of Jews in Palestine led to the massacre of hundreds of Palestinian Arabs and the flight of thousands into neighboring countries. Finally the United Nations, with the backing of the United States, passed a resolution partitioning Palestine into two independent states and consequently setting up a permanent hostile environment between Israel and the Arab nations. The subsequent armed conflict between Jews and Arabs resulted in the first of many defeats for the Arabs, and nearly eight hundred thousand Palestinians immediately became refugees from their homeland, a number that soon grew to over one million. Middle East historian Ussama Makdisi in presenting the Arab-Israeli conflict from the Arab standpoint has brought considerable focus to the humiliation of Arabs in the wake of America's "perverse blindness to the wreckage of an Arab society entailed by the creation of Israel."[45]

In the decades after the partitioning of Palestine, America's involvement in the Middle East became oriented around a cold war mentality in which communism in general and the Soviet Union in particular were seen as the primary threat to the United States. With its eye primarily on Middle Eastern oil as a resource to ensure national security, and seeking to gain every advantage possible over the Soviet Union in the Middle East, it became even more desirable for America to have a strong, centrally located ally in Israel. America took on a double-headed policy of appeasing Arab states in a limited way while also supporting Israel to a great extent.

In this atmosphere, a young devout Egyptian Muslim, Sayyid Qutb, came to despise the policies of the Western world. His visits to America in 1948 and 1950 reinforced his perception of America as materialistic, decadent, sexually permissive, and racist, and his writings contained severe condemnations of America. Eventually he was imprisoned, tortured, and hanged by a brutal Nasser-led Egyptian government that did not abide independent thinking and expression, but his work was later to have a considerable influence on what was to become the leadership of al-Qaeda.

As the state of Israel evolved into a strong military ally of the United States (with substantial American financial and military aid), America came to be seen by the Arabs as an enemy that stole both their oil and their land. The land was as sacred to Muslims as it was to Jews, each religion seeing itself as God's proprietors on earth. In 1971, the Syrian poet Adonis wrote lines that expressed a predominant Arab sentiment: "A woman—the statue of a woman / lifting in one hand a rag called liberty by / a document called history, and with the other / hand suffocating a child called earth."[46]

In 1967, Palestine became a victim of an explosion in Israeli-Arab relations culminating in the Six Days War and the resulting occupation of East Jerusalem, the West Bank, and Gaza, along with their two million Palestinian Arab residents. Walter Rostow, Under Secretary of State under President Lyndon Johnson, came up with a formula for peace that became the basis for UN Resolution 242. The resolution called for Israeli withdrawal from occupied Arab lands and a vaguely worded "just settlement" of the Palestinian refugee problem in return for Arab recognition of all states in the area and a commitment to exist in peace within previously established boundaries. Palestinian self-determination was ignored, however, with the result that the Palestine Liberation Organization (PLO), which had originally been tied to Egypt, came under the direction of Yasser Arafat, the leader of the

Syrian-backed al-Fatah organization, who vowed to carry on hostilities against Israel. At the time of the Middle East Peace Conference in December 1973, there were no Israeli settlements, but any chance for substantial agreements was lost because the PLO, seen as a terrorist organization, was excluded.

America had come to be recognized by Arabs as inextricably linked to Israel and thus linked to Israel's hostility in the co-opting of land and power in Palestine. Egypt's leader Gamal Abdel Nasser had declared in 1960, "Every bullet fired to kill an Arab was paid for by America," and a Palestinian liberation journal in Beirut stated unequivocally, "America is Israel, and Israel is America."[47] War broke out again in 1973, this time involving Israel, Egypt, and Syria. Israel was again victorious due to a massive influx of American arms and supplies sent under the direction of President Richard Nixon, who, fearful of a cold war defeat, wanted to do "whatever it takes to save Israel."[48] In retaliation for America's overt support of Israel, Arab countries withheld oil resources and cut off oil supplies to the United States. The UN again intervened with an ineffectual resolution, followed by Secretary of State Henry Kissinger's arrangement of unsteady agreements between Israel and the Arab world, which nevertheless achieved the American goal of a renewed flow of Arab oil to America.

In 1982, the Israeli army invaded Lebanon for the sake of eradicating the PLO as a competitor for the West Bank and Gaza. The PLO had been striking at Israeli settlements in the Galilee area, and Ariel Sharon, wanting to eliminate the PLO once and for all, initiated a brutal attack on Beirut that killed and maimed hundreds of civilians. Eight hundred Palestinian refugees were subsequently massacred by a right-wing Lebanese militia directly enabled by Sharon and indirectly by American inaction.[49] Sharon was forced to step down due to international pressure. President Ronald Reagan sent marines to Beirut, and in April 1983 the extremist Islamic Lebanese group Hezbollah bombed the American embassy. Subsequently, 241 American service men were killed by another Hezbollah bomb. By February of 1984, fearful of American over-involvement, Reagan pulled all troops out of Beirut. A precarious peace regarding the Israeli-Palestinian question ensued, but America's massive financial and military support of Israel (now the number one recipient of American foreign aid), along with continued Jewish settlement in occupied territories, continued to anger the Arab world.

In ensuing years, two negotiated agreements between Israel and Arabs accomplished little in defusing hostility over Palestine. President Jimmy Carter brokered an agreement between Israel and Egypt at Camp David in which Israel withdrew from Sinai, but which also granted continued Israeli settlement in the West Bank. Fifteen years later President Bill Clinton oversaw the signing of an accord worked out secretly between Prime Minister Rabin of Israel and Yasser Arafat of the PLO, but the negotiations about general principles would ultimately bring about little change in the hostile environment between Palestine and Israel. A subsequent effort by Clinton to bring about an agreement between Arafat and Israel led by Ehud Barak turned out to be disadvantageous toward Arabs, as were the previous two. Palestine would be granted statehood on the condition that Israel would continue to control the infrastructure and borders, and large chunks of the West Bank were to go to Israel. In 2001, President George W. Bush carried his pro-Israeli orientation to an extreme by supporting Ariel Sharon's offensive against Palestinians in the West Bank in which thousands were killed or captured. Bush later endorsed the creation of a Palestinian state but would increasingly turn away from the Palestinian cause as Israel established more settlements in occupied territories. President Obama at first called for a Palestinian state and then resisted Palestine's bid for statehood through the UN.

Although it is true that the divided political condition of the Palestinians as well as the obstinacy of its leadership made negotiations difficult, there have been consistent blind spots on the part of America as to the essential needs of Palestinians. The first is the need, not just for statehood, but for liberation from the oppression of an occupational force and the freedom to live with basic rights that come with sovereignty including the freedom to move at will. The second is the right of Palestinian refugees to return to their homeland, and the third is the right to be free of the continuous encroachment of new Jewish settlements. In the wake of the Arab Spring movement in 2011, in his loudly applauded speech to the American Congress, Israeli Prime Minister Netanyahu praised young Arabs for their demand for dignity and their desire for liberty. Ironically, lost to both Netanyahu and the Americans forgetful of the words from Exodus, "Do not oppress the stranger, for you know the soul of the stranger, for you were strangers in the land of Egypt" (23:9), was the fact that Israel would not honor the same needs in Palestinians.

The picture that emerges from this history of American attitudes and actions regarding Jews in Palestine reveals a bias against anything that could be considered in line with the ideal of democracy and self-determination for all people. America has often been inconsistent in its efforts to bring about peace and at the same time consistent in its support of Jews at the expense of Palestinians. Through this approach, America has been successful in achieving control in the Middle East, but at the cost of alienating a large portion of the Arab population.

In addition to its alliance with Israel, America's support of governments that are compliant toward American interests yet autocratic and oppressive toward their own people has caused ire among many Middle Eastern Arabs and led to a vision of America as the "Great Satan" by extremists such as Ayatollah Khomeini and bin Laden. One of the biggest debacles in American Middle Eastern policy was its support of the shah of Iran, whom President Eisenhower installed after the CIA had orchestrated the overthrow of Tehran's left-leaning government. The shah systematically persecuted his people until he was eventually overthrown by an internal popular revolt. This revolt shocked American policy makers, such as President Carter, who did not understand the viewpoint of the majority of Iranian people and their resentment toward the influence of the United States. In January of 1979, Shiites under the Ayatollah Khomeini took control in Tehran while Khomeini labeled the United States as the "oppressor" and the "plunderer." Giving voice to Iranian anti-American sentiments he stated, "America is the number one enemy of the deprived and oppressed people of the world."[50] The overthrow of the shah and the eventual takeover of the government by the Shia led to a more generalized suspicion on the part of American officials toward Islamic government.

Later that year, the American embassy in Tehran was taken over by Iranian students who captured sixty-four Americans and took them hostage, leading to a highly publicized and humiliating standoff for the United States. Again an old pattern asserted itself in American–Middle Eastern relations dating back to the Barbary pirates, wherein the United States itself is held as a form of hostage in its ineffectiveness. President Carter eventually worked out the release of the hostages by the unfreezing of Iranian bank accounts before his term expired.

America's wishy-washy policy in the Middle East was best exemplified during President Ronald Reagan's administration. In an unsuccessful attempt to gain compliance from Tehran, Reagan authorized the sale of weapons to the regime in Iran, a state that had sponsored terrorist hostage-taking activities in Lebanon. At the same time, Reagan was also arming Iran's sworn enemy Saddam Hussein in Iraq, a dictator who had taken and maintained control in his country through bloodshed and the use of America-tolerated chemical weapons against his enemies. Reagan's administration also gave support to *mujahideen* or "holy warriors" in Afghanistan fighting against the Soviet Union. After the Soviets withdrew, America pulled back from its help of Afghanistan, leaving it available eventually for a takeover by the thuggish Taliban. Likewise, Reagan first helped evacuate the PLO who were under assault from Israel in Beirut, then boycotted them, then went back to engagement in diplomatic dialogue. All told, Reagan alternately befriended and antagonized five different Arab parties in the Middle East, against three of whom America would later go to war. The fumbling of the Reagan administration eventually led to America's armed conflict with Iraq in the Gulf War, its retaliation against the Taliban and al-Qaeda after 9/11, and the continued hostility between Israel and the Palestinians.

The inconsistency and untrustworthiness of Reagan's policies were carried over into the subsequent administration of George H. W. Bush, which left the Kurds in the north of Iraq and the Iraqi Shiites in the south helpless against Hussein's retaliation against them after having been promised American support. In the aftermath of the Gulf War, America put millions of Iraqis at risk by prohibiting the importation of generators or any substance deemed useful for industrial or military purposes. As a result of American sanctions, tens of thousands of Iraqi children died while the general population dealt with malnutrition and various social disruptions. America's continued presence in Saudi Arabia after the Gulf War evoked the rage of militant Saudi holy warriors, such as Osama bin Laden, over America's continued presence in Saudi Arabia. In 1996, bin Laden issued a fatwa in which he declared war on America's occupation of "the Land of the Two Holy Places." He declared,

> It should not be hidden from you that the people of Islam had suffered from aggression, iniquity and injustice imposed on them by the Zionist-Crusaders alliance and their collaborators; to the extent that the Muslims' blood became the cheapest and their wealth as loot in the hands of the enemies. Their blood was spilled in Palestine and Iraq. The horrifying pictures of the massacre of Qana, in Lebanon are still fresh in our memory.[51]

A second fatwa in 1998 asserted that to "kill the Americans and their allies—civilian and military—is an individual duty for every Muslim."[52]

The legacy of the father, George H. W. Bush, was carried out by his son, George W. Bush, who responded to the 9/11 attacks with an invasion of Afghanistan that was successful in routing out the Taliban but unsuccessful in capturing its primary target, bin Laden. Then, for the second time, America essentially abandoned Afghanistan, this time in favor of a full-scale war in Iraq backed by a large majority in Congress, liberal and conservative alike, which was deemed justifiable by the Bush administration in the name of national security regarding Hussein's potential use of weapons of mass destruction. This assertion was proven groundless as it would have been before war was undertaken if the administration had given UN inspectors the chance to complete their work. The American incursion into Iraq would cost Iraq a good deal of its traditional culture, its infrastructure, hundreds of thousands of Iraqi lives, as well as tens of thousands of American lives and trillions of dollars before America would begin its withdrawal almost a decade later.

In summary, America's actions and attitudes since its beginnings in regard to the Middle East have been marked by a self-declared superiority and self-interest compounded by a profound lack of understanding of a culture whose core values were different and a lack of trustworthiness when alliances had been formed. Although America introduced educational and medical facilities in the Middle East, they were established with the aim of influencing the local inhabitants to Christian and republican values that had little to do with the Islamic tribal culture they were meant to serve. From the billions of barrels of oil America has taken from the Middle East, very little benefit has come to the indigenous populations, and instead American corporate and governmental aid dollars have gone primarily to support oppressive regimes. In regard to the crucial political issue of conflicting Israeli and Palestinian claims upon "the Land of the Two Holy Places," America has basically denied the Palestinians a right to their homeland and to basic freedoms and been wholly unsympathetic to the Palestinian experience of displacement and oppression.

The clearest statement of the folly and self-destructive nature of American actions in the Middle East comes from its own Defense Department in the form of the report of the 2004 Task Force on Strategic Communication.

> Muslims do not "hate our freedom," but rather, they hate our policies. The overwhelming majority voice their objections to what they see as one-sided support in favor of Israel and against Palestinian rights, and the longstanding, ever increasing support for what Muslims collectively see as tyrannies, most notably Egypt, Saudi Arabia, Jordon, Pakistan and the Gulf states. Thus when American public diplomacy talks about bringing democracy to Islamic societies, this is seen as no more than self-serving hypocrisy.[53]

When terrorists attacked the twin towers in 2001, President Bush set the tone for America's retaliation by framing the attack as an act of war evoking memories and thinking patterns of World War II which would justify an American "war" effort. In fact, the attacks were not acts of war, but crimes committed by terrorists representing a movement in the world political scheme that emerged after the Cold War as a new form of opposition to the United States and its values, that of militant fundamentalist Islam. As the Middle East has been revealed as a likely stronghold for anti-American sentiment giving rise to attacks by representatives of this movement, terrorism itself may now be seen as a universal phenomenon with religious underpinnings analogous to the Judeo-Christian narrative underlying the American psyche.

Notes

1. In the background of this exploration lies an archetypal pattern of mythical and historical conflict between the West and the Middle East. Sam Naifeh has compiled a historical list of military encounters in his paper, "Xenia's Journey through the Iliad and the Odyssey,"

presented at IAAP XVII in Cape Town, South Africa, August 16, 2007, which is included in the following list of East-West conflicts:

Trojan War, 1250 BCE
Athens versus Persia, 470 BCE
Alexander versus Persia, 330 BCE
Rome versus Asia Minor, 214–101 BCE
Africa versus Islam, 750 CE
Spain versus Islam, 1036 CE
European Crusades versus Asia Minor (including the massacre
of Muslims and Jews by Crusaders in 1099), 1095–1291 CE
Europe versus Genghis Kahn, 1206 CE
Europe versus Turkey, 1423–1503
France versus Algeria, 1830
UK versus Egypt, 1882
UK versus Turkey, 1915
Europe versus Egypt, 1956
USA versus Iraq, 2002–2010

2. Michael B. Oren, *Power, Faith, and Fantasy: America in the Middle East 1776 to the Present* (New York: W. W. Norton, 2007), 18.

3. *Ibid.*, 29.

4. *Ibid.*, 27.

5. Alexander Hamilton, James Madison, and John Jay, *The Federalist Papers*, with an introduction and commentary by Gary Wills (New York: Bantam, 2003), 147, 249.

6. Oren, *Power, Faith, and Fantasy*, 54.

7. *Ibid.*, 55.

8. *Ibid.*, 74.

9. *Ibid.*, 74.

10. *Ibid.*, 95.

11. *Ibid.*, 140.

12. *Ibid.*, 199.

13. Ussama Makdisi, *Faith Misplaced: The Broken Promise of U.S.-Arab Relations: 1820–2001* (New York: Public Affairs, 2010), 81–82. It is noteworthy that this is the same ambivalent attitude taken by the Obama administration in regard to the populist overthrow of the regime of President Hosni Mubarak in Egypt in spring 2011.

14. Oren, *Power, Faith, and Fantasy*, 153.

15. *Ibid.*, 216.

16. *Ibid.*, 242.

17. *Ibid.*, 321.

18. *Ibid.*, 74.

19. *Ibid.*, 110.

20. *Ibid.*, 153-4.

21. *Ibid.*, 198.

22. *Ibid.*, 241.

23. *Ibid.*, 318.

24. *Ibid.*, 385.

25. *Ibid.*, 86.

26. *Ibid.*, 131.

27. *Ibid.*, 214.

28. *Ibid.*, 128.

29. American relations with Egypt had improved with the Union's efforts to enhance Egypt's trade in cotton along with Isma'il's positive impression of Union weaponry and industry during the war.

30. Oren, *Power, Faith, and Fantasy*, 208.

31. *Ibid.*, 235.

32. *Ibid.*, 234-5.

33. *Ibid.*, 249.

34. The first three can be readily seen as emanating from a mythical narrative in which America as God's latter-day nation pursues the promised land of global domination. The aspect of guilt, however, would need to be seen in terms of a "cultural complex." Jungian analysts Thomas Singer and Sam Kimbles have contributed a great deal to the expansion of psychological thinking by extending the idea of an unconscious interior life to the culture itself, which they see in terms of the cultural complex. See S. L. Kimbles, "The Cultural Complex and the Myth of Invisibility," in *The Vision Thing*, ed. T. Singer (London: Routledge, 2000); T. Singer, "The Cultural Complex and Archetypal Defenses of the Collective Spirit: Baby Zeus, Elian Gonzales, Constantine's Sword, and Other Holy Wars," *San Francisco Jung Institute Library Journal*, 20 (4):4–28; T. Singer and S. L. Kimbles, eds., *The Cultural Complex: Contemporary Jungian Perspectives on Psyche and Society* (New York: Routledge, 2004); S. L. Kimbles, "Social Suffering through Cultural Mourning, Cultural Melancholia, and Cultural Complexes," in *Spring: A Journal of Archetype and Culture,* vol. 78, *Politics and the American Soul* (2007); T. Singer, "A Personal Reflection on

Politics and the American Soul," in *Spring: A Journal of Archetype and Culture,* vol. 78, *Politics and the American Soul* (2007).

Following the general direction of Singer and Kimbles's thought, one might describe a complex as a portion of the unconscious psyche, born of the experience of a singular traumatic event or repetitive experiences over time, which holds a consistent quality of feeling and pattern of actions in the face of encounters with the world that carry associations to the original experience(s). The American cultural complex of guilt in relation to a Jewish homeland in Palestine could then be ascribed to the underlying experience of guilt felt by America as a nation in the face of images and knowledge of the Holocaust perpetrated by Germany under the leadership of Adolph Hitler onto Jewish people.

35. This fundamentalist fantasy has persisted throughout the years so that in the early twenty-first century some of the largest contributors to humanitarian causes in Israel are fundamentalist Christians.

36. Oren, *Power, Faith, and Fantasy*, 141–42.

37. *Ibid.*, 221.

38. *Ibid.*, 357.

39. *Ibid.*, 359.

40. *Ibid.*, 364.

41. *Ibid.*, 366.

42. *Ibid.*, 365.

43. Makdisi, *Faith Misplaced*, 143.

44. Oren, *Power, Faith, and Fantasy*, 488.

45. Makdisi, *Faith Misplaced*, 202.

46. *Ibid.*, 290.

47. *Ibid.*, 257, 285.

48. Oren, *Power, Faith, and Fantasy*, 533.

49. See Seth Anziska, "A Preventable Massacre," *New York Times*, September 17, 2012, p. A23.

50. *Ibid.*, 324.

51. Makdisi, *Faith Misplaced*, 340.

52. *Ibid.*, 341.

53. *Ibid.*, 359–60.

13

The Soul of Terror /
The Terror of Soul

For Beauty's nothing
but beginning of Terror we're still just able to bear.
—Rainer Maria Rilke

In 1926 Max Ernst painted a tableau of the Virgin Mary in an
outsized, angular, cubist mode in which she is dressed mostly in
red and physically dominates the picture in a terrifying way. The
image depicts Mary spanking her young son, Jesus, perhaps in
punishment for his cruel treatment of his peers.[1] Legend has it that
as a child Jesus was instructed by his mother to include other
children in his play. When he asked three children to play with
him, they all refused because of his low birth. Jesus retaliated by
first creating a bridge of sunbeams crossing over a body of water
and then crossing the bridge. When the children tried to follow,
he caused the bridge to disappear, and the children drowned. This
story of Jesus indicates comparable themes and holds allusions to
aspects of what we would now call terrorism: beating as prelude to
flagellation and crucifixion symbolizing sacrifice, betrayal from an
unlikely or seemingly innocent source, and show of violence as a move
toward rectifying political injustice.

Likewise, Jesus's life can be seen through the lens of terrorist biography. He was born amidst a cultural setting of violence in which children were slaughtered. As a youth he disobeyed his parents and argued with the church elders. As a young man, he gave up his trade as a carpenter to become a vagabond teacher of spiritual/political doctrine. In the mode of suicidal terrorist, Jesus died as a willing martyr.[2] His burial was not successful, and subsequent interpretations of his teachings led to centuries of oppression, torture, and bloodshed. Jesus's life, as well as his iconic death, was a symbolic message, meant as hyperbole and enacted for a larger audience.

As part of his message, Jesus used violent metaphors and acted violently. His righteous anger created havoc from within the temple (literally "turning the tables"), and he subsequently prophesized the temple's destruction. He instructed his followers to sell their robes and buy swords. "Think not that I am come to send peace on earth: I came not to send peace, but a sword," Jesus told his followers. "For I am come to set a man at variance against his father, and the daughter against her mother, and the daughter in law against her mother in law."[3]

Jesus's call to his followers to awaken and give up their lives carried an implicit ontological message of terror that burst through the hierarchical authority of political and religious order, as well as slicing through the comfort of a mundane consciousness regarding everyday life. He held his life to be a weapon in itself, and as the cutting edge, he was singular in his orientation, tolerating no deviance and leaving no other choice but faith in God through himself alone. He urged his followers to give up all thoughts of present and future security, to live every moment as if it were their last, and to dedicate their life to him. His "day" was declared to come as a "thief in the night," and finally, as the King of Kings, he is depicted as bringing about the destruction of the known world with a sword emerging from his mouth, dressed in garments dipped in blood.

Beginning an exploration of terror by seeing Jesus, held by many as the arch representative of peace, as a terrorist in his own way demonstrates how terrorism works in a paradoxical manner. Terrorism operates from *within* a structure of comfort and security in order to undermine that very structure through spiritualized violent action meant as political message for a specific audience. Leaving a focus on the core character of America, its myth brings home to America a universal potential which it sees as its absolute opposite in terms of values—the violence of militaristic, fundamentalist Islam. Terrorism as a phenomenon emerges from an underlying layer of the psyche common to *all* of humanity.

The word "political" comes from the Greek word for city, *polis*, which originally referred to a "ring-wall." The political theorist Hannah Arendt takes Aristotle's reference to man as *zoon politikon* or "political animal" as an indication that humans are fundamentally social beings. For the ancient Greeks and Romans, "to live" was to be among men. "No human life, not even the life of the hermit in nature's wilderness, is possible without a world which directly or indirectly testifies to the presence of other human beings."[4]

Arendt uses the word "action" to indicate that specifically human activity which has to do solely with the need for social organization. The *polis*, as opposed to the private realm, provides the public space where such action can be undertaken. Political activity is beyond necessity, separated from the household where futility exists in the struggle for survival.[5] The *polis* is where individual excellence (*arete*) can be shown, the present memorialized, and immortality approached through a form of organized remembrance. The political world is a *thiasos*, a community based on a notion of theater in which the internal is made real through the process of seeing and being seen. For Plato, this action is a matter of creation, fabrication, or craftsmanship.[6] The essence of political life becomes a show or display that is a "making," a making of appearance for an other in the service of remembrance. Here, Arendt locates violence in political life. Violence, says Arendt, "without which no fabrication could ever come to pass," plays an essential role in the political realm.[7] In essence, political life provides a mold or role in which the terrorist can fit. The terrorist acts in a violently performative manner in the service of a higher cause, not for the sake of winning ground, but for the purpose of persuading or being seen by the community of humans and gods that make up his or her world.

The notion of terrorism can be expanded by seeing its history in the background of three contemporary English words that are directly or indirectly related to terrorism—"thug," "zealot," and "assassin."

"Thug" was the name given to members of a terrorist group in India that existed from as early as the thirteenth century until the nineteenth century. The word originally meant "deceiver." In everyday life, thugs were models of propriety, known for such virtues as industry, temperance, generosity, kindliness, and trustworthiness. In their shadow life, they were followers of the earth goddess Kali (literally "Black Time"), the great divinity of life and death, sustenance and destruction. As members of a secret sect, they believed that Kali demanded blood in order to keep the world in balance. A thug would choose his victim from among fellow Hindu travelers on the road, gain an intimate connection with the traveler through the guise of companionship, and then strangle the victim with a handkerchief. The corpse was then gashed and gutted, and the blood and organs buried in the earth as a sacrifice to Kali.[8]

"Zealot" was the name given to a group of Jewish terrorists operating in the Holy Land in the centuries of Roman occupation.[9] The Zealots and another terrorist group, the Sicarii, targeted Roman or Jewish individuals whose high station of government official, priest, or landowner served to maintain the status quo. According to Flavius Josephus, an ancient Hebrew historian, these groups frequently committed murder in broad daylight, often on holy days when Jerusalem was crowded with pilgrims. With daggers concealed in their cloaks, the Zealots and the Sicarii mingled with the crowds undetected. When their victims fell to the ground, their murderers would join in the general frenzy around the crime and then make their escape in the midst of the ensuing panic.[10] "The panic created was more alarming than the calamity itself; everyone, as on the battlefield, hourly expected death," Flavius Josephus wrote, speaking of a period of daily murders following the first assassination of a high priest. "Men kept watch at a distance on their enemies and would not trust even their friends when they approached."[11]

The word "assassin" comes from the name of a group of Muslim terrorists operating during the twelfth century. This Shiite sect rebelled against the rival Sunni rulers, who wanted to purify Islam and return it to a single fundamentalist community in the form of a state. The assassins placed young men in the service of religious or political leaders in power, and over the years the young men would acquire the trust of their masters. At an appropriate occasion, usually on Muslim holy days in a highly public place, the man in service would stab his master with a dagger in full public view with the complete expectation of being killed himself. In this way the first of the suicidal martyrs of later centuries would be rewarded with an afterlife in paradise.

A pattern emerges from these three originating terrorist agencies in which violence performed by a religious group is enacted from an unlikely close-up position and carried out in a ritualistic manner meant as symbolic gesture to create an effect serving a larger spiritual/political truth. Out of the origins of terror in three religious traditions we see the inevitable connection between violence and the sacred.

James Hillman has said that through religion a warrior class serves the human condition and through the virtues of the warrior—courage, persistence, nobility, honor, loyalty—war finds its place in the human psyche.[12] The terrorist would claim these virtues in taking on the aspect of the archetypal holy warrior. The roots of this role lie in ancient Hindu mythology where we can see in a passage from the Bhagavad Gita a paradigm for righteous warfare out of which holy terror emerges. In the text, the hero, Arjuna, surveys the field of impending battle before he enters it and loses heart. He cannot tolerate the loss of innocent life and the splitting of family and friends that war involves. The god Krishna tells him he is confused.

> [Y]our sorrow is for nothing. The truly wise mourn
>   neither for the living nor for the dead.
> There was never a time when I did not exist, nor you
>   nor any of these kings. Nor is there any future in
>   which we shall cease to be.
> Just as the dweller in this body passes through
>   childhood, youth, and old age, so at death he
>   merely passes into another kind of body . . . .
> Bodies are said to die, but that which possesses the body
>   is eternal. It cannot be limited, or destroyed.
>   Therefore you must fight . . . .
> Die, and you win heaven.[13]

Here, before the advent of the three great religions of the Middle East, the agenda of the terrorist is laid out: We live a timeless existence. He who slays, slays not; he who is slain, is not slain. The fight for the higher cause, in and of itself, renders the warrior ultimately victorious.

The history of warfare in the name of God in both the Judeo-Christian and the Islamic traditions serves as further background context for the connection of violence with the sacred inherent in the psyche of the terrorist.[14] The Old Testament is filled with accounts of military struggles of the children of God: Abraham struck an enemy encampment at night with a small group of men in a guerilla attack. Moses served as a military leader when he was still an Egyptian. While the children of Israel followed Moses through the desert, his followers, the sons of Levi, slaughtered the three thousand Israelites who chose to worship the golden calf. God swore to the children of Israel that the promised land would be theirs as they conducted "holy war" in his name, saying, "I will send forth my *terror* before you, and I will cast into panic all the peoples among whom you pass, and I will cause all thy enemies to flee before you."[15] Joshua sacked the cities of Jericho and Ai and established the precedent of carrying into battle the Ark of the Covenant or *shekinah*, "the place where God dwells."

For the Israelites, God lived on the battleground, whether through commando raids such as those perfected by Gideon or individual acts of terrorism such as those of the heroines, Jael, who drove a stake through the head of an enemy commander while he slept, and Judith, who seduced an enemy general and beheaded him in his sleep. Samson pulled down the Philistines' world trade tower, David conducted insurrectionist military raids against established authority, and both David and Saul used conventional warfare as a part of their centralized rule. Believing that their Lord was "a man of war," the children of Israel engaged in genocide at Jericho in his name.[16] The word "Israel" came to mean "God fights," and one of the psalms in praise of God is a song of revenge against the Babylonians: "Happy shall be he who takes your little ones and dasheth them against the stones."[17] War in the name of God was inherent to the life of the Israelites.

In 610 A.D., Muhammad received the revelation of the Qur'an, left his home in Mecca, and became a military leader intent on establishing theocratic rule. Echoing Jesus, he declared, "Behold! God sent me with a sword, just before the Hour, and placed my daily sustenance beneath the shadow of my spear, and humiliation and contempt upon those who oppose me."[18] He established a stronghold in Medina and through various military campaigns conquered Mecca and most of western Arabia before his death in 632. In the early stages of Islam the entire Muslim community served a single ruler, an ideal for which contemporary Muslims still strive. From the beginning the Muslim world, as did its counterpart the Judaic world, considered religion, government, and war to be intrinsically connected.

The fundamentalist Islamic terrorist takes a wide view of the notion of holy war. The word "Islam," in fact, is a cognate to the word for peace, *salam*, which is related to the Hebrew *shalom*. Allah is merciful and compassionate, and he forbids the slaying of a soul which he has made sacred. "We will provide you and them; and that you approach not any indecency outward or inward, and that you slay not the soul God has forbidden." But there is a catch, "except by right."[19] Violence is condoned in defending home and faith. Jihad, meaning "striving toward the light," is sanctioned "to suppress tyranny, insure the right of the individual to home and freedom within his own nation, prevent persecution in religion, and guarantee freedom of belief to all people."[20] Jihad came to indicate a political as well as religious act, the armed struggle for the defense or advancement of Muslim power in government in the face of the threat of infidels. The Qur'an reads,

> When you meet the unbelievers, smite their necks,
> And those who are slain in the way of God, He
> Will not send their works astray.
> He will guide them, and dispose their minds aright,
> And He will admit them to Paradise.[21]

The Qur'an contains detailed accounts of how, where, and when to fight. The battle is always in the name of God, with an emphasis on discipline, persistence, patience, and self-sacrifice, all qualities claimed by militant Islamic fundamentalist terrorists. The Qur'an reflects its Hindu predecessor, the Bhagavad Gita, in its admonition to the holy warrior to kill and be killed in order to receive eternal life in heaven. The central tenets are the same: that God himself is to be feared, not the enemy infidels; that life on earth is a delusion; and that the true life awaits the believer in the paradisiacal afterworld.

For Muslims following the Qur'an, the Day of Apocalypse is always already at hand. The Qur'an embodies a sense of time different from the linear notion of beginning, middle, end—a chronology that frequently can be perplexing to Westerners. In the Qur'an, only the present moment is real. The hour is but a twinkling of the eye, as God is continually creating each point in time and space at each moment. Written in an imagistic style rather than as a straight chronological narrative, the Qur'an moves from talking about the Day of Judgment as future—"Upon that day . . . the Trumpet shall be blown (echoing Joshua) . . . and upon that day We shall present Gehenna (Hell) to the unbelievers,"[22]—to announcing the Day of Judgment in the present tense—"The Hour has drawn nigh: the moon is split."[23] The Islamic terrorist is living the present as if it were the last day, and what others call terrorism is only one more act in a war that is occurring right now in the perpetual struggle for the soul of Islam.

A review of three major religions shows that the sacred is inherently violent, and those who consider themselves on the side of God can be seen through a fundamentalist lens to be licensed by their holy scripture to "smite the necks" of those they believe to be unbelievers.[24] What makes the terrorist different from the conventional warrior or the guerilla warrior is that the goal of the terrorist is not a military victory, rather a triumph of propaganda. The terrorist acts for a larger audience, both earthly and divine. Terrorists think through representational images and stage events that make symbolic statements. The terrorist is a performance artist, creating a spectacle for an effect that will outlast immediate consequences and leave the audience shaken.

For the Greeks, terror existed in a condition expressed in the word *tromokratia,* where there is no order, and control is beyond human means. The word "terror" is derived from the Latin *terrere,* which means "to cause to tremble." "Tremble" comes from *tremere,* referring to tremor, specifically the trembling of the earth. *Terrere* is derived from its root, *terra* or earth, which in turn comes from a Greek word, *tremos,* which again means "quaking" or "quivering" like the earth disrupted. *Tremos* is the root of the English word "trauma." Etymological origins reveal the earth itself as a source of terror.

The Greeks had a god for earthquakes, Poseidon in his earth-father form, called Old Earth Shaker. In the Judeo-Christian tradition, God speaks through the shaking of the earth: "Yet once, it is a little while and I will shake the heavens . . . and the earth and the sea and the dry land; And I will shake all nations."[25] Every Christmas and Easter, the bass in Handel's *Messiah,* standing in for the voice of God, sings the word "shake" in vibrating sixteenth notes telling us in effect that the Lord will act as a terrorist. God shakes the world in many ways—

through famine, pestilence, flood, and fire—but ultimately through the coming of his Son, the Messiah. The idea is echoed in the Gospels as well, when the coming of Christ is indicated by the shaking of both heaven and earth. Where the water is troubled, there is God. Where there is terror, there is God.

The root of the word "religion," the Latin *religio*, means to "bend back," as if toward a more fundamental plane of existence. When we are terrorized, our foundations tremble, and we are shaken back to our roots. Traumatized with a glimpse of infinity, with a dismembered identity, we become "fundamental," shaken to our foundational being.

The theologian Rudolph Otto, in exploring the irrational aspect of the divine, described the holy as a *mysterium tremendum*, a tremendous mystery that acts like a terrorist.

> It may burst in sudden eruption up from the depths of the soul with spasms and convulsions, or lead to the strangest excitements, to intoxicated frenzy, to transport, and to ecstasy. It has its wild and demonic forms and can sink to an almost grisly horror and shuddering. It has its crude, barbaric antecedents and early manifestations, and again it may be developed into something beautiful and pure and glorious. It may become the hushed, trembling, and speechless humility of the creature in the presence of—whom or what? In the presence of that which is a *mystery* inexpressible and above all creatures.[26]

Even the goddess of love and beauty, Aphrodite, carries an aspect of terror as those involved where love goes wrong can attest. She was born from the severed genitals of Uranus and the chaos of primeval waters. In Hesiod's account her children were Terror and Fear. She was called the "black one," also known as "Aphrodite of the Grave" and "Grave Robber," and she wrecked terrible revenges on those who defied her. Claire Lejeune writes,

> This Beauty is sovereign, because it is unforeseeable and inescapable. Against its possible victory, our defeat, we arm ourselves; we turn from terror to terrorism. The ultimate object of human fear is Beauty; nothing is more disarming, more ravishing, than its eruption in our lives.[27]

The sense of the irrational as connected with the divine carries over into the seeming irrationality of terrorists and our sense of them as diabolical, but the devil, as Fallen Angel, has a dual character. The Greek word *diabolein* means to "tear apart," an action characteristic of the Judeo-Christian God. The psalm promising destruction of the heathen declares, "Thou shalt break them with a rod of iron: thou shalt dash them in pieces like a potter's vessel."[28] Ferocity or fury is in the character of Lucifer, but "Lucifer" means the "light bringer." The word "Satan" means "one who obstructs," or "accuser," but Satan was originally considered to have been sent to earth by the Lord to carry spirit energies that organize natural processes, that is, to "enspirit" the earth. In this sense the possessed mentality of terrorists can be thought of as mediation by the divine, or in William Blake's words, "Terror, the human form divine."

The literary critic Terry Eagleton has written, "Like God, the Real . . . is the unfathomable wedge of otherness at the heart of identity which makes us what we are, yet which—because it involves desire— also prevents us from being truly identical with ourselves."[29] One way the divine makes itself visible as terror in human form is through the chaos hidden within all human gestures toward order. Mythically, chaos marks the beginning, and order emerges only from its turbulent ground. All gods, as creatures of excess, surpass human understanding. Institutional human structures as those of religion, economics, and justice, necessarily created through will, inevitably involve transgression and violation as earthly matters are pressed by the spirit of will to give shape to what is ultimately ineffable.

The concept used by philosophers of the Enlightenment to indicate the unfathomable wedge of otherness is that of the sublime. In 1757 Edmund Burke, the English philosopher, wrote a treatise on aesthetics, *Philosophical Enquiry into the Origin of Our Ideas on the Sublime and the Beautiful,* in which he associated the sublime with terror. For Burke, the sublime was impressive, vast, ruggedly magnificent, infinitely fearsome, inducing feelings of wonder, astonishment, and awe. Eagleton describes it as "any power which is perilous, shattering, ravishing, traumatic, excessive, exhilarating, dwarfing, astonishing, uncontainable, overwhelming, boundless, obscure, terrifying, enthralling, and uplifting . . . a glimpse of infinity which dissolves our identity and shakes us to our roots."[30] From this perspective terror, as intricately connected with the sublime, is the base of all power, and by extension most significantly religious, economic, and political power.

This idea was later echoed across the English Channel with the temporary founding of another Western democracy through what is paradoxically known as the Reign of Terror. One of the architects of that bloodbath, Robespierre, looked to terror as a consequence of the general principle of democracy applied to the needs of the nation.

> The mainspring of popular government in time of war is both virtue and terror: virtue without which terror is fateful: terror without which virtue is helpless. Terror is nothing but prompt, severe and inflexible justice: It is thus emanation and emanation of virtue.[31]

Tocqueville, whose grandfather was beheaded during the Reign of Terror, envisioned the potential banality of mind he saw in the future of American democracy as a "terror which depresses and enervates the heart," giving voice to the violence which underlay the attitude of comfortable self-interest engendered by the seeming order of its cultural institutions.[32] Eagleton, Burke, Robespierre, and Tocqueville are all giving voice to the idea that what we look to as security inevitably carries its own pathos.[33] It is the life energy of this invisible violence, the other of social order, which cultures throughout the ages have symbolized through blood as sacrifice.

There is no single symbol that stands out more in the imagery of terrorism than that of blood—blood spilled, spattered, or stained, given by donors in post-9/11 New York, covering bodies in the marketplaces of the Middle East, or ritually poured out in libations by Indian thugs. Universally, divinity demands something from humans, and the terrorist reminds us that the sacred is sealed in blood. The Hebrew god Yahweh honors the offerings of the hunter Abel and not the farmer Cain. God wants blood. Abel becomes Cain's sacrifice. God gets blood. God demands a blood sacrifice from Abraham and eventually gets it. The Hebrew words for "to make a covenant," *karat berit*, mean literally to "cut" a deal. The cut of circumcision becomes a covenant. God cuts words into stone for Moses. Moses cuts an animal in two, passes fire between its parts, and casts the blood toward the people. Through the "blood of the covenant" God's children live for him, and bloodletting in the name of God carries over to transgressors who would be given by Him "into the hand of them that seek their life; and their dead bodies shall be for meat unto the fowls of heaven, and to the beasts of the earth."[34]

Blood is symbolic of sacrifice that is associated with the word "sacred," representing the mode of giving back to the gods, reciprocating their favor. The root of the word "sacred," the Latin *sacer*, means "holy," "belonging to gods," but also "devoted to deity for destruction," "accursed," "detestable," and "criminal." The Greek root *ieros* means "holy," but also relates to death and taboo animals. The root syllable *sac* also refers to the last spinal bone, the sacrum, called the "holy bone," which gives rise to our word "sacroiliac." The notion of sacred means to get to the bottom of things, the dirty side of life, which borders on death as well as on the divine. The sacred is the sack or pouch that carries the gore and guts of the animal as well as the head of the slain enemy offered in sacrifice. Blood represents life having passed through death to become sacred. The suicidal terrorist performs and provides a double sacrifice, himself and his victim.

The institutionalized Hindu worship of Kali featured a great temple festival in which hundreds of animals were slaughtered and the blood let into a deep pit filled with fresh sand that sucked up the blood and then was buried in the earth to create fertility.

> Today the temple of Kali at the Kalighat in Calcutta is famous for its daily blood sacrifices; it is no doubt the bloodiest temple on earth. At the time of the great autumn pilgrimages to the annual festival . . . some eight hundred goats are slaughtered in three days. The temple serves simply as a slaughterhouse . . . For to the Goddess is due the life blood of all creatures—since it is she who has bestowed it.[35]

Pouring blood libations into the earth is a universal ritual practice; earth wants blood, earth gets blood. Life and death come from the same source.

Divinity, both heavenly and earthly, evokes terror through a call for blood mirrored in the actions of the terrorist. The terrorist brings us to body and a violent propensity for body rending which lies in the domain known by some as the "feminine." Archetypally, the terrorist can be seen as a form of son-lover to the great earth goddess. In the myth of Adonis, the young man becomes the beloved of Aphrodite. Against her wishes he goes out on a hunt and is gored to death by a boar, and Aphrodite is thrown into grief. In ancient Egypt, Adonis was associated with the corn god, and at the harvest, women of the community would shave their heads or prostitute themselves in lamentation for the dismembered god seen in the sickled, ground grain. In the ancient Middle Eastern cultures, the son-lover was Attis and the goddess Cybele. Attis was thought to have castrated himself and on the Day of Blood, a high priest would cut his arms while lower priests would dance in ecstasy, gashing their bodies and spattering blood on the alters. In Syria, laymen would be moved by the dances of eunuch priests to castrate themselves and spend their lives dressed in female attire. The Egyptian god Osiris, consort to his sister Isis, was dismembered by his brother Set in the form of a boar. Set scattered the pieces of Osiris's body, but Isis, in mourning, gathered them, reforming the god. In an ancient Egyptian festival, human sacrifice was performed in imitation of the violent death of Osiris, and pieces of the body scattered while farmers beat their breasts in lamentation. An alchemical text, the *Turba*, describes the interaction of the son with "my mother who is my enemy," but who also "gathers together all my divided and scattered limbs."[36]

Seeing through the images of Jesus's crucifixion and the Pieta, as well as terrorist bombings with scenes of grief and mourning, we can detect the savage violence and lamentation in the ancient rites and rituals of the archetypal mother and her son-lover. One of the great plays of the Western world, *The Bacchae* by Euripides, tells of the terrible god, Dionysus, as ur-terrorist and gives dramatic form to the rites of dismemberment of the son-lover.

Terror gives way to a larger image of the conjunction of life with death, fertility with dismemberment, intimacy with violence, and the sublime with the uncertain. Through the vivid spectacle of terror as a body-rending spectacle of red blood amidst bits of bone and flesh, all in order to appease the gods, the form of another divinity emerges. It is a youthful, effeminate face, now bearded, now beardless, framed by an entwined serpent, revealing the god who exposes the joy of terror and the terror of joy, Dionysus. He was the invigorating and ravishing god of wine, divinity of the drumbeat and the dance, but also of human savagery and lust for blood from within intimate settings. The classicist W. F. Otto characterized him as "the god of the most blessed ecstasy and the most enraptured love," as well as "the persecuted god, the suffering and dying god, and all whom he loved, all who attended him had to share his tragic fate."[37]

In the terrorist we see Dionysus, god of fluidity, wine, and blood, dismemberment, dance, and theater. As "the Great Loosener," he liberates from cares, but he also dismembers. He dissolves form and notions of linear progression, transgressing over boundaries, licensed and unruly, emancipated from the ground of reason to the passions of the animal and the guile of the serpent.

> And the inner force of this dual reality is so great that he appears among men like a storm, he staggers them, and he tames their opposition with the whip of madness. All tradition, all order must be shattered. Life becomes suddenly an ecstasy—an ecstasy of blessedness, but an ecstasy, no less, of terror.[38]

Intimate and alien, suddenly appearing and disappearing, Dionysus presides over what Terry Eagleton describes as

> that orgy of un-meaning, before the dawn of subjectivity itself, in which bloody stumps and mangled bits of bodies whirl in some frightful dance of death. It is a dark parody of carnival— jubilant merging and exchange of bodies which like carnival itself is never far from the graveyard. The orgy dissolves distinctions between bodies, and thus prefigures the indifferent leveling of death.[39]

Of all the gods the "most terrible, although most gentle, to mankind," the dual aspect of Dionysus is evident in the stories of his birth. In one version, Zeus, in the form of a snake, fathered Dionysus through union with the goddess of the underworld, Persephone. In jealousy, Zeus's wife Hera had the infant torn into pieces by the Titans. Zeus swallowed the heart and fathered the child a second time with the human female Semele. After being impregnated by Zeus, Semele was tricked by the still-jealous Hera into getting Zeus to grant any wish. In her naïveté, Semele wished to see Zeus in his true form. Being human she could not survive the sight of the god in his divinity and burst into flame. Zeus again rescued the infant, carried him to term in his thigh, and born again, Dionysus was given to foster parents to be raised for a time as a girl.

In *The Bacchae*, Dionysus, disguised as an effeminate foreigner from the east, enters the city of Thebes and, finding himself without honor, casts a spell upon the women so that they leave their looms and shuttles, take to the hills, and are initiated into his mysteries. Dionysus demands to be worshipped as a god, but the young king Pentheus refuses his request. Pentheus is an arrogant man who is intolerant of tradition and disdainful of any power—except that which he derives from his station as king. He has nothing but contempt for tradition and a hidden fear of anything other. When he hears of the havoc being wrought in his city, Pentheus can only think by way of rigid forms and insists on meeting the challenge of Dionysus with the conventional symbols of man-made power: manacles, chains, traps, nets, hangings, and prison cells.

Pentheus is the embodiment of *amathia*, the condition of self-unknowing where action is performed from an inaccessible, ungovernable ignorance of self and of necessity. When Dionysus is taken prisoner, he turns into a terrorist, crying, "Let the earthquake come! Shatter the floor of the world!"[40] He causes the palace to be razed to the ground, and the chorus cries in dismay as it goes up in flame ignited by a thunderbolt. Dionysus's female followers, the maenads, which include Pentheus's mother Agave, wear serpents as headbands and dance to drums and flutes as they descend upon the city to honor their god.

> O city,
> With boughs of oak and fir,
> Come dance the dance of god!
> Fringe your skins of dappled fawn
> With tufts of twisted wool!
> Handle with holy care
> The violent wand of god!
> And let the dance begin![41]

As the god of madness, Dionysus's appearance calls into question the very nature of sanity. In the background of the question we can see the relativistic essence of terrorism. Pentheus sees the revels of Dionysus as a kind of mad possession, but from Dionysus's standpoint, ordinary life—the shuttle and the loom—is in itself a kind of madness. The elders of the city consider it crazy of Pentheus not to pay attention to the traditional relationship of men and gods, while he takes them for lunatic old men in suggesting he give up his power.

Dionysus turns our perspectives inside out and gives us double vision. After he has come to possess Pentheus, Dionysus calls him out to be seen. Pentheus, king of Thebes, emerges wearing a dress and wig of long blonde curls, now a cross-dresser with dual identity. He stammers,

> I seem to see two suns blazing in the heavens,
> And now two Thebes, two cities, and each
> With seven gates. And you—you are a bull.[42]

Dionysus frames this vision as the recognition of a god, the bull, unlike previously when Pentheus was "blind." Dionysus teaches us to see with multiple eyes, the dual vision as the gaze of imagination—not literal, not abstract—but material and spiritual at once.

Dionysus lures Pentheus into following him into the hills to witness the revels of the women. The god becomes the poet of revenge as the women who were hunted by Pentheus turn and become the hunters, their ecstatic desire echoed by the chorus.

> When shall I dance once more
> With bare feet the all-night dances,
> Tossing my head for joy
> In the damp air, in the dew,
> As a running fawn might frisk
> For the green joy of the wide fields,
>
> . . . leaping
> to frisk, leaping for joy,
> gay with the green of the leaves,
> to dance for joy in the forest,
> to dance where the darkness is deepest,
> where no man is.[43]

Pentheus is finally treed like an animal and falls to his death by dismemberment at the hands of his crazed mother foaming at the mouth as she tears the limbs and head from her child's torso.

Euripides's play tells us that the life force, *zoe*, embodied in Dionysus carries its own violent surprise which comes bursting forth as if from out of the earth. Its chaos cuts through the rational barriers of personal ego and collective order based upon reason in the service of certainty. Dionysus asks his followers to abandon homeland security and demands his place among the psychological necessities we call gods. Openness to the terrible powers of this surreptitious daimon winding its way across the earth brings a form of compassion for life and also reflects a kind of wisdom of uncertainty.

> The gods have many shapes.
> The gods bring many things
> To their accomplishment.
> And what was most expected
> Has not been accomplished.
> But god has found his way
> For what no man expected.[44]

The ways of the gods are not the ways of humans. "What is most expected" is not accomplished, and instead what is "found," an ecstatic dance of explosive terror shattering established form and conventional assumptions, is "what no man expected." Augustine confesses that God is "one who fills me with terror and burning love: with terror in so much as I am utterly other than it, with love in that I am akin to it."[45] Jean-Paul Sartre extends this idea to the formation of human identity which cannot be separated from surrounding world. We are who we are, always in relation to an other. A terrorist is inherently terrifying because, like Dionysus, he or she works from a place of intimacy or close proximity to the subject—a fellow airplane traveler, a friendly shopper in the marketplace, a quiet passerby at the customs gate—in order to achieve his or her violent ends which call into question one's very identity. Does the innocent appearance of the concealed bomber reflect my own aggression or my innocence?

If social structures conceal their terror, and terror its order, then Pentheus embodies the terror of the state, and Dionysus the order of ritual within chaos. Ultimately, what makes terrorism most terrifying is that the terrorist is at once something totally other than his or her subject and at the same time akin to it. The terrorist and victim always reflect a trace of each other, at some level complicit in the act. Terrorism becomes an autoimmune crisis, as Jacques Derrida characterizes it, an aspect of a system turned against itself. Finally, terrorism serves to turn the tables on our values, pulling out our underlying secrets in a maneuver presented by John Milton in his character, Satan, the fallen angel who declares, "Evil, be thou my good."

The book has come full circle from 9/11 by leaving the core which is essential to America and delving into the universal strata of the human psyche to find a mirror of America in its other. Just as core character finds its visibility in its everyday attitudes, behaviors, and imagery, so also does it find its ultimate source in an archetypal bedrock. Just as the archetypal lays out parameters for the possibilities of transformation that are given within each segment of human being, so does national myth provide a sense of finitude and limits for change within an essential structure of identity.

Notes

1. See Leo Steinberg, "Max Ernst's Blasphemy," *New York Review of Books*, September 22, 2005, 85.

2. Jesus's death was a sacrifice in the tradition of the scapegoat or *pharmakon,* the figure that is cast into the desert carrying the sins of the community.

3. Matthew 10:34.

4. Hannah Arendt, *The Human Condition* (Chicago: University of Chicago Press, 1958), 22.

5. The container that was central to the rites of Vesta, goddess of the hearth, was the *futile,* a vessel that could not stand without tipping over.

6. "Our first task . . . is to mold the model of a happy state." From "Republic," in *The Collected Dialogues of Plato*, edited by Edith Hamilton and Huntington Cairns (Princeton, NJ: Princeton University Press, 2005), 420.

7. Arendt, *The Human Condition*, 228.

8. The myth upon which this practice was based states that Kali at one time had killed a gigantic monster that devoured humans. Kali killed the monster with her sword, but the drops of blood simply turned into more monsters. The more she killed, the more were formed from subsequent drops of blood. Kali solved the problem of multiplying demons by licking up the blood of their wounds.

9. The criminal Barabbas, who was released by Pilate according to the Roman custom of letting a prisoner go at the time of the Jewish holiday, a reverse form of scapegoating, is thought by some to have been a Zealot. Ironically, Jesus took his place on the cross.

10. The origin of the ideology and tactics of the Zealots and Sicarii extended back to the time of Moses, when the children of Israel were still wandering in the desert. Phineas, a high priest, was incensed by the unfaithful and licentious acts of God's children. Taking the law into his own hands, he murdered a tribal chief and his concubine with the head of his spear which he used as a dagger (*sica*). This act prepared the way for God to command the Holy War (*herem*) against the Canaanites for possession of the promised land.

11. As quoted by David C. Rapaport in "Fear and Trembling: Terrorism in Three Religious Traditions," *American Political Science Review*, 78, 670.

12. "Wars are not only man-made; they bear witness also to something essentially human that transcends the human, invoking powers more than the human can fully grasp. Not only do gods battle among themselves and against other foreign gods, they sanctify human wars, and they participate in those wars by divine intervention." James Hillman, "Wars, Arms, Rams, Mars: On the Love of War," in *Facing Apocalypse*, ed. Valerie Andrews, Robert Bosnak, and Karen Walter Goodwin (Dallas: Spring Publications, 1987), 120.

13. *The Song of God: Bhagavad-Gita*, trans. Swami Prabhavananda and Christopher Isherwood, introduction by Aldus Huxley (New York: New American Library, 1951), 36–39.

14. The right of just war was advocated by Cicero, St. Ambrose, and St. Augustine, as well as Mohammed, and has been exercised throughout Judeo-Christian as well as Islamic history.

15. Exodus 23:27.

16. Exodus 15:3; Joshua 6:21.

17. Psalms 137:9.

18. As quoted by Robert Jewett and John Shelton Lawrence, *Captain America and the Crusade against Evil: The Dilemma of Zealous Nationalism* (Grand Rapids, MI: William B. Eerdmans, 2003), 155.

19. Qur'an I, VI:152. All quotes from the Qur'an are taken from *The Koran Interpreted*, trans. A. J. Arberry (New York: Simon and Schuster, 1955).

20. Azzam, Abd-al-Rahman, *The Eternal Message of Muhammad* (New York: New American Library, 1964), 129.

21. Qur'an, II, 47:4–8.

22. Qur'an, I, 18:98–100.

23. Qur'an, II, 54:1.

24. Regina Schwartz, in *The Curse of Cain: The Violent Legacy of Monotheism* (New York: University Press, 1997), has made the point that when a religion is monotheistic, the people identifying on the one hand with God and with land on the other, violence is the inevitable result.

25. Haggai 2:6–7.

26. Rudolf Otto, *The Idea of the Holy*, trans. John W. Harvey (New York: Oxford University Press, 1958), 12–13.

27. As quoted in Ginette Paris, *Pagan Meditations* (Dallas: Spring, 1987), 157.

28. In Handel's *Messiah* the very next word after this declaration is "Hallelujah," again an indication of a celebration of God's violence.

29. Terry Eagleton, *Holy Terror* (London: Oxford University Press, 2005), 43.

30. Eagleton, *Holy Terror*, 44.

31. Andrew Sinclair, *An Anatomy of Terror: A History of Terrorism* (New York: Macmillan, 2003), 76.

32. Alexis de Tocqueville, *Democracy in America*, vol. 2 (New York: Vintage Books, 1990), 330.

33. An excellent example is the subtle "violence" manifested in the architecture and regimentation of American high school life, which evokes terrorism like that of the Columbine episode in Colorado in 1999.

34. Exodus 24:8; Jeremiah 34:20.

35. As quoted by Erich Neumann, *The Great Mother* (Princeton, NJ: Princeton University Press, 1963), 152.

36. C. G. Jung, *Mysterium Coniunctionis* (Princeton, NJ: Princeton University Press, 1970), 21.

37. Walter F. Otto, *Dionysus: Myth and Cult*, trans. Robert B. Palmer (Bloomington: Indiana University Press, 1965), 49.

38. Otto, *Dionysus: Myth and Cult*, 78.

39. Eagleton, *Holy Terror*, 3–4.

40. Quotes from *The Bacchae* are taken from *Euripides V* of the *Complete Greek Tragedies,* ed. David Grene and Richmond Lattimore (New York: Washington Square Press, 1968), 186, line 585.

41. *The Bacchae*, 165–6.
42. *The Bacchae*, 202.
43. *The Bacchae*, 200–1.
44. *The Bacchae*, 227.
45. As quoted in Eagleton, *Holy Terror*, 72.

14

Epilogue:
The Limits of Change

The purpose of this book has been to present an essential image of America. In this light, the question of change inevitably comes up. Can a myth be changed? Or can a new myth be made? The concept of change is a vital part of America's unchanging central vision of progress. In addition, the flow of a counterculture has historically run against the mainstream while striving for change—Roger Williams and Anne Hutchinson in Puritan Boston, Tom Paine in Revolutionary America, Andrew Jackson with his fight against the National Bank, the turn-of-the-century populism and the Progressive movement, the labor movement, women's suffrage, the New Deal, the civil rights and antiwar movements of the 1960s, feminism, Occupy Wall Street, and so on. Shifts do occur, usually over time, such as in the betterment of conditions for factory workers and the rights of women and minorities, and sometimes overnight, such as the democratization inherent in the computerized communication revolution. But within each shift there are operating, to a greater or lesser extent, the vestiges of the myth—self-interest, hierarchy of internal political structure, intolerance of difference, emphasis on the new at the expense of the lasting, quest for domination. Third parties are outspent at election time; communes succumb to power struggles; revolutionaries acquire a book deal, a movie, or a business card. Like microorganisms sharing the same culture in the petri dish, everyone operates from within the makeup and limits of the central myth.

Myth is the narrative and image of the tacit assumptions upon which a group is founded and a collective consciousness is certified. This essence will evolve into many derivatives, but at the core will be the kernel that determines the parameters of a particular mode of being. All collective human being has its fundament, the limits of existence determined by the enveloping, invisible patterns of its core. Myth is the final word or primary collage of images, the story, which opens up the complexity of the configuration in its fullest sense. Myth cannot be escaped or altered and does not tell us how to. Rather it is an invisible background that opens consciousness up to questioning and a deepening of understanding.

Again, the classical meaning of the word "myth," from the Greek *mythos*, has associations to "story," "plot," "that which is spoken," or "the word in its finality." Yet, as James Hillman reminds us, the root *mu* contains etymological connotations to words that speak of the opposite, that which cannot be spoken—"mute," "mum," "mumble," "closed as a mystery" (Greek *myein*), "dumb" (Sanskrit, *muka*). In other words, myth has to do with the interface of the known and the unknown, human and immortal. Myth takes up the ultimate contradictions of revealing and concealing that make up human consciousness and gives them image or intelligibility. Precisely because myth is unknowable, it leaves open the unknown.

Myth has to do not only with those patterns that are and are not seen or spoken but with the way in which they are seen and spoken. *Myth is the very structure through which we comprehend, speak, and act.* Myth is always already lived prior to any cognizance or consciousness, and therefore always informing that particular cognizance or consciousness, thus never really "known," let alone "changed" or "created" anew. Myth is neither good nor bad, positive or negative; it simply is.

Hillman has called the ontological foundation which myth provides "mythic certitude," as opposed to a sense of certainty derived from reason. He talks about the "risk" involved in mythic thinking when he says, "[Mythical] certitude gives neither peace nor help for pain nor prophetic assurance nor rule of law."[1] In other words, a mythic ground already gives rise to an anxiety, and what passes for change is often the discharge of this anxiety. What can be accomplished is the intuition of the mythic form, and thereby a sense of its limits, an action toward consciousness that already involves a transformation in ways of seeing. A change in a mode of perceiving by its very nature changes the corresponding action patterns. Abraham Lincoln implied this when he pointed out in his Second Inaugural Address that Americans may be the children of God, but as such the war that they had just been through could be seen as punishment by God for the sin of slavery.

American myth may not be changeable, as such; rather it can be deepened through consciousness resulting in the recognition of alternatives within parameters. Self-interest may be achieved by including a window to the other, progress may be seen in terms of sustainability, regeneration with profit may become an orientation toward energy and relationship with the environment, looking backward to history may allow for advancement, leadership may be provided "from behind," and domination may occur with enlightenment. In order for true change to come about and be recognized on its own terms and within its own limits, the necessity of the changeless calls for a sensitive awareness.

Note

1. James Hillman, "On Mythical Certitude," in "Myth: Theory and Behavior," Institute of Philosophic Studies, University of Dallas, Spring 1981, unpublished, section 3, p. 6.

Index

Weber, Max, 56–57
Webster, Daniel, 23, 89
Wein, Lawrence, 7
well-being, physical or material, 14,
    17, 35. *See also* materialism
Wells, H. G., 114
West Bank, 204–206
Westermann, William, 200
western territory, 84–85
westward expansion (western
    frontier), 85–86, 94
White Heat (film), 189
White, John, 43
Wiesner, Jerome, 186
Williams, Roger, 73, 237
Wills, Gary, 21
Wilson, Francis Huntington, 197
Wilson, Woodrow, xii, 25, 39–40,
    106–109, 115, 124, 198,
    201–202
    as cosmic hero, 112–115
    and democracy, 111, 114
    Fourteen Points, 112, 202
    identification with Jesus (divinity),
        109–110, 114
    and the white race, 110
    and World War I, 111
Winthrop, John, 51–52, 54, 58, 60,
    74, 116
Wister, Owen, *The Virginian,* 101
Wittgenstein, Ludwig, 155
Wolfowitz, Paul, 120
Wolin, Sheldon, 16, 158
work, 21, 89–90
    as vehicle for salvation, 56–57. *See
        also* Puritan work ethic
world peace, 112, 120
World Trade Center, 5–8, 13
    collapse, 9
World War I, 111, 200–201
World War II, 180–181, 183,
    186–187, 203, 210

Wright, Lawrence, 11n6

Y
Yale, William, 202
Yamasaki, Minoru, 7–8, 12n20

Z
Zahn, Paula, 137
zeal, 187–188, 193, 198
zealot, 217–218, 232–233
Zeus, 228
Zionism, in America, 201–202
Zuschlag, Richard, 135

About the Author

Ronald Schenk, Ph.D., received his master's degree in social work from Washington University, St. Louis, Missouri, and initial training in psychoanalytic psychotherapy in New Haven, Connecticut. He lived and worked with the Navajo before earning a Ph.D. in psychology at the University of Dallas, specializing in phenomenology. He trained in Jungian analysis with the Inter-Regional Society of Jungian Analysts and has served as senior training analyst and president of the society. He is currently in private practice in Dallas and Houston, Texas. His interests lie in clinical training, cultural psychology, and postmodernism. He has published several essays and is the author of *The Soul of Beauty: A Psychological Investigation of Appearance* (1992), *Dark Light: The Appearance of Death in Everyday Life* (2001), and *The Sunken Quest, The Wasted Fisher, The Pregnant Fish: Postmodern Reflections on Depth Psychology* (2001).

CPSIA information can be obtained at www.ICGtesting.com
Printed in the USA
BVOW06s0126300416

445807BV00009B/109/P